The Forms of Autobiography

The

Forms of

Autobiography

Episodes in the History of a Literary Genre

William C. Spengemann

Yale University Press
New Haven and London

Designed by James J. Johnson
and set in VIP Caledonia type by
United Printing Services, Inc., New Haven, Conn.
Printed in the United States of America by
Edwards Brothers Inc., Ann Arbor, Mich.

Library of Congress Cataloging in Publication Data

Spengemann, William C.
   The forms of autobiography.

   Bibliography: p.
   Includes index.
   1. Autobiography.   I. Title.
CT25.S63   1980   808.8'0351   79–22575
ISBN 0–300–02473–8 (cloth)
        0–300–02886–5 (paper)

11   10   9   8   7   6   5   4   3   2

FOR NAN

Contents

Acknowledgments

Among the many people who have had chunks of this book fall on them at one stage or another in its glacial progress toward completion, I wish particularly to thank L. Rod Lundquist, Albert B. Friedman, Quincy Howe, Anne Fisher, Margaret Boegmann, Thomas McFarland, Norman Council, and James M. Cox for their encouragement and advice. Important contributions to the bibliographical essay came from Ms. Boegmann, Marylynne Slayen, and especially Gary Westfahl, whose scholarly resourcefulness and care saved me many hours and many potential embarrassments. Catherine Tramz typed the copy with her usual care, and Sally Serafim edited it with keen discernment. Regarding the tact, kindness, and good sense displayed by Ellen Graham throughout the editorial process, I can only say that every author should have such a friend.

Introduction

The years that have slipped by since I began work on this little book have seen autobiography move from the borderlands of literary study to a place much nearer the privileged center traditionally occupied by fiction, poetry, and the drama. Had I written this introduction even five years ago, I could have begun, as was then the custom among critics of autobiography, by lamenting the scholarly neglect of this worthy literature. Now that the genre has become critically respectable, not to say fashionable, however, prefaces like this one are obliged to open on a softer note, with some acknowledgment of the great deal that has already been said on the subject, as well as some justification for adding yet another handful of pages to the steadily mounting pile.

While the recent flurry of books and articles on autobiography has abundantly answered the old plea for more work in the field, the volume of that response has raised a new problem: the more the genre gets written about, the less agreement there seems to be on what it properly includes. Back in the days when very few people even thought about this question, those who did might quarrel over the admissibility of letters, journals, memoirs, and verse-narratives, but they generally agreed that an autobiography had to offer an at least ostensibly factual account of the writer's own life—that it had to be, in short, a self-written biography. As the number of people writing about autobiography has swelled, however, the boundaries of the genre have expanded proportionately until there is now virtually no written form that has not either been included in some study of autobiography or else been subjected to autobiographical interpretation. What was once a rather clearly demarcated territory, populated almost exclusively by such self-identifying texts as John Stuart Mill's *Autobiography* and Jonathan Edwards's *Personal Narrative*, has become an unbounded sprawl, in which the poetry of T. S. Eliot and William Carlos Williams, the novels of Stendhal and Proust, the plays of Tennessee Williams, and even Henry James's prefaces have found a place.

These efforts to expand the boundaries of autobiography have split critical opinion into two schools of thought concerning its permissible methods. On the one side are those critics who continue to insist that autobiography must employ biographical—which is to say historical rather than fictional—materials. On the other side, there are those who assert the right of autobiographers to present themselves in whatever form they may find appropriate and necessary. Whether a particular study takes up the subject of autobiography itself, or uses autobiographies as a source of information about some other subject (the idea of individualism, for example), or simply treats some literary work as an autobiography, it will adopt, either implicitly or explicitly, one of these two theoretical positions, which will in turn condition everything else the writer has to say.

Both of these approaches to autobiography seem to me to have a good deal to recommend them. The idea of autobiography obviously cannot be separated completely from self-biography. However one chooses to define the genre, its universally recognized classics were all written in this mode, and anyone who wishes to redefine autobiography must begin by redefining the essential character of these acknowledged models. But neither can the idea of autobiography be identified with self-biography. The various poems, novels, and plays that have recently been inserted into the genre—all of which, significantly, are either modern or else particularly susceptible to modernist interpretation—do seem, despite their fictiveness, to address the same problems of self-definition that have taxed autobiographers ever since Augustine discovered that the self is a hard ground to plough. Indeed, the modernist movement away from representational discourse toward self-enacting, self-reflexive verbal structures and the critical theories that have been devised to explain this movement conspire to make the very idea of literary modernism seem synonymous with that of autobiography.

Insofar as both of these views of autobiography conform to our experience with actual texts both are right. What we need, therefore, is a theory, or rather a description, of autobiography that will recognize both its perduring relation to the self-biographical mode and its apparently increasing tendency to assume fictive forms in the modern era. Instead of identifying autobiography with self-written biography because it has usually been written in that form or denying the generic importance of that convention because autobiography has often been written in other forms, we need to understand the conditions that have led different autobiographers at different times to write about themselves in different ways. In other words, we must view autobiography historically, not as one thing that writers have done again and again, but as the pattern described by the various things they have done in response to changing ideas about the nature of the self, the ways in which the self may be apprehended, and the proper methods of reporting those apprehensions.

Introduction

The evolution of autobiographical forms outlined in the following chapters begins with *The Confessions of St. Augustine*, a work that meets even the strictest formal prescriptions for the genre, and concludes with *The Scarlet Letter*, a work that retains no vestige of the self-biographical mode. My aim is to demonstrate the generic kinship between these formally diverse works by locating them both within a single evolving tradition that arose in the early Middle Ages and arrived at the conclusions of its own internal logic in the nineteenth century. Chapter one analyzes the form of Augustine's *Confessions* in some detail, partly because this work is generally acknowledged to be both a true autobiography and the first of its kind, but mainly because this seminal document employs in succession all three of the forms—historical, philosophical, and poetic—that autobiography would assume in the course of its development over the next fifteen hundred years. Following the essay on *The Confessions* are three chapters: one on the development of historical autobiography in the Renaissance and the Enlightenment, one on the transition to philosophical autobiography in the later eighteenth century, and one on the emergence of poetic autobiography in the nineteenth century. By applying the formal paradigm provided in Augustine's *Confessions* to a number of ostensibly representative, but at any rate familiar, works, these three chapters attempt to chart the formal permutations that, all together, constitute what autobiography is.

A word or two needs to be said at this point regarding my selection of texts for discussion. Although this book treats its subject historically, it does not pretend to survey the vast library of autobiographical writing. On the contrary, I have chosen for extended analysis only as many works as I needed to describe the movement of autobiography from the biographical to the fictive mode. This is not to contend that the works I have chosen are necessarily the first to do what I describe them as doing. Few of my readers will be unable to name for each formal category an autobiography written earlier than those I discuss, and fewer still will excuse my failure to acknowledge their favorites. Since I do not maintain that the formal evolution of autobigraphy was unilinear, proceeding directly through any particular sequence of texts, I have felt free to single out works that illustrate most clearly what seem to me the crucial episodes in the larger movement that is my subject.

Some of my readers may also feel that the evolution I am proposing does not really evolve, since the "earlier" forms, historical and philosophical autobiography, are still being written, while poetic autobiography, the "latest" stage of development, is present in Augustine's *Confessions*, at the very beginning of the movement. My response to the first part of this objection would be that no theory of evolution requires mutant forms to supplant the strains from which they arise; they simply add to the existing stock of forms available for use. Although not everything done today has always been done, it is probably fair to say that everything that has ever been done is still being done, somewhere. In any event, I take each of the three autobiographical forms to be characteristic of the period to which I have assigned it, even though it may not be the form most often used in that period. What I call historical autobiography seems to me to accord perfectly with the climate of opinion regarding the self that prevailed from the Middle Ages to the Enlightenment, philosophic autobiography to reflect the changes in that climate which occurred around the turn of the nineteenth century, and poetic autobiography to express the radically altered conditions that resulted from the ideological upheavals of the nineteenth century. Only St. Augustine remains a true anomaly in this pattern, accomplishing the entire course of autobiographical change in a single work written at its very beginning. Concerning this recusant fact, I will simply observe that it is the subsequent evolution of autobiography that gives Augustine his preeminence, in retrospect. If later autobiographers like Dante, Rousseau, and Carlyle had not employed the very different forms they did, we would doubtless be unable to recognize the formal movement that makes *The Confessions* so proleptic.

And that brings me to my final word concerning the selection of texts analyzed in the chapters ahead. Although a good deal has been asserted already about the proliferation of autobiographical forms in the twentieth century, this study concludes with an analysis of *The Scarlet Letter*, my prime example of poetic autobiography. Where, the reader may well ask, do we account for the autobiographical experiments of Yeats and Proust, of T. S. Eliot, William Carlos Williams, Robert Lowell, and Sylvia Plath? Although the reader's satisfaction on this point will depend on the persuasiveness of the chapters ahead, I will say here that, however various critics have defined autobiography, their ability to recognize one has always depended on some evidence that the writer's self is either the primary subject or the principal object of the verbal action. In the former case, the self is seen to exist independent of whatever the writer says on its behalf, and the verbal action seeks either to describe that self historically, or analyze it philosophically, or express it poetically. In the latter case, the self is seen to depend for its existence upon the verbal action, which therefore describes its own poetic creation. Historical self-explanation, philosophical self-scrutiny, poetic self-expression, and poetic self-invention—these are, so far as I know, the only procedures available to autobiography, and the list was exhausted by the time Hawthorne finished *The Scarlet Letter*. Unless I am greatly mistaken in this formulation (a possibility of which I am perfectly aware), then, all subsequent autobiographies may be described in terms of one or more of these formal strategies. Although historical, philosophic, and poetic autobiographies are still being written today, the generic evolution that produced these divergent forms and so relates them to each other—the movement outlined in this book—was complete a century ago.

I

The Formal Paradigm

The Confessions of St. Augustine

The structure of Augustine's *Confessions* is tripartite. In Books I through IX, the Augustine who has already received the gift of faith stands upon the fixed point of an immutable truth and looks back, or rather *down*, upon the sinful life he led between his birth and his conversion. To dramatize the importance of conversion, Augustine draws a sharp distinction between his old, unregenerate self, who could see his life only from an ever-shifting perspective within it, and his new converted self, who sees that life as an eternally complete moral design with all its parts existing simultaneously in timeless space. The religious significance of the conversion, the accuracy of the meanings he assigns to his past life, the whole lesson of the narrative in fact, depend upon the narrator's ability to persuade himself and the reader that he has attained this timeless wisdom, and can now see the true, eternal pattern of his false, temporal life.

Once the narrative arrives at the moment of conversion, however, and the old Augustine gives way to the new, the narrator ceases to recount his past life and begins a meditative inquiry into three topics: memory, time, and the Creation. In this second part of *The Confessions*, Books X through XII, the narrator no longer surveys his temporal life

1

from a point outside it; he moves through the temporal process of meditation in search of some timeless wisdom beyond. No longer do we have two Augustines, one trapped in time and the other standing outside it. Now, the Augustine who lives the life and the one who recounts it are the same person, and that person finds himself once again in an uncertain, temporal condition, between past conversion and the ultimate redemption he seeks. If the import of part one depended upon the narrator's standing still in the presence of an unchanging truth already known, the success of part two depends on his ability to move rapidly through his changing thoughts toward a truth which is yet unknown.

The Confessions then conclude with Book XIII, which continues the meditation upon the Creation, but in quite a different spirit. Here again, the Augustine who acts and the one who reflects and explains are the same person, a faithful but still time-bound mortal in search of truth. Instead of pursuing his quest for complete understanding along the temporal path of inquiry, however, the narrator now confesses directly to God his conviction that faith itself is wisdom. Although time, change, and ignorance are the inescapable conditions of our mortality, when redeemed by faith, time can symbolize eternity, inquiry can adumbrate knowledge, corruption can mirror grace, the created can glimpse its creator, and the conditional can find, in the fleeting instant, its absolute ground.

While it is possible to see these three parts as integrally related elements in a single, coherent structure—with each part representing one stage in the soul's progress from a sinful indifference to God, through an awakened desire for redemption, to the realization that wisdom and salvation lie in faith alone—the narrative mode and theological ideas of each succeeding part appear to invalidate, or at least to qualify, the assumptions behind the structure and doctrine of each preceding part. The abrupt change in the narrator's function and circumstances after the conversion calls into question the authority he assumed in Books I through IX, since he does not seem to know now what he professed to know then: the ultimate purpose and meaning of his life. Nor do the inquiries he conducts in the second part quite explain how he finally manages to achieve the assurances he proclaims in part three, where he stops his inquiry and asserts his belief that faith in ultimate redemption offers the ecstatic repose of redemption itself and that a confession of faith in the existence of the truth will satisfy his appetite for wisdom as completely as would wisdom actually achieved. If the faith he confesses in part three is meant to depend upon certain assurances gained through the inquiries of part two, these investigations must appear incomplete, since they touch upon only a few of the many possible questions that might be supposed to stand in the way of a full profession of faith. Then, too, the profession of faith must appear somewhat fortuitous, an evasion of the problems that the inquiry either does not raise or does not solve. If, on the other hand, part three is not meant to arise out of conclusions reached in part two, but is to be understood as a state of spiritual wisdom beyond the reach of intellectual inquiry, then part two must appear gratuitous, a somewhat pointless exercise of the intelligence in quest of a wisdom that only faith can bring. Viewed in relation to part three, in fact, the curious questionings of part two rather closely resemble the foolish ambitions and intellectual pretensions of the old Augustine of part one, who wandered lost in his mortal state until he stopped trying to find wisdom through his unaided intelligence and learned to find it in unquestioning resignation to the inscrutable will of God.

While *The Confessions* as a whole may be said to dramatize the quest of a time-bound, mortal soul in search of rest,

3

each of the three parts stipulates a different resting place or end to its action. The narrative mode of part one, with its firmly situated narrator and its wandering protagonist, posits conversion as the point where the agitated protagonist will come to rest in the enlightened narrator, and the action will stop. But when the previously unmoving narrator begins his own quest for knowledge in Book X, the unconditioned ground of rest is displaced from the narrator to a point somewhere beyond him, and the *telos* of the action is removed from conversion to that ultimate wisdom which presumably lies at the end of inquiry. Once portrayed as an ending achieved prior to the writing of the autobiography, conversion is now portrayed as the beginning of a process whose end must be achieved by way of the autobiography itself. And while the end of part one was foreknown and clearly defined from the beginning by a narrator who had already achieved it, the end of part two remains necessarily shadowy and undefined to the narrator who has yet to achieve it. Then, when persistent inquiry into the mysteries of the mind and the Creation bring him no closer to that ultimate knowledge which is his goal, when questions succeed only in raising even more perplexing questions, the narrator redefines his goal once again, substituting faith in the existence of unknowable answers for the answers themselves. In part two, faithful meditation was seen as the means to an end outside itself and derived its value from that end. In part three, faithful meditation, the ongoing process of confession, becomes its own end, its own resting place, its own reward.

These changes in narrative mode and structure signal attendant shifts in the underlying doctrine of *The Confessions*. Although all three parts hold firmly to the essential idea that true knowledge comes from faith alone, the narrator of part one represents himself as having already attained full knowledge through the faith that came to him at the moment of his conversion. The reader is therefore surprised to see him embark on a quest for additional, more complete knowledge in part two and then to see him substitute faith for knowledge in part three. The case seems to be that while the doctrine of *credo ut intellegam* remains unchanged throughout *The Confessions*, the precise relation of faith to knowledge is subtly but significantly different in each of the three parts. In part one, the narrator's faith appears to have already brought him the knowledge he needs to interpret correctly the pattern and purpose of his life. In part two, faith becomes the instrument by which such knowledge is to be attained, the posture of the soul most conducive to its attainment, and the one proper guide to the truth, which lies beyond faith. And in part three, faith is identified with knowledge, suggesting that he who has faith has the truth in effect, even though he may not be able to grasp it intellectually or to articulate it in the limited language of men.

These alterations in the meaning of the central doctrine are something more than variations upon a single unchanging idea. They constitute a change in the fundamental conception of *The Confessions*, and the meaning of the word "confession" itself changes in concert with them. In part one, confession is at once a conceptual act (the arrangement of temporally scattered events into their one, true, eternal design), a penitential act (the painful recollection of old errors), and an act of thanksgiving to God for having guided Augustine all during his faithless early life and finally having delivered him into his present belief and knowledge. In part two, confession is no longer a revelation of the self to God, who already knows everything, but a revelation of the self to the self, an act of self-knowledge, a process of discovering the true meaning of one's life. And in part three, confession is neither a profession of knowledge as in part one, nor a mode of inquiry as in part two, but an assertion of faith in the efficacy of faith itself.

Insofar as these correlative changes in the form and doctrine of *The Confessions* do not permit us to see the three parts as elements in a single preconceived structure, they incline us to see each succeeding part as a response to problems created by the preceding one, and they oblige us to identify in each section the particular difficulties which the following one attempts to address and resolve. The structure of *The Confessions*, in other words, must be seen, not simply as an imitation of doctrinal ideas that precede it and remain unchanged throughout, but as a form unfolding out of complications which emerged in the course of composition. The narrative mode of part one raises questions about the assumed relations between memory and truth, time and eternity, the created and the Creator, on which that form is based; and these questions become the subject of inquiry in part two. The further complexities brought to light by the investigations of part two and by its narrative form necessitate the formal and doctrinal revisions that characterize part three. The structure and argument of each part leads directly to those of the next, even as each succeeding part calls into question the narrative mode and ideological assumptions of the one preceding.

I I

The narrative mode of Books I through IX has been employed by so many autobiographers of so many different ideological persuasions over the centuries that we are apt to forget that its origins lie in a very special set of beliefs and assumptions. The mode is grounded ultimately in the conviction that the retrospective narrator can see his life from a point outside it, that his view is not subject to the limiting conditions of the life he is recounting. While the past self, the protagonist, can see each event in his life only in its ever-changing relation to a past which is being continually reshaped by the addition of new experience in the present, and to future expectations which experience is continually revising, the narrator can see each past event in its fixed relation to a past which has presumably achieved its final form. Because the narrator does not stand within the temporal span of the action he is reporting, because he does not stand in time at all, his perspective is not altered by new experience. He contemplates each past event from the same, unmoving point, the point of immutable truth. In these first nine books, it is faith and faith alone that gives the narrator this timeless vision of his temporal life, enabling him to survey his past wanderings from a stationary, exterior point, and preventing his memory from wandering along those old paths that once led him away from the truth. What the narrator sees from this ecstatic ground is nothing less than the eternal form of the life he once lived moment by moment, the true meaning of his false life.

Since the narrative is above all the story of Augustine's conversion, of his awakening to the faith that taught him the truth, the converted narrator and the unconverted protagonist are distinguished primarily on the basis of their faith and their consequent knowledge of the divine purpose behind the life. The narrator draws this distinction sharply at the moment of the protagonist's birth. Upon asserting his present conviction that good things come from God, he immediately explains, "This I came to know later. . . . [T]hen all I knew was how to suck, to be contented with bodily pain; that was all."* From this point in the narrative until

---

* *The Confessions of St. Augustine*, trans. Rex Warner (New York, 1963), p. 21. Subsequent references to this translation appear in parentheses in the text.

the moment of conversion, when the protagonist suddenly awakens to the true meaning of his life and thus becomes the narrator, Augustine maintains this clear division between past ignorance and present knowledge, elucidating the true significance of acts which he failed to understand previously. "At that time," he says, "I was ignorant of these things and unaware of them. On all sides they were striking me in the eye, but still I did not see them" (62); and again, "At that time I did not know this and I loved these lower beauties and I was sinking down to the depths" (82). So penetrating is the narrator's redeemed perception, compared to the protagonist's blindness, in fact, that he can now discern not only the ultimate significance of past acts but their true causes as well. While the protagonist believes that he is going to the Manichees to find the truth, the narrator knows that he really went in order to become disillusioned with them (107–08).

The extent and completeness of the narrator's knowledge give him a command of his past life that is truly Godlike; and although he never commits the impiety of confusing himself with God, his position and function in the narrative are formally analogous to God's role in the universe. Early in the narrative, Augustine makes God the eternal repository of all things that are lost in time: *"For Thou are most high and art not changed,* and this Today does not come to an end in you; and yet it does come to an end in you, since all times are in you; for they would have no way of succeeding each other, if they were not all contained in you. And since *Thy years do not fail,* your years are Today. And how many of our years and of our father's years have passed through this Today of yours, receiving from it the pattern and form of the existence which they had. . . . But *Thou are still the same,* and all things of tomorrow and after tomorrow, all things of yesterday and before yesterday, you will accomplish today and you have accomplished today" (23). God's eternal being gives reality, sequence, pattern, and meaning to all things known and unknown, remembered and forgotten, past and future.

God is thus the paradigm memory, the ideal to which the narrator aspires as he struggles to give past events an eternal presence, pattern, and meaning by passing them through the "most high" and unchanging medium of his own divinely instructed intelligence. To the unconverted protagonist, things seem to come and go or else to change so rapidly that he cannot grasp their eternal form. But the narrator stands above change with God, of whom he says, "you are always the same, and as to those things which do not always exist or do not always exist in the same way, you know all of them, always and in the same way" (165). Even his language aspires continually to divinity, as he labors to maintain a level of discourse that will move smoothly in and out of Scriptural quotation with no syntactic break or tonal seam, and thus to demonstrate rhetorically the consonance of his own words with the divine Word.

From his enlightened, unmoving position above the action of his story, the narrator gives to the protagonist's fallen life a literary form which aspires to imitate the eternal form given to the objects and events of the material world by the omniscient, unmoving mind of God. "I want to call back to mind my past impurities and the carnal corruptions of my soul," he says, "not because I love them, but so that I may love you, my God. . . . And gathering myself together from the scattered fragments into which I was broken and dissipated during all that time when, being turned away from you, the One, I lost myself in the distractions of the many" (40). The form of this gathering is repeatedly associated with the divine form; implicitly in the narrator's apostrophe to God as "the one from whom is every manner of form,

9

you, most beautiful, the creator of beauty in all things, you who by your law lay down for all things the rule" (24); and somewhat more explicitly in those passages where Augustine uses the form of words to illustrate the principle of eternal form. Concerning material things, the narrator says in prayer, "So much you have given to them, namely to be parts of a structure in which the parts are not all in existence at the same time; instead, by fading and by replacing each other, they all together constitute the universe of which they are all parts. Our own speech, too, which is constructed out of meaningful sounds, follows the same principles. There could never be a complete sentence unless one word, as soon as the syllables had been sounded, ceased to be in order to make room for the next" (79). The words and the material objects or temporal events they signify all pass away, but the forms of those words together, like the form of all things and events together, is eternal and divine.

Because the divine form is the absolute ground of reality, and is in no way contingent upon its material, historical content, it is sufficient in itself. Nevertheless, the totality of divine being includes all those conditional objects and events which it informs, and insofar as the narrative seeks to imitate the divine totality it must not only expound the eternal truth but also explain the relation between truth and error. Recalling how faith reconciled him to the existence of evil things, the narrator says, "So I no longer desired better things. I had envisaged all things in their totality, and, with a sounder judgment, I realized that while higher things are certainly better than lower things, all things together are better than higher things by themselves" (152). Doctrinally, the narrative establishes the relation between truth and error, higher and lower things, by asserting that the truth now known to the narrator was always present and available to the protagonist, who simply refused to see it. "And where was I when I was seeking for you," he asks. "You were there, in front of me; but I had gone away even from myself. I could not even find myself, much less find you" (91).

The form of the narrative imitates this doctrinal relation by making the narrator something more than a voice of recollection, recounting past events. As the voice of that truth which was available to the protagonist from the beginning, he in fact represents the eternally ambient truth in which the protagonist lives his false life. Monica's dream about her son's eventual conversion, the bishop's counsel of patience (67-68), and the narrator's stated belief that God was "doing everything in the order which [He] had predestined it" (103), indicate that his conversion was foreordained—which is to say, eternally true. Consequently, the converted narrator, who embodies that truth, exists complete throughout the narrative, standing alongside the fallen self as the voice of the eternally present truth to which the fallen self must awaken. Once again, narrator and protagonist are separated primarily by faith, not by time. Although the narrator is obviously older than the protagonist, his knowledge is not attributed to his age or his past experience, to wisdom achieved in time, but to the faith which he could have embraced at any time.

Augustine's stated intention to explain the relation between truth and error, requires that the protagonist's false life occur entirely within the context of the narrator's truth. That life must be presented consistently as an example of error, impiety, infidelity and personal insufficiency, never as something of interest or value in itself. Events from the life are chosen solely for their suitability as illustrations of the narrator's pronouncements or as topics of exegesis. The pear-stealing, for example, receives the attention it does, not because it is exciting, not even because it was an especially vicious act, and certainly not because it taught the protagonist a valuable lesson, but simply because it gives the narrator an opportunity to discuss at length an important doctrinal truth about the sinner's love for sin itself. The protagonist is seldom permitted to speak in his own voice. When he does, he merely displays the negligence and self-seeking that are at once the cause and effect of his sickness, and his statements are immediately condemned by the narrator: "So I used to speak and so the winds blew and shifted and drove my heart this way and that and time went by and I was slow in turning to the Lord" (129). What he is allowed to say, moreover, makes him appear far more meanly inclined than we might suppose the young Augustine actually was, given his life-long passion for the good.

It is not enough to say that such self-hatred is conventional in spiritual autobiography; after all, Augustine established the convention. The point is that the highly unflattering portrait of the protagonist is dictated entirely by Augustine's determination to maintain the proper doctrinal relation between truth and error, showing them to be radically divergent paths, both of which were open to the protagonist at all times. Undue attention to the protagonist's less ignoble desires and inclinations, or to the sinner's own view of his situation at the time, might suggest that the path of error led him to the truth in time, that he made his way through error to the truth. Because faith alone is the way to the truth, all his previous efforts, lacking faith, must be shown to have been incapable of producing good results.

Although the chronological ordering of narrative events implies a temporal development in the protagonist, then, the idea that he came to his conversion in time is explicitly denied again and again. The primary cause of all things is the eternal will of God working through temporal causes, to which the unredeemed intelligence mistakenly ascribes prime causality. Aware of his spiritual sickness, the protagonist believes that he will become well in time: "A minute, just a minute, just a little time longer." But, as the narrator knows, "there was no limit to the minutes and the little time longer went a long way" (169). Time does not lead to the truth, only to vanity and sorrow: ". . . time came and went from one day to another, and in its coming and going it gave me other things to hope for and other things to remember, and gradually patched me up again with the sort of pleasures which I had known before. To these pleasures my great sorrow began to give way. But, though its place was not taken by other sorrows, it was taken by things which would cause other sorrows" (77–78). In the fruitless opinion of worldly men, wisdom comes with maturity, as boys give up their childish games for the sober business of adulthood. But to the intelligence that is instructed by faith, childish games and adult occupations appear equally foolish, the one giving rise in time to the other. Wickedness is a turning away from God. In no way can it be construed as a path to God. Lust does not lead to satiety and from there to continence. Lust leads only to more lust; continence alone will produce continence, and that requires faith. Learning does not lead to faith, as his mother wrongly believes. Faith alone brings wisdom, and his learning does him far more harm than good. Illumined by eternal faith, all temporal things are good. Without faith, all temporal things are damned, and damned things do not lead to faith. One damned thing leads to another.

Conversion, then, is an awakening to the truth that has been present from the beginning—doctrinally in the ambient spirit of God's eternal truth and formally in the *persona* of the narrator. It is not an arrival at some wisdom that has been waiting for him down the path of his life in time. When he says that he remained in sin nine years after his mother's prophetic dream, he does not mean that nine years were required for his conversion, but only that he waited nine years to do what he could, and should, have done immediately. Looking back on the twelve years that followed his first reading of Cicero, he ruefully notes that he was in worse spiritual health at the end of that period than he was at its beginning. Although conversion is an event, it is utterly unlike all previous events in his sinful life, for it does not occur in time and space. It is a turning, but not from one part of the material world to another. It is a turning from the sensual world of matter to the world of spiritual ideas. It is a rising, but as he says in Book XIII, "... it is not in space that we sink down and are raised up again" (320). Conversion is a movement, but a movement without duration or extension: "For to be in darkness of affection is to be far from you. We do not go from you or return to you on foot or by spatial measurement. ... In lust, therefore, that is to say, in darkness of affection is the real distance from your face" (36). The way to God, "is not by ship or chariot or on foot; the distance is not so great as that which I had come from the house to the place where we were sitting. All I had to do was to will to go there, and I would not only go but would immediately arrive" (175). Because conversion is an event of a different order, it is removed from the chain of temporal causality that bound together his sinful life. If conversion were the result of his past acts, those acts would participate in the good they had caused. But the redeemed self does not evolve from the fallen self. Conversion divides the life in two, severing all connections between the mortal and the immortal soul. "It was no longer I myself" who went on sinning after having glimpsed the truth, the narrator says, "since there to a great extent I was rather suffering things against my will than doing them voluntarily" (168). At the moment of conversion, a new man is born.

Augustine portrays that birth as an acquisition of both faith and self-knowledge, equating these two in a subtle paraphrase of St. Paul's well known figure of the enigmatic mirror. Construing faith as a form of knowledge, Paul had said that in our imperfect state we see (something un-named, presumably the truth or God) through a mystify-ing medium, but that in the state of perfection we will see (it) face to face and know (it) even as we are known (by some-one again unnamed and again presumably God). Where Paul leaves the object undesignated, Augustine interpolates "myself," making self-knowledge the result of conversion and the definitive attribute of faith. Describing the hour of his conversion, the narrator says, "But you, Lord, . . . were turning me around so that I could see myself; you took me from behind my own back, which was where I had put myself during the time when I did not want to be ob-served by myself, and you set me in front of my own face so that I could see how foul a sight I was . . ." (173). Infi-delity limits the sinner's self-knowledge to an always un-certain prospect. The knowing self stands behind the experiencing self on the path of time, drawing from each successive experience certain tentative inferences about the truth which will have to be revised in the light of subse-quent, unforeseeable experiences.

The converted narrator's self-knowledge, on the other hand, is complete, for the knowing self stands in front of the experiencing self, where he can see not only those things that have already happened but also those things that will happen in the future. He can thus correctly interpret each experience in relation to the entire pattern of the life. Once again, form and doctrine are inextricably entwined. Con-version completes both the doctrinal lesson of faith and the form that was projected by the initial distinction between the self-deluded protagonist and the self-aware narrator. When the protagonist gives way to the narrator, his story ends. At the same instant, the narrator is born to tell the story already told. The end joins the beginning to form an endless circle, which is at once the figure described by the narrative, the symbol of a mortal life made eternal by faith, and the mystical emblem of God.

III

The circle is no sooner joined, however, than it is broken. Book X begins with these richly suggestive although somewhat cryptic words: "Cognoscam te, cognitor meus, cognoscam, sicut et cognitus sum." As in the foregoing narrative of conversion, self-knowledge is identified both with a knowledge of God and with God-like knowledge, for the passage seems to mean, "Let me know you, God, and my true self in the way that you know me."* What is distinctive

---

* Warner translates this passage, "Let me know thee, my known; *let me know Thee even as I am known*" (210), leaving the phrase *cognitor meus* somewhat obscure. "My known" cannot refer to God, for in the very next clause Augustine asks God to reveal Himself. William Watts and Edward Pusey take *cognitor meus* to refer specifically to God: "Let me know Thee, O Lord, who Knowest me." J. G. Pilkington follows Augustine more closely, leaving the referent of *cognitor meus* unspecified. And yet he, too, implies that the phrase refers mainly to God: "Let me know Thee, O Thou who knowest me." Since *cognitor meus* may be literally translated "my knower," Warner's "my known" may be a printer's error. On the other hand, Watt's and Pusey's interpolation, "O Lord," and Pilkington's capitalization of the words "Thee, O Thou," seem to rob Augustine's phrase of its subtle ambiguity by designating a single specific reference for it. Literally translated, the entire passage reads, "Let me know you, my knower; let me know you even as I am known." Since the main subject of Book X is self-knowledge, and since Augustine consistently equates self-knowledge with knowledge of God (which is, in turn, the ability to know things the way God knows them), *cognitor meus* seems to refer at once to God (who knows everything, especially Augustine's true self) and to the true, hidden self Augustine struggles throughout his book to know. If so, the passage may be interpreted, "Let me know God and my true self exactly as God does."

about this passage is, first, the implied association between God and the true self, which are the paired objects of Augustine's quest; and second, the narrator's rather clear suggestion that he does not yet know either himself or God. In part one, the narrator associated his God-like *knowledge* with divinity, his known self with mortality. But here, he reverses the order of association, linking the unknown self to divinity and portraying his present knowledge as mortal. Before, he knew the eternal truth that preceded and governed his mortal experience, and he could see how his past experience exemplified that truth, because conversion had turned him around to see his false self "face to face." Now, that truth, which is also his true self, lies enshrouded in "a sad kind of darkness . . . , what is inside the mind is mostly hidden and remains hidden until revealed by experience . . ." (241).

When the faithless protagonist was his subject, the narrator could stand on the eternal, unchanging ground of faith and survey the sinner's wanderings without participating in them. But now that the narrator is his own subject, he finds himself back in the condition of the old sinner, looking up through his present experience toward the gradually unfolding truth, rather than down through the complete truth at his past experience. The present narrator is still distinguishable from the old protagonist: he knows what perfection is and desires it, whereas the former sinner either did not know it or else did not desire it even when he knew it. Nevertheless, the substitution of his present, unknown self for his past, known self dramatically alters his situation and authority, suggesting that his previous knowledge was not absolute but only appeared so in comparison with the sinner's utter self-delusion. He may have been able to see his past self "face to face" and know what lay in store for it, but his present self and its destiny remain an enigma to him: "and in this life . . . no one ought to feel sure that, just as he has been worse and become better, he may not also, after having become better, become worse" (241).

Conversion, it now appears, is not the alpha and omega of his spiritual life, the point where the beginning and end of mortal time meet in an eternal circle that is already historically complete. It is only one point on a much larger, as yet incomplete circle that began in God before birth and will end in heavenly salvation after death. And while the narrator of part one could stand at the beginning and end of the smaller circle because he had already gone around it himself, the narrator of part two is still moving away from his starting point along a path whose ultimate, divine curvature he can at best dimly perceive. *"Certainly now we see through a glass darkly*, and not yet *face to face,"* he says, completely reversing his earlier position; "and so long as I am on pilgrimage away from you, I am more present to my self than to you; yet I know that you are not in any way subject to violence, whereas I do not know in any case what temptations I can and what I cannot resist. . . . And what I do not know remains unknown to me until *my darkness be made as the noonday* in your countenance" (214). Conversion is no longer an event outside time, but simply one more event—albeit a highly significant one—in a spiritual life that extends through time from birth to final judgment. And although the narrator previously insisted that conversion was always available to the protagonist, it now appears to be a stage of spiritual development which had to be approached gradually through certain necessary preliminary stages.

This redefinition of conversion throws a strange light back on the narrator's arguments in part one. In the first place, it makes his comprehensive view of the protagonist's life seem less a gift of eternal grace than the product of natural memory, less a conspectus from a point outside time than a retrospect from a point later in time. This relocation of the narrator's vantage-point, in turn, seriously impairs the rationale which allowed him to stand alongside the protagonist throughout the action as an eternal presence. For if the narrator emerged in time, he is separated from the protagonist by time, and not just by faith. The two *personae* do not exist simultaneously in an eternal order of things, one in time and the other out of it. The voice of the narrator follows that of the protagonist in time, and the two can be brought together only in the narrator's memory, which also operates in time.

In addition, if the truth represented by the narrative voice did in fact emerge in time, and was therefore not always available to the protagonist, the narrator had no basis for condemning the protagonist's failure to embrace conversion before he did. On the contrary, the narrator should have dealt mercifully with the sinner's blind gropings, as he now begs God to deal with his own. And finally, if conversion is now to be seen as a temporal experience, not essentially different from those that precede and follow it, it is connected to all other events in the historical order of things; and all those earlier events suddenly assume a causal significance that was denied them previously. Indeed, when we re-examine part one from this new perspective, we can see scattered throughout the narrative suggestions that the conversion did not occur outside the order of temporal causality, but was at least partially contingent on previous events and therefore had to follow them.

In Book VI, the narrator takes his accustomed doctrinal stand on the issue of worldly activity, employing a highly significant metaphor to illustrate his contention:

Where are you going over those rough paths? Where are you going? The good that you love is from Him; but its goodness and sweetness is only because you are

looking toward Him; it will rightly turn to bitterness if
what is from Him is wrongly loved, He Himself being
left out of the account. What are you aiming at, then, by
going on and on walking along these difficult and
tiring ways? There is no rest to be found where you are
looking for it. Seek what you seek, but it is not there
where you are seeking. You seek a happy life in the
country of death. [81–82]

Because travel occurs in time and space, it leads only to
more wandering, more time, and eventually to death. Peace
and happiness can be found only at home: "Let us return
now to you, Lord, so that we may not be overturned, because our good is with you, living and without any defect,
since you yourself are our good. And we need not be afraid
of having no place to which we may return. We of our own
accord fell from that place. And our home, which is your
eternity, does not fall down when we are away from it" (89).
Here and throughout part one, travel stands for fruitless human ambition, home for spiritual resignation to the eternal
will of God. Cast in these metaphors, secular action and
spiritual repose are irreconcilable opposites.

This sharp doctrinal distinction is considerably blurred
in Book V, however. Motivated by worldly ambition, the
protagonist travels from Carthage to Rome, abandoning his
home and his mother, whom the narrator repeatedly calls
the medium of God's voice, the temple of his faith, his anchor against the tide of error; and with whom he identifies
the true church, "the mother of us all" (28). Theoretically
the voyage should do him no good, since it takes him away
from his own heart, where God dwells, and since the narrator sees clearly that the traveler's ambitions are vain. At the
same time, however, the narrator also sees that, although
the protagonist went for false reasons, the true cause of his
going was God's eternal plan for his salvation, working

through the secondary causes of the voyage. From his privileged vantage-point beyond conversion, the narrator perceives that God was "dragging me away by the force of my own desires in order that these desires might be brought to an end" (101).

While this assignment of eternal causes to worldly activity reaffirms the often-stated doctrinal distinction between true, eternal causes and apparent, historical causes, it also has the effect of making temporal actions seem instrumental, perhaps even necessary, to the attainment of eternal truths. He *must* leave his mother physically in order to return to her in spirit, for it is not until he gets to Rome and discovers the folly of his ambitions that he realizes the truth she has been trying unsuccessfully to tell him all along. Although the ambition itself eventually proved vain, it nevertheless served a divine purpose in the end. Desire did not lead to more desire in this case, as the narrator has so often said it must, but to an end of desire. Inevitably the question arises: if this past desire led to a cessation of desire and to conversion, might not one's present desires, although perhaps vain in themselves, also lead to an end which, although not yet known, will also prove eternal and divine once it is achieved? It is a question that will occur repeatedly to the inquisitive narrator of part two as he pursues his quest for knowledge.

The distinction between eternal causes and historical causes, between the absolute and the contingent, is no easier to maintain in the narrative of a life, it seems, than it is in life itself. Whenever the narrator attempts to explain in retrospect the divine purposes that lay behind historical events he runs the risk of suggesting that the truth is somehow contingent on those events. In order to justify the existence of error in the world, he says, "For there must also be heresies, that the approved may be made manifest among the weak" (156), implying that error is not just useful but necessary to the revelation of the truth. If he had died from his illness in Rome, he says, he would have gone to hell because his false idea of God denied him the benefits of divine mercy. God's mercy is thus made to appear contingent on Augustine's conception of Him, and ultimate causality is once again displaced from the eternal to the historical realm. But God healed him, he goes on, "so that I might live for a more certain health" (104), again implying that his conversion somehow depended on his living longer.

However often the narrator may deny on principle the spiritual efficacy of faithless action, many of the protagonist's errors have eventual good results. In some cases, the good lies hidden in a single mistake. Faustus the Manichee, the narrator says, "who to many people had been a snare of death, now began, without willing it or knowing it, to unloosen the snare in which I had been caught" (99). And in other cases, the good arises from the temporal sequence of actions. According to the narrator's arguments, he could have embraced the truth revealed in Scripture at any time. In fact, his full understanding of the Scriptures when he did read them was at least facilitated by, if not entirely dependent upon, his earlier reading of the Platonists.

To the extent that eternal truth is made to seem contingent on temporal events, the protagonist appears to proceed gradually toward the truth through the lessons of experience rather than to awaken suddenly from his misleading experience into a full understanding of the truth. The narrator's efforts to maintain the doctrinal distinction between human error and divine truth while he is explaining the eternal design hidden in past error, lead him at times to deny the value of experience and ascribe all saving power to faith, and at other times to make faith seem the fruit of experience. When Alypius surrenders to temptation at the gladiatorial games, the narrator attributes his subsequent rescue entirely to God's "merciful hand," leaving the sin no part to play in Alypius's eventual conversion. But in the very next sentence he says, "Nevertheless, this [experience] was already being stored up in his memory for future healing" (124), suggesting that the sin itself was instrumental in the cure. Similarly, he believes that God let Alypius be falsely arrested in order to teach him an important lesson about the limitations of human judgment, and that from this mistake Alypius "went away a wiser and more experienced man" (126).

Insofar as experience contributes to faithful understanding, of course, faith must follow experience. The narrator recalls that he, Alypius, and Nebridius hated their vain lives and longed for true happiness; ". . . yet still we did not forsake these things, because there was no dawning gleam of a certainty to which we could hold once these things had been forsaken" (127). Although he subsequently blames himself for having refused to turn toward the light that he says was already present, the gleam referred to here seems to be not his own faith but that other light, from God, which is not yet available; for, after condemning his own negligence, he says, "So there we were until you . . . came to our help in secret and wonderful ways" (131). And after describing one of the false opinions he held at that time, he says to God, "However, you had not yet enlightened my darkness" (137).

Here again, the narrator's elucidations of the divine purposes that governed the protagonist's improper acts effectually deny his repeated assertion that sinful experience cannot possibly produce good results. For, if an eternally predestined conversion informs the mistakes that preceded it in time, it also *justifies* those mistakes—not only in the theological sense that it *redeems* them, the way Christ's

23

eternal sacrifice redeemed the sins that men committed before he lived, but also in the psychological sense that it *makes them important*, the way any state of human understanding lends significance after the fact to the unwitting mistakes that contributed to it. Although the narrator portrays his understanding as a form of eternal wisdom gained through faith, then, it often appears to be nothing more than hindsight gained through experience. He calls his mother's dream of his eventual conversion "prophetic" and her dream of his impending marriage "fantastical," not because he can now see in the two visions some essential difference that he should have seen then, but simply because events proved the one right and the other wrong. The more the narrator explains the eternal significance of his past errors, the more he implies that those errors gave rise to his present understanding of God's purposes.

As the protagonist approaches his predestined conversion, the narrator finds it increasingly difficult to draw the distinctions between ignorance and wisdom that were so evident when the protagonist was younger and so much less enlightened than the narrator. Unlike the egregiously faithless actions of his youth, which attested only to his worthlessness, the events that immediately precede conversion appear to move the protagonist closer to the moment of his redemption. Suddenly, he is no longer wandering away from the God who resides at home; he is a pilgrim, following the way to God, a wanderer with God as his guide. Even when the narrator resumes his condemnatory attitude toward the protagonist's faithless and therefore fruitless wanderings, his metaphors betray an unaccustomed indecision about the ultimate value of actions which were followed so closely by the great moment of conversion. "What tortuous ways these were," he says, "and how hopeless was the plight of my foolhardy soul which hoped

to have something better if it went away from you." But
here immediately follows the suggestion that God was di-
recting his sinful wanderings toward the point of his redemption: ". . . you set our feet in your way and speak
kindly to us and say: 'Run and I will hold you and I will
bring you through and there also I will hold you' " (134).
Little wonder that, having made understanding seem the
result of a development over time rather than a belated
awakening to an ever-present truth, the narrator is led to
look back upon his benighted past and ask, "But where
had this ability been for all those years?" (184).

IV

Such controversions of stated doctrine do not indicate
Augustine's disbelief in the doctrine so much as they betray
a fundamental antipathy between his other-worldly theology and his artistic method. Having elected to arrange the
events of his narrative in chronological order, ending with
conversion, he can hardly help but create the impression
that they are causally linked to the ultimate event in the
series, however much he might have wished to deny this
causality. Furthermore, the events themselves have a powerful attraction, if not for the theologian who hates the
infidelity they represent, then at least for the narrative artist who has taken the pains required to depict them accurately and forcefully. Disparage his sins as he will, they are
his subject. They constitute the life he is striving to depict,
and they make the narrative both necessary and possible.

The narrator obliquely addresses this very problem in
Book VII, when, commenting on the parable of the Prodigal
Son, he asks, "What is it in the soul, then, which makes it
take more delight in the finding or recovery of things it
loves than in the continual possession of them?" (165). The

examples that follow—the general who triumphs after a hard battle, the sailor rescued from a storm, the sick person made well, the pleasure that comes of eating or drinking after great hunger and thirst—all bear out his conclusion: "Everywhere we find that the more pain there is first, the more joy there is after" (166). A conversion that is preceded by a sinful life is more interesting, even more valuable, than uninterrupted grace. The created universe "alternates between deprivation and fulfillment, discord and harmony" (166), and it is this polarity, which has its being in God, that makes life go on. An eternal union with God, prized above all things by the theologian, would deprive the man of his life and the artist of his art. Art is at once the legacy of the Fall and its mitigation; it both testifies to our imperfection and gives us a vision of perfection, lending savor and value to that perfect state which, it seems, would be meaningless, or at least incomprehensible, without sin and suffering.

This theologically questionable, if not downright heretical suggestion, that divine perfection somehow depends upon imperfection, and the implied association between fallen life and art, help to explain the narrator's rather shrill anti-aestheticism in the early books. Recalling his early schooling, he laments the time he wasted studying fiction instead of facts, drama instead of history and philosophy, eloquence instead of truth. He describes the imagination as a kind of wandering and associates its products with the letter that killeth and with human words, which, occurring serially in time, betray our mortal condition. Opposed to the imagination is the memory, which, by making the past present, seems the psychological analogue of divine knowledge, that ever-present reality in which all times exist simultaneously. Thus equated with divine form and with the redeemded soul, the memory is associated with the spirit that giveth life and with the divine Word.

26

Throughout the early books, this emphasis on form and truth at the expense of substance and error evidences Augustine's determination to avoid the enticements of art, imagination, and experience, to hold his ecstatic ground and, by recollecting the events of his past life, to "re-collect" them into their eternal form. By the time he has brought his narrative to the point of conversion, however, and has opened his inquiry into the topics of time and memory, he has already begun to question many of the assumptions on which the narrative and its form rest. In Book XI, he notices that the act of composition has its own time: "I do know that I am saying these things in time, that I have been speaking for a long time and that this 'long time' is only long because of the passage of time" (277–78). And in Book X, he understands that recollection is at least partly a creative act, that memory is less a mirror of the world than a source of something new added to the world: ". . . by the act of thought we are, as it were, collecting together things which the memory did contain, though in a disorganized and scattered way, and by giving them our close attention we are arranging for them to be as it were stored up ready to hand in that same memory where they previously lay hidden, neglected, and dispersed . . ." (221).

The mind that remembers past experience is not immune to present experiences as it remembers. Pursuing a particularly difficult line of inquiry, the narrator says to his mind, "Do not interrupt me, or rather, do not let yourself be interrupted by the thronging of your impressions" (281). The mind, he realizes, is not God-like: "When a man is singing or hearing a song that he knows, his feelings vary and his sense is distracted as the result of his expectations of the words to come and his memory of the words that are past. But nothing of this kind happens to [God], the inimitably eternal creator of minds" (284). Without the advantage of retrospect, the mind loses its resemblance to eternal form, to the spirit that giveth life, and to the divine Word. Instead of arranging words according to the known form of truth, it seeks the truth through fallen words. "In the lowliness of my language," the narrator of part two says, "I confess to your highness" (284). Once a profession of known truth, that confession now takes the form of a question, one that bears heavily upon the assurances which informed the first part of *The Confessions* and would rise to trouble those reflective autobiographers who sought to employ that form in later centuries: "Can we not hold the mind and fix it firm so that it may stand still for a moment and for a moment lay hold upon the splendor of eternity which stands forever . . . ?" (265).

This question lies at the heart of the meditative inquiry in part two, and all other issues—the investigations into the nature of memory and time, the commentary on *Genesis*—are subsidiary to it. It arises from the suggestions in part one that the narrator and his wisdom evolved directly out of the protagonist and his errors, and are therefore still in a state of development and not in that state of repose he equates with grace. The narrator of part one set out to tell how he achieved his present repose through conversion in the past. But in doing so, he became increasingly aware that the memory is not static and purely reflective, but active and creative. Part two, then, must analyze the memory in its relation to time and eternity in order to discover in it some evident connection with the absolute.

As the inquiry proceeds, however, the narrator begins to suspect that the analysis itself is being conducted by a mind in motion—searching, speculating, questioning, imagining—wandering, in short. Because the narrator of part one represented himself as occupying an unmoving position above the wandering protagoinst, he said, "It is not the time now to be asking questions but for making my confession to you" (76). To ask a question would have been to imply that the mind is not at rest in the truth, but actively in search of it. But now that conversion has erased the distinction between the narrator and his subject and he finds himself a pilgrim in a strange land, searching for his true home, questions are his proper mode of discourse. "I am asking questions, Father," he says, "not making statements. My God, govern me and direct me" (270). When the narrator stood outside time and the protagonist stood in it, time and eternity were absolutely opposed entities: the one leading to death, the other to eternal life. But now that the narrator finds himself moving through time in his quest for eternity, he interprets time according to the Platonic theory of emanation, making time a degree of non-being that has emanated from complete being and is continually returning to its source. "It appears that we cannot truly say that time exists," he argues, "except in the sense that it is tending toward [its own] non-existence" (268), which is to say, toward eternity. By following his path in time, he hopes to arrive at eternity and not at death.

Similarly, when the unconverted protagonist was a wanderer in search of creature happiness and worldly wisdom, the curiosity that drove him on was roundly condemned. Not only did it lead him into false paths, it reflected his disbelief in God, for an unholy desire for knowledge implies that if one does not know something it will not be known. But the present inquiry presupposes a desire to discover what is hidden, and this change of value underscores the increasing subjectivity of *The Confessions* in part two. In the first part, the narrator saw the world laid out before him in its eternal, objective form, the way God sees it from above. Now he sees the world only as it unfolds moment by moment in his own inquiring, speculating mind—where it owes its shape, indeed its very being, to the concepts he is able to form about it as he explores its secret, unknown avenues and obscure cul-de-sacs.

Trapped in time, condemned to partial knowledge, driven by his desire for truth, and left with only his lowly language to pursue his investigations, the narrator begins to suspect that what he repeatedly said about the protagonist's wanderings applies equally to his own. Questions do not lead to truth, but only to more questions. Desire leads to more desire, words to more words. Having filled page after page with commentary on the first few verses of the Scriptures, he understands that mortal words can never grasp the eternal truth: "See, Lord my God, how much I have written on these few words! Really, how much! What strength of ours, what length of time would be enough to comment in this way on all your Scriptures!" (314).

His present activity has not been undertaken out of any love for activity itself, but only in order that it may be ended. The purpose of his inquiry is not to fill up pages with words, for words betray his imperfection. The knowledge which is grace requires no words; it is silence. As he says, ". . . the poverty of human understanding shows an exuberance of words, since inquiry has more to say than discovery, asking takes longer than obtaining, and the hand that knocks does more work than the hand that receives" (285). Up to this point, the aim of *The Confessions* has never been to perpetuate itself, but to complete itself—by arriving at its foregone conclusion in part one and by reaching an as yet unachieved but passionately desired end in part two. Time, movement, desire, and words were condemned in part one because they bespoke the protagonist's infidelity, and they are tolerable now only insofar as they promise to bring about their own cessation. Once they show signs of perpetuating themselves indefinitely, however, they lose their value as instruments of knowledge, as the necessary means to an end, and become an end in themselves.

At this point, Augustine is faced with the problem of how to bring about the end he has always desired but has twice failed to achieve, once through recollection and once through inquiry. From the beginning, words have subverted his doctrinal intentions, creating movement where he sought to maintain repose in part one, raising questions where he longed for answers in part two. Unless he can find a way to reconcile his vagrant words with the eternal Word, neither continued utterance nor silence will give him the repose he seeks. If he simply stops talking, he will leave the problem unsolved. And if he goes on talking, he will only complicate it further. Somehow, he must make his words express silence, duration express eternity, imperfection express perfection, desire express fulfillment. With no way to escape his limitations, in sum, he must turn them into virtues.

His solution to his problem amounts to nothing less than a complete disavowal of his original anti-aestheticism and a vindication of those artistic impulses which threatened to subvert the stated doctrines of part one by giving the protagonist's worldly experiences an importance of their own. Having discovered that he can neither fix the mind and hold it fast while remembering the past, nor follow its movement to a point where movement stops, he terminates his inquiry and turns to a third mode of confession: an impassioned avowal of his belief that the truth exists even though he cannot know it and that faith in its existence is tantamount to full knowledge of it. In effect, this protestation of the faith that is knowledge *imagines* the absolute that the memory could not hold and the intellect could not reach. As he expresses his faith in words, singing the song of ecstasy, he experiences poetically something akin to a state of grace. His words are no longer merely signs of depravity, as they were in part one, or the feckless instruments of his search for the ever-elusive truth, as in part two. Spoken words are now the means by which grace is realized, instantaneously, in the present moment. If words were previously necessary only because grace had not yet come, the experience of grace now seems to depend upon their continued utterance. Grace may be everlasting in that eternal realm where time and words do not exist. But in this world, grace endures only as long as it is enacted imaginatively in a form of words. Once the enemy of doctrinal truth, art has become the sole means of realizing the truth that doctrine preaches but does not tell us how to achieve.

V

St. Augustine set the problem for all subsequent autobiography: How can the self know itself? By surveying in the memory its completed past actions from an unmoving point above or beyond them? By moving inquisitively through its own memories and ideas to some conclusion about them? Or by performing a sequence of symbolic actions through which the ineffable self can be realized? For these three methods of self-knowledge, Augustine devised three autobiographical forms—historical self-recollection, philosophical self-exploration, and poetic self-expression—from which every subsequent autobiographer would select the one most appropriate to his own situation. What is more, the sequence of forms in *The Confessions* and the reasons behind its formal modulations from history, to philosophy, to poetry rehearse the entire development of the genre from the Middle Ages to the modern era.

If we will think of autobiography in terms of the problem of self-knowledge that Augustine gave it to solve, in

terms of the historical, philosophical, and poetic forms he
applied to this problem, and in terms of the organic relation
among these three forms in his *Confessions*, we will find it
somewhat easier to follow the genre beyond the point
where it leaves the straight highway of self-history for the
sinuous path of introspection and the thickets of poetry and
fiction in the nineteenth century. Augustine wanted his
Confessions to answer, once and for all, the questions that
must confront anyone who seeks to know the absolute truth
about himself and to portray his life as an example of that
truth. But he did not answer those questions; he passed
them on to all those later autobiographers who were
reflective enough to share his feeling that the self is "a
piece of difficult ground, not to be worked over without
much sweat" (226). Standing well along in the autobiographical tradition that begins with Augustine, Henry
Thoreau managed to capture in a single metaphor the restless spirit of Augustine's *Confessions*, the evolving tradition that leads from the *Confessions* to *The Scarlet Letter*,
and the critical attitude that these materials require us to assume toward them, when he said in *A Week on the Concord
and Merrimack Rivers*, "Every sacred book, successively,
seems to have been accepted in the faith that it was to be
the final resting place of the sojourning soul; but after all, it
is but a caravansary which supplies refreshment to the traveller, and directs him further on his way to Isphahan or
Bagdat."

2

Historical Autobiography

La vita nuova

The purpose of Dante's *La vita nuova*, like that of Augustine's narrative of his conversion, is to reconcile the autobiographer's past life with what he takes to be the absolute truth by showing how the apparently peculiar events of that life actually participated in the eternal plan of reality and how that divine scheme actually informed each event in his individual career. In both works, a narrator who knows the truth retraces the course of his life from a time when he did not know the truth to the moment when he arrived at his present state of enlightenment. As this narrator recounts each biographical event, he explains its place in the total pattern described by previous and subsequent events and, hence, its particular relation to the larger truth which informs that pattern.

Similar as they are in purpose and method, there is yet a significant difference between these two historical autobiographies. Although knowledge of the truth distinguishes narrator from protagonist in both works, that distinction is absolute in part one of *The Confessions* and only relative in *La vita nuova*. Because the truth comes to Augustine in a flash at the moment of conversion, when the sinner dies and a new man is born, it divides his life in two. Accord-

ingly, his protagonist and narrator are two essentially different people, the one adrift in mortal error, the other secure
in eternal truth. For Dante, however, the truth emerges
gradually from a number of experiences scattered through
his life. Instead of pursuing a horizontal course and then
turning abruptly heavenward, his spiritual career follows a
steadily upward path from relative ignorance, through a
series of enlightening experiences, to eventual possession
of the truth. Consequently, his narrator and protagonist are
essentially the same person at different stages of enlightenment, which is to say at different points in time, rather than
two different people, one out of time and the other in it.

These two important revisions of Augustine's historical
form—the relocation of the source of the narrator's knowledge about the protagonist's life from somewhere outside
that life to the life itself, and the concomitant relocation of
the narrator, from a timeless ground above the protagonist's
life to a point further along in the time of that life—have a
number of significant effects upon Dante's narrative as a
whole. In the first place, they incline Dante to regard his
past life far less harshly than Augustine did his youthful
failings. Because Augustine's protagonist, lacking faith, can
do nothing, say nothing, of any spiritual consequence, his
actions are treated with unremitting contempt. Whereas
Augustine's protagonist simply lacks the truth that his narrator possesses, however, Dante's protagonist enacts the
truth that his narrator understands, and these actions lead
directly to the narrator's understanding. Consequently,
while the narrator occasionally laments his earlier carnality
and ignorance, he also feels an understandable affection for
even those follies which contributed their mite to his present fund of wisdom. If Augustine felt obliged to deny that
his recollections were prompted in any way by love for his

past sins, Dante's love for Beatrice and for the actions inspired by her provide the main impetus behind *La vita nuova*.

Dante's attribution of the narrator's knowledge to the protagonist's experiences has the additional effect of giving to the action of his autobiography a share of the emphasis that Augustine had placed almost entirely upon form. Insofar as details of the writer's life provide the action of historical autobiography, while the stipulated truth about that life resides mainly in its form, the task of reconciling the individual life with the truth amounts to reconciling action and form. Because Augustine's false life has value only when contemplated through the form of truth, and even then primarily as an example of error, action and form are reconciled entirely on the ground of form. The action of Dante's life, however, is justified not only by its place in the formal design of truth, but by its being the medium through which that design is manifested. Instead of explaining the truth behind the protagonist's errors, as Augustine's narrator does, thus emphasizing the difference between them, Dante's narrator allows the form of truth to emerge gradually from the protagonist's experiences, merely hinting occasionally at the formal pattern which he can see now but could not see then. In this sense, Dante's narrative method imitates the process of his enlightenment, allowing the form to unfold with the action, exactly as the truth arose from the events of his life.

This displacement of emphasis from the narrator's present knowledge to the process of his awakening also tends to make the narrative more naturalistic, less purely allegorical, than part one of *The Confessions*. While it may seem odd, on the face of it, to call Dante a less allegorical writer than Augustine, it is nonetheless true that Augustine strives continually to deny any ultimate spiritual significance to the temporal, causal connections among the events of his faithless life. Whatever divine meaning any particular event does possess stems entirely from its direct, vertical relation to the absolute truth, not from its place in a horizontal sequence of causes and effects; and that allegorical meaning is supplied entirely by the narrator, who alone is in a position to know it. In *La vita nuova*, on the other hand, the divine meaning of events resides in the pattern described by their temporal, causal sequence—in the actions of the protagonist as well as in the explanations of the narrator. To be sure, the pattern which emerges from this sequence is one of stunning allegorical complexity. The point remains, however, that the alien realms of biographical event and religious truth, which Augustine brought together solely on the ground of transcendent meaning, are united in *La vita nuova* upon a common ground, where the natural is as much at home as the divine, and naturalism can be trusted to unveil its allegorical meaning.

If Dante's redaction of Augustine's historical form has perceptible effects upon the tone, the relation of action to form, and the representative mode of *La vita nuova*, these alterations also raise a number of doctrinal and artistic problems—problems which Augustine devised the form to solve and which Dante must now confront anew. By ascribing his present wisdom to the succession of his past experiences, he seriously complicates the task of deciding which of those experiences to include in the autobiography. Because the only consequence of Augustine's faithless actions is error, he is not obliged to trace out every turning in that temporal path. One event will do as well as another to illustrate the truth that faithless acts are spiritually impotent. For Dante, however, as for any historical autobiographer who makes his present knowledge the effect of causally connected experiences in his past, each event is a link in the chain that binds past to present. Since he cannot possibly include all of his experiences, he must decide which ones are the most important, the most telling, or the most interesting. But since every one is at least theoretically of equal consequence, any selection must appear somewhat arbitrary, a decision based as much upon personal or aesthetic criteria as upon the strict demands of truth.

The ascription of knowledge to past experience rather than to instantaneous revelation makes it similarly difficult for the historical autobiographer to distinguish the truth from whatever his experience has happened to teach him. In part one of *The Confessions*, the truth is portrayed as being primarily transcendent—"beyond" the protagonist, who lacks the faith he needs to participate in it—and immanent only in the sense that the converted narrator can see how the truth accounts even for his previous errors. In *La vita nuova*, on the other hand, the truth is transcendent mainly in that it remains unknown to the protagonist, who has not yet performed all the actions that will eventually reveal it to him, and immanent in the very important sense that his actions are true even though he does not know it. By emphasizing the immanence as well as the transcendence of truth, Dante manages to avoid Augustine's paradox about worthless experience which is yet true. At the same time, however, he offers the even more troublesome suggestion that any experience, however vicious, may be justified if it contributes to what one comes eventually to consider the truth. For the historical autobiographer whose experiences include direct providential revelations, of course, there remains a sure way to distinguish between truth and error; and Dante makes his several dream-visions the principal source of his knowledge. And yet, even among these luxuries of belief the spectre of moral bewilderment is dimly visible. For, the divine messages Dante receives seem as much to depend upon his mundane experience as to enlighten it, remaining cryptic until subsequent experience clarifies their meaning.

Of all the difficulties raised by Dante's alteration of Augustine's historical form, perhaps the most important is that of freeing the autobiography from the limiting conditions of the life it professes to explain. Insofar as historical autobiography seeks to connect the writer's past with his present, to show how he changed from the man he was into the man he now is, the autobiographer must find some way to redeem the time he takes to tell his story. For, unless he can erase that narrative time, it will always lie between his present and past selves, moving the present ahead even as the past races to overtake it. Instead of gathering his past experiences into their true and timeless form, the narrative will enact further experiences in the moving present, experiences which will themselves have to be collected and explained before the person who began the autobiography can be connected with the one who completed it.

Customarily, historical autobiography achieves this necessary effect of timelessness by permitting the protagonist to become the narrator who tells the story of how the protagonist becomes the narrator. By this strategy, the beginning and end of the narrative time-span are joined in an eternally repeating loop. In order for the protagonist to become the narrator, of course, the narrator must stand still as the protagonist moves toward him, whether that movement is instantaneous, as in part one of Augustine's *Confessions*, or gradual, as in *La vita nuova*. For Augustine, the merging of protagonist into narrator creates no problems. He devised the historical form to dramatize his belief that the convert stands out of time. To overtake the converted narrator, therefore, the sinning protagonist need only cease his wanderings and rise on the wings of faith into that timeless state that has always been available to him. But Dante's narrator and protagonist both exist in time. As a result, although the narrator, whose dream-visions and love for Beatrice anchor him to the truth, appears to "wait" for the protagonist to become him, something quite different and quite striking happens at the conclusion of the narrative.

To dramatize his idea of gradual spiritual development, Dante distinguishes sharply between his narrator and protagonist at the beginning of the narrative and then narrows this distance gradually as the story proceeds and the protagonist draws closer to the narrator in age, experience, wisdom, and spiritual health. The narrator speaks "now" of events that occurred "then." Although he lives in time, his soul rests in unmoving reason. Accordingly, he speaks in prose, the exoteric language of understanding. The protagonist, in contrast, is a poet whose esoteric language expresses the restlessness of a heart impelled by desire. Given these distinctions between the two *personae*, the reader justly expects desire to give way to reason, action to understanding, movement to rest, heart to soul, poetry to prose, as the narrative approaches its conclusion. What actually happens, however, is that the two *personae* merge, not on the narrator's fixed ground of rational prose, but in the final sonnet, on the protagonist's moving ground of impulsive poetry. Instead of the protagonist's becoming the narrator who tells the story of *La vita nuova*, the narrator becomes the protagonist, the man who will go on to write *The Divine Comedy*. At that moment, the autobiography ceases to be a re-collection of events from the completed past into a timeless design, a prelude to itself, and becomes an event in the ongoing present, a regathering of the poet's spiritual resources in preparation for the writing of his masterpiece.

Surprising as it is when it happens, this transformation

of narrator into protagonist appears upon reflection to have been nearly inevitable from the beginning. Although the narrator repeatedly suggests that prose and reason are better than poetry and desire, the stable and moving faculties are not really in conflict. Reason is not an alternative to desire, it is the perfection of desire. The protagonist does not come to reason by abandoning desire, but rather by pursuing his desires along the upward path lined out by Beatrice's return to heaven. In fact, he becomes most rational when he ceases to equate desire with mortal life and begins to desire the death that will reunite him with Beatrice. What is more, to the extent that the narrator's comprehension arises from the protagonist's acts and so depends upon them, prose understanding appears less important, ultimately, than poetic desire. The narrator may understand the import of the protagonist's desires, but understanding will not lead him to Beatrice, who still exists beyond him at the close of the narrative. Only the continued movement of pure desire can negotiate that passage.

By the same token, prose may elucidate the divine meanings hidden in secular poems, but the spiritual puissance of the poems does not depend upon the narrator's interpretations of them. On the contrary, the reconciliation of time and eternity, which Augustine effected through his narrator's understanding that temporal things are eternally true, is accomplished in *La vita nuova* by the protagonist's poems alone. Poetry contains within itself both impelling desire and steady truth, the former in its material content, the latter in its spiritual form of music and figure. The sonnets on the death of the beautiful lady spring from carnal motives, but they also contain a divine truth, for they not only foreshadow Beatrice's death, they can also be applied to that temporally distant yet eternally present event. And while the narrator explains in prose this poetic truth, the truth does not depend upon either his understanding or his explanation of it. Indeed, because the truth is ultimately a mystery, there are elements that the understanding cannot grasp, and although the narrator once said that he would never employ a poetic figure that he could not translate into prose, as the narrative approaches its conclusion he becomes increasingly reluctant to diminish the magic of the poems by paraphrasing them.

Having attributed the narrator's understanding to the protagonist's impelling desires, prosaic comprehension to poetic action, throughout the narrative, Dante can hardly relinquish at its conclusion the virtues which have proved so beneficial. Although the narrator understands the meaning of the protagonist's actions, the value of those actions does not depend upon the narrator's understanding of them. Set in motion by his desires and guided aright by the object of those desires, the protagonist was both on his way to the truth and in possession of the truth long before he ever realized it. Prose adds nothing of any ultimate consequence to poetry. Poetry is itself both the key to treasure and the treasure, the way to Beatrice and Beatrice realized. Understanding and prose, therefore, have value not as the goal of action but as a stage in a process that must continue, a regrouping of forces preparatory to further action. The autobiography, similarly, has value not as a final account of the life but as a prosaic gathering of poetic resources from the past in preparation for an even more important, entirely poetic movement into the future.

Dante's extension of value from the narrator to the protagonist, from the truth that art illustrates to the art that reveals the truth, from the formal design that precedes and governs action to the energetic action that generates form, reflects that growing faith in the value of individual human action which is generally taken to characterize the spirit of the Renaissance and to distinguish it from the temper of the Middle Ages. More specifically, Dante's interpretation of Augustine's historical form reflects his own particular situation. Whereas Augustine's protagonist is sunk in sin, the younger Dante has already entered upon his new life by the time *La vita nuova* opens. While this attention to spiritual growth after conversion may be taken as still further evidence of the Renaissance interest in virtuous human action, the comparative spiritual health of Beatrice's lover also accounts for the value that Dante places upon his experiences. Then, too, Dante was first of all a poet, albeit one with strong theological interests, rather than a theologian with artistic leanings, and so we are not altogether surprised to discover in his poems a cognitive and spiritual power far beyond that given to doctrine or even to the sacraments by his autobiography.

But, however one chooses to account for shift in emphasis that makes *La vita nuova* so different from the first nine books of Augustine's *Confessions*, the point remains that Dante's work marks an important stage in an artistic and ideological development that would make the historical form more and more problematical for reflective autobiographers in the centuries to come. Augustine had grounded that form upon his belief in the ability of the divinely instructed memory to stand still and lend the changeful past the enduring form of truth. Although Dante's narrator cannot himself occupy the fixed point of truth, the center of the circle, he has yet an access to that still point through Beatrice and his dream-visions. And, as Augustine could stand upon the eternal center to see the temporal circumference of time move about him, the moving arc of Dante's life reveals the center which both directs and is implicit in that movement. In both cases, the historical form has depended upon the writer's unquestioned faith in the accessibility of the truth. It remains to be seen what problems the form presented to those later autobiographers who abandoned not only Augustine's doctrine of the new man but also Dante's belief in Providential revelation and sought to derive the narrator's knowledge from human experience alone.

Grace Abounding . . .

When *Grace Abounding* is read alongside part one of Augustine's *Confessions* and *La vita nuova*, its most salient features appear as exacerbations of the formal differences between those two earlier historical autobiographies —continuing the drift, so noticeable in Dante's narrative, away from Augustine's emphasis upon the static design of known truth, toward a concentration upon the dynamic process of experience through which the truth becomes known. Discernible in every aspect of Bunyan's autobiography, this shift of narrative gravity is most strikingly evident in the frequency of his mystical experiences. The truth reveals itself directly to the protagonist only once in *The Confessions*, at the instant of conversion that separates the old life from the new; five times in *La vita nuova*, through the dreams that punctuate Dante's new life with Beatrice; and ten times in *Grace Abounding*, in a series of visions that begins far back in Bunyan's sinful youth and continues throughout his long search for redemption.

Although the number itself is not significant (as it was in *La vita nuova*) the multiplication of divine messages has the effect of flattening the curve of that upward path along which the protagonist climbs from ignorance and sin toward the narrator's gracious wisdom, making his upward movement seem a gradual inclination rather than an instantaneous elevation or a flight of clearly demarcated stairs. Distributed as they are over the entire course of his life, furthermore, these ecstatic moments necessarily occur in series with the protagonist's more mundane experiences. And since his natural actions often seem to trigger his revelations as well as to derive instruction from them, all of his experiences, worldly and divine, go together to form a temporal sequence of largely undifferentiated and equally consequential moments leading to grace. Most important of all, because his first vision occurs in his sinful youth, apparently as a result of his sinfulness, the spiritual significance that Augustine and Dante restricted to their new lives after conversion is extended to Bunyan's earliest and most unregenerate actions. If the temporal and eternal realms are sharply divided in *The Confessions* by Augustine's instantaneous conversion, and are symbolically merged in *La vita nuova* only after Dante has given himself to Beatrice and only in those temporal actions which are redeemed by her eternal spirit, the worlds of sin and grace, of error and truth, are inextricably intertwined in *Grace Abounding*. No event is utterly devoid of truth; none is denied its effect upon the protagonist's uneven but inexorable progress toward redemption.

Like Augustine and Dante, Bunyan repeatedly insists that the true meaning, the reality, of his life is eternal; that its apparent duration and causal sequence are only the secondary effects of God's prime motion. Where this doctrine is formally demonstrated in the presiding authority of Augustine's narrator, however, and in the symbolic pattern that emerges from the action of *La vita nuova*, it is merely asserted in *Grace Abounding*. Apart from these explicit reminders, the dominant impression created by Bunyan's narrative is that of an almost purely naturalistic world, one in which events derive their significance more from their relation to each other than from their direct, individual relation to some transcendent reality. Although the protagonist's difficult passage from sin to grace is seen in retrospect to have occurred in three distinct phases—conviction of his sinfulness, faith in Christ's power and willingness to save him, and union with God—this three-stage pattern is offered so late in the narrative that it seems more an afterthought than a preconceived design, and so offhandedly that it seems far less important to the narrator than the specific experiences it purports to explain. What is more, when viewed in retrospect, each stage in this ostensibly timeless pattern is seen to be a necessary precondition of the one that follows. Until the protagonist acknowledges the extent of his wickedness, he feels no need for Christ's help. But once he realizes that he is really unsavable, extraordinary faith becomes both necessary and possible. This faith, in turn, enables him to understand the power and the method—the sense—of redemption in Christ, and that understanding locates his soul, his true self, at God's right hand.

Then, too, each of these necessarily sequential stages comprises a number of still shorter but equally determinative steps. The conviction of sinfulness that will precipitate his faith in Christ, for example, arises from a long train of causally related experiences. His reading of the books in his wife's library leads him to join the church, where he learns the meaning of guilt from a sermon and conceives the plan to align his life with Scripture. That plan leads him to leave off cursing, which causes him to feel a false pride in his outwardly good behavior as he measures his improvement against the settled wickedness of a former companion. But it also prompts him to take up the Bible on his own, which enables him to apprehend the difference between ordinary and extraordinary faith, to face the question of his own faith, to realize that faith is necessary for true understanding, and finally to understand that he is utterly un-

worthy of redemption. The entire course of the protagonist's conversion breaks down into so many constituent
parts, in fact, that, as often as Bunyan may attach especial
importance to God's providential intervention in the natural course of his life, his mystical experiences seem no more
consequential than his early vices or his lucky meeting with
two converted women. Arranged in this causal sequence,
all experiences partake equally in his ultimate deliverance.

By assigning some portion of responsibility for redemption to every event in his past, rather than simply to one
extraordinary experience, as Augustine did, or to certain especially hallowed occasions, as Dante did, Bunyan lends to
his protagonist's sinful life an emphasis that Dante would
have considered unpoetic and Augustine would have found
downright impious. Because Augustine's sinful life contains no truth within itself, his narrative moves almost entirely in the redeemed present, abstracting from the past
only those occasional details that will serve to illustrate the
eternal truth. Since *La vita nuova* begins with Dante's conversion, he can recite verbatim the early poems which express the spiritually immature but still regenerate condition
of his past life. But even here, interest in the past extends
only to those carefully selected moments which contribute
to the eternal pattern that is Dante's ultimate concern. In
Grace Abounding, however, the narrative attention falls almost entirely upon the past, that succession of moments in
which eternity is presumed to inhere. With this shift of emphasis from the truth that life illustrates to the life that
embodies the truth, from memory's abiding form to its ever-
changing content, the theological suavity of Augustine's
Confessions and the symbolic ingenuity of *La vita nuova*
give way to Bunyan's novelistic density and bustle. The
complete rendition of the autobiographer's life, which
consisted for Augustine in a complete statement of the truth

about that life, has come to require a complete record of events from the life.

Bunyan's concentration upon the details of his past life reflects the Dissenter's belief that the truth resides primarily in the religious life, rather than in some formulated theology, and is therefore a matter of individual experience and personal conviction, rather than the property of some external authority to which the individual must conform. The doctrines that explain Augustine's life lay outside that life and outside *The Confessions*, in a theological system which the life and the autobiography merely exemplified; and Dante based the informing pattern of *La vita nuova* upon the established symbology of the Christian sacraments. Insofar as Bunyan comes to the truth by severing himself from the established church, however, and since his highly idiosyncratic readings of Scripture seem to be experiences in their own right rather than doctrinally authorized interpretations of his experience, the truth about his life is available only in the record of that life, in *Grace Abounding*. If *The Confessions* and *La vita nuova* may be called "why do it" books, in that they seek to excite the reader's desire for truths that are available elsewhere—in the Scriptures or in the Church—*Grace Abounding* is a "how to do it" book, providing in its history of a unique life not only some persuasive reasons for the reader to convert but a model of conversion that ostensibly exists nowhere else—a record of gropings, wrong-doings, and backslidings that Bunyan had to stumble through on his way to grace but that the reader, armed with Bunyan's hard-earned knowledge, can learn to avoid. In effect, Bunyan portrays his life as a source, not merely an example, of truth, as if he were the first man ever to be saved, the discoverer of some hitherto unvisited land whose existence he did not even suspect until he stumbled upon it and whose location is recorded nowhere except in the narrative of his own vagrant but ultimately successful expedition.

Bunyan's identification of the truth with his own peculiar experiences comes very close to erasing altogether that dividing-line between the autobiography and the life it recounts which had been so clear to Augustine and had become somewhat less distinct with Dante's suggestion, in his closing chapter, that *La vita nuova* occupies an important place in his still developing poetic career. Augustine's first nine books are the record of a completed spiritual transformation. *La vita nuova* recounts an important phase of a spiritual development that is still in process. But with Bunyan's statement that "it is profitable for Christians to be often calling to mind the very beginnings of grace with their souls," autobiography ceases to be a formal comprehension of completed past actions and becomes, itself, a present action with its own consequences for the writer's future spiritual condition and eventual salvation. Since salvation constitutes Bunyan's greatest good, the recollection of his sins, so hateful to Augustine, is as pleasurable to him as the recollection of the redeemed life was to Dante. To the extent that Bunyan's spiritual progress depends upon his recollections, however, the autobiographical act is far more important to him than it was to either Augustine or Dante. As an instrument of redemption, *Grace Abounding* takes upon itself a very large share of that responsibility for the writer's spiritual well-being and attendant wisdom which Augustine gave entirely to God and Dante gave primarily to Beatrice.

Bunyan's inclusion of the writing of his autobiography among the more important events in the life it depicts marks the point in the development of the genre where historical form modulates into philosophical form—the point Augustine had reached, centuries earlier, upon discovering that the act of recollection is subject to the same temporal conditions that governed the events being recollected. From the beginning, historical autobiography had depended upon, or at least reflected, a number of assumptions about men's place in the world, about the way men apprehend the truth, and about human character, all of which had come into question during the two intellectually tumultuous centuries that preceded *Grace Abounding*. With the rapid proliferation of possibilities for individual action that attended such literally earthshaking events as the Protestant Reformation, the discovery of the New World, and the scientific revolution, that medieval other-worldliness and spiritual quietism which are reflected in Augustine's devotion to truth's eternal form, had given way everywhere to that more secular, more adventurous spirit which underlies Bunyan's obvious affection for truth's temporal manifestation in human activity. This revolutionary period had also seen the epistemological primacy that Augustine gave to divine revelation move gradually toward the dialectical process of observation and reflection that is dramatized in Bunyan's portrait of a mind arriving at its own conclusions through its own experiences. And in consequence of these changes in the climate of opinion, that typological view of human behavior which, regarding each individual life as simply one more example of God's eternal plan for salvation, had persuaded Augustine to sketch his life in a few broad, representative strokes, was replaced by those ideas of individual uniqueness and psychological complexity which reveal themselves in Bunyan's painstaking record of his most commonplace experiences.

In giving more attention to the excitements of the soul's worldly pilgrimage than to its heavenly destination, more importance to personal religious experience than to the doctrines which authorize that experience, and at least as much significance to the details of an individual life as to the universal truths which presumably govern that life, *Grace Abounding* appears to have abandoned the assumptions that make historical autobiography possible. Still, the harmonies of enabling belief remain clearly audible behind the realistic clatter of Bunyan's narrative. Like many of his contemporaries, Bunyan could afford to indulge his taste for secular event, individual peculiarity, and temporal processes simply because the divine superstructure that had given shape to the Christian life ever since the Middle Ages remained largely intact in the late seventeenth century, at least to the eyes of simple faith. The ordering theological system upon which Augustine had to insist because he was busily erecting it, Bunyan tended to take for granted because it had stood for a thousand years and so might be trusted to stand for a thousand more without the sort of theological maintenance that many Dissenters considered the unnecessary, even impious, tinkering of wool-gathering schoolmen. Secure in the largely personal conviction that this eternal structure undergirds every temporal event, Bunyan might concentrate his efforts upon the content of his life and let its form take care of itself. And yet, this conviction that the truth informs whatever happens lies uncomfortably close to the suspicion that whatever happens is the truth. Untended by believers like Bunyan and besieged by a growing army of skeptics in the century ahead, the structure of belief upon which all previous historical autobiographers had formed their recollections fell into disrepair, leaving Benjamin Franklin with the task of replacing it with an edifice built from his recollections alone.

The Autobiography of Benjamin Franklin

Bunyan's presentation of his life as a primary source of his reader's knowledge about the divine truths which inform that life lends an unprecedented importance to the public, didactic function of historical autobiography. While the form had always served an exoteric as well as an esoteric purpose, its social effects had usually been a by-product of its primarily devotional office. By justifying their own lives in the light of absolute truth, Augustine and Dante established their membership in a community of persons whose lives were justified in the same truth. What these historical autobiographers take to be the truth thus constitutes both the ground of their own true being and the basis of true consanguinity. Augustine's attainment of true being, which he located in God, out of time, automatically removes him from the false society of worldly persons and initiates him into the true community of the faithful. Dante's discovery that his true being resides at once in the spiritual Beatrice and in the carnal desire he feels for her makes him one both with her and with those who love her as he does. In both cases, membership in the true community depends upon and arises from the autobiographer's attainment of true being, which remains the primary concern of his narrative.

As the locus of true being shifts from Augustine's predominantly transcendent order to the immanent pattern described by Bunyan's temporal life, however, and individual experience becomes increasingly necessary to a knowledge of the truth, the devotional aims of historical autobiography become less important than the public purpose of conveying the lessons of individual experience to men who might not otherwise know them. We note that Augustine addresses his narrative primarily to God, the ground of his true being, while men are allowed to overhear this devotional colloquy. But, since Beatrice is a personal acquaintance of Dante's as well as an avatar of divine love, Dante addresses *La vita nuova* both to her and to an audience of men, who will learn to know and love her only through the experiences recounted in his narrative. And since Bunyan's own experiences are the principal medium through which the absolute truth makes itself known in the world, God overhears the narrative that is addressed primarily to Bunyan's parishioners.

With Franklin's *Autobiography*, the locus of true being has come to reside entirely in the temporal world of individual and collective history. Whereas the life-span surveyed in part one of Augustine's *Confessions* begins in God, before birth, and ends in God, after conversion; and Dante's life begins when he meets Beatrice and will end when he rejoins her in heaven; and Bunyan's life begins with the earliest workings of grace upon him and will end with his heavenly salvation; Franklin's life begins in the historical past, with his ancestry, and extends into the future, toward that posterity whom Franklin addresses in the name of his "son." What is more, Franklin's idea of true being, the life of Reason, is itself the product of history rather than its eternal, governing law. Not only does Reason manifest itself solely in Franklin's temporal experience, without the aid of any immediate revelations, but as a state of mind it does not seem to exist prior to his becoming a reasonable man.

Although the attainment of Reason appears to justify all the unreasonable actions that preceded it, conferring a semblance of value and purpose upon events that seemed largely fortuitous when they happened, and although Reason persuades Franklin that it is the true goal of human history, it does not appear to confer upon Franklin either a sense of true being or membership in the true community. The problem appears to be that, having arisen out of his own life, Reason will remain peculiar to his experience and will not become universal until all men have become reasonable. Whereas Augustine, Dante, and Bunyan became members of the true society upon achieving true being, Franklin's achievement of true being depends upon the creation of a reasonable society in which he can become a member. And insofar as Reason is the product of his peculiar experience, the creation of that community will depend upon his readers' imitating his life. Consequently, the *Autobiography* is addressed entirely to his fellow men, and especially to posterity, whom he enjoins to follow his example and so construct that perfect condition which his success has persuaded him to consider the truth. The aim of the *Autobiography*, therefore, is not so much to explain how his life is justified by some universal principle as to justify his life by persuading others to make its conclusions universal. If Augustine's *Confessions* offer an example of the truths revealed in Scripture, and *La vita nuova* offers a poetic analogue of Scripture, and *Grace Abounding* offers a source of divine truth that is as reliable as Scripture, Franklin's *Autobiography* offers itself as a Scripture, the only one available to an audience that had overthrown all forms of traditional authority and replaced them with the authority of personal conviction. By imitating his success, men can fulfill his prophecy and bring about the rule of human Reason, that earthly heaven in which Franklin will have his immortality.

Franklin's attempts to bring about through a historical autobiography the kind of universal order upon which the form had traditionally depended raises certain difficulties that none of his predecessors had been required to face. Augustine, Dante, and Bunyan had employed the form to dramatize their belief that an eternal truth guided their lives from the beginning and that this truth had revealed itself directly to them at one or more points in their spiritual progress. But since Reason does not exist, to all intents and purposes, until one attains it, it cannot reveal itself to the unreasonable Franklin the way faith reveals itself to the faithless Augustine, or divine love reveals itself to the carnal Dante, or grace reveals itself to the sinful Bunyan. As a result, Franklin finds it impossible to explain how he happened to arrive at Reason rather than somewhere else. At times he attributes his success to "foresight," the ability to see one's true destiny ahead in time and thus to avoid those "errata" which cause him to lose sight of his proper goal. At other times, however, he ascribes this success to the quite different faculty of "hindsight," the ability to learn from his mistakes, which in this case seem to have fostered rather than impeded his progress. Betraying a similar indecision about the value of experience, he assigns credit for his present reasonableness sometimes to "character"—an innate configuration of the soul, akin to innocence, which will eventually become manifest if he can preserve it from the taint of experience—and sometimes to experience itself, which molds character into an eventual shape that did not precede experience. This fundamental question of historical autobiography remains unsettled throughout the narrative as Franklin vacillates between the notion that his life operated under the direction of Providence or a Guardian Angel—agents of a prevenient design—and the contradictory idea that his success is purely the undesigned result of luck or chance.

Franklin's inability to account for the happy issue of his life undermines all his efforts to represent the conclusions of his experience as being universally true and hence applicable to every life, rather than peculiar to his own case. Depending as they do upon his own experience, the truths he wishes to convey are virtually impossible to separate from the individual life that generated them. Because Augustine's temporal experience had no direct bearing whatsoever upon the eternal truth, he could have explained that

55

truth without ever mentioning his own life. By making his love for Beatrice an allegory of the soul's relation to Christ, Dante could describe his own progress toward the truth without suggesting that men could be saved only by loving Beatrice. And, although Bunyan's truth reveals itself primarily through his apparently unique experiences, his several visions indicate that this truth exists independent of that experience and so remains the same for all believers. But Franklin's idea of Reason remains so closely tied to his particular experiences that he can neither make his success seem generally attainable without de-emphasizing the uniqueness of his life nor do justice to that unusually fortunate life without making its truth seem relevant to that life alone.

On the one hand, his didactic purpose prompts him to explain how the unreasonable, idiosyncratic youth became a reasonable, exemplary adult by overcoming the selfishness that alienates him for society and by aligning his self-interest with the larger, public interest. On the other hand, Franklin's evident feeling that this wayward boy was father to the successful man, coupled with his expressed desire to relive in the autobiography the life that has turned out so well, makes the highly particularized boy a far more memorable, more completely realized figure than the rather bland and featureless adult he becomes as he sheds his distinctive, alienating traits. At the same time, the reader cannot help but feel that the supposedly peculiar boy, compelling though he is as a fictional character, is really a quite typical figure, a prodigal son, and that the ostensibly representative adult is in fact a highly unusual and inimitable man. Had the *Autobiography* been true to Franklin's remarkable career, we feel, it would have failed in its attempt to set an example for posterity. But, in pursuing that aim, it had to suppress both the facts of the life and Franklin's own nonetheless evident pride in his unusual accomplishments.

Although Franklin's avowedly secular, historical, and social biases have led many critics to call his the first truly modern autobiography, and although countless autobiographers have imitated his model in the last two hundred years, it is really something of an anachronism, a holdover from a vanished age when enlightened people believed in the kind of world that makes historical autobiography possible. As a necessarily foredoomed attempt to employ that form without its enabling beliefs, it marks the end rather than the beginning of an era in the long evolution of autobiographical form. Historical autobiography had undergone significant changes over the centuries since Augustine wrote his narrative of conversion, and these changes all reflect an ideological development that leads straight to Franklin's reliance upon the cognitive and creative power of individual experience. Instead of devising an autobiographical form that would honor that faith in the individual and accurately represent a world in which the individual life arrives at its own conclusions, however, Franklin tried to avoid the problems implicit in the doctrine of self-reliance by writing a historical autobiography in which the lessons of individual experience assume the role traditionally taken by revealed, eternal truth.

Augustine depicted the individual life as an allegory of eternal truths which do not require temporal experience to reveal them. Dante portrayed that life as both emblematic of eternal truth and instrumental in the truth's becoming known, and Bunyan presented it as necessary to a realization of a truth which is nonetheless eternal. Since Franklin clearly regards the individual life as the only source of a truth which may become universal in time, he might be expected to portray that life at least as realistically as Bunyan did, as a series of events consequential in themselves. Instead, Franklin represents it as an allegory of Reason, even though Reason is the temporal product and not the guiding principle of that life. Similarly, Augustine conferred moral authority entirely upon his narrator, who knows the truth; Dante distributed that authority evenly between the narrator who understands the truth and the protagonist who enacts it unwittingly; and Bunyan reposed authority mainly in his protagonist, whose experiences gradually reveal what the narrator knows. In Franklin's case, this authority rightfully belongs to his protagonist, whose experiences create a truth that does not seem to precede them. But Franklin places it almost entirely in his narrator, allowing that persona to preside autobiographically over a life in which he could not have played a part.

In the matter of biographical detail, Augustine selected only a few events from his life, since for him every experience bore the same negative relation to God's self-sufficient truth. Although an equally small number of biographical details are reported in *La vita nuova*, Dante chose them both for their hidden symbolic relation to the eternal truth and also because they contributed to his eventual understanding of that truth. And the myriad details that fill *Grace Abounding* were selected entirely on the basis of their contribution to Bunyan's eventual understanding of the truth that guided his life all along. Since Franklin attributes his attainment of Reason entirely to the fortunate sequence of his own experiences, we might justly expect him to report those experiences in great detail, with comparatively little attempt at selection. Instead, he relates only those events from his past which can be interpreted —valued or condemned—in the light of Reason, as if that truth had been in force at the time those events took place. In sum, since Augustine had placed the emphasis of his *Confessions* entirely upon its doctrinal form, which precedes and governs its artistic action; and Dante had placed equal emphasis upon the theologically symbolic form of *La vita nuova* and the poetic action in which that form unfolds; and Bunyan had placed his emphasis primarily upon the novelistic action that adduces the doctrinal form of *Grace Abounding*; Franklin should have emphasized almost entirely the narrative action upon which the didactic form of his *Autobiography* seems to depend. Instead, he concentrates primarily upon its explanatory form, in an apparent effort to imitate artistically the assurances once conferred by the very doctrines he has repudiated.

In one important respect, Franklin's *Autobiography* does continue the line of development that runs from Augustine through Dante and Bunyan. Starting with the *Confessions*, historical autobiography had displayed an ever-increasing tension between the narrator's statements about the truth and the implications of the life that supposedly illustrates those statements. Although Augustine says repeatedly that faithless experience contributes nothing to redemption, the chronological ordering of those experiences and the narrator's explanation of the eternal truths that underlie the protagonist's errors tend to contradict this doctrinal argument, making some of the protagonist's most faithless acts seem both necessary and valuable to his conversion. Dante's narrator insists that prosaic understanding is better than poetic action, but poetry alone has the power both to reconcile the eternal and temporal realms and to move Dante toward his desired reunion with Beatrice. And although Bunyan often insists that union with God is the rightful purpose and sole justification of life, his sinful separation from God receives most of his attention, and his connection with his parishioners remains his prime concern.

In Franklin's *Autobiography* this conflict between statement and action has become extreme. Franklin's repudiation of all revealed truth in the name of self-reliance bound him to accept the conclusions of personal experience, whatever these might be. And yet, his apparent fear that without some universal principle to direct it toward a common goal experience might lead each individual to a different truth and society as a whole to anarchy, persuaded him to treat his own life as the source and model of a principle which could become universal if every man would only relinquish his own individuality and follow Franklin's example. Determined to present his life as generally imitable, he had to deny the very individualism upon which his lesson rests, suppressing the accomplishments which had made his own life so remarkable, so satisfactory, and so potentially interesting as a subject for autobiography. At the same time, however, his desire to relive in the autobiography the unique and highly atypical success of that life caused him—no less than the reader, apparently—to lose interest in the autobiography at the point where the reprehensible oddities of youth must give way to the exemplary conformity of adulthood.

Historical autobiography was invented to demonstrate the consonance of an individual life with an absolute, eternal law already in force and known through some immediate source outside the life that illustrates it. Fashioned to these purposes, the form could neither make the conclusions of an individual life seem universally applicable without misrepresenting the individual life, nor represent that life accurately without compromising the universality of its conclusions. Having decided to do without those cognitive instruments by which historical autobiographers had learned the truth that explained their lives, and left with only their own experiences as a source of knowledge about the meaning and purpose of their lives, modern autobiographers would have to devise a form more appropriate to their vision of reality and to their unprecedented needs, one that could acknowledge both the authority and the inescapable consequences, the delights and dangers, of the truly original life.

3

Philosophical Autobiography

The Confessions of Jean-Jacques Rousseau

Rousseau's *Confessions* bring to its logical conclusion the development of historical autobiography lined out in the preceding chapter. The life portrayed is now altogether unique, and significant precisely to the extent that it is unique. "I am like no one in the whole world," Rousseau says. "I may be no better, but at least I am different." Typifying nothing but itself, his life is the sum of his own peculiar experiences and can be rendered only in terms of those experiences. Insofar as the life purports to represent no universal principles about life in general, furthermore, its pattern consists primarily in the causal relations among its own events. Instead of turning on a single ecstatic point, as did Augustine's typically Christian life, or rising through a number of more or less clearly demarcated representative stages, as did the lives of Dante, Bunyan, and even Franklin, Rousseau's life proceeds horizontally from one remembered event to the next. Since all events participate equally in the formation of his life, all have equal value, and none can be omitted if the self-portrait is to be complete. Accordingly, the life portrayed is now almost completely naturalistic, its destiny completely secular. Addressed exclusively to Rousseau's "fellow men," the *Confessions* aim to secure for their author a place of honor in history. Moreover, the truth—the ground of the autobiographer's true being and the basis of his kinship with others—is now totally subjective. For Rousseau, the conviction of self and the test of truth consists in "feeling," an intangible which lacks not only the external support that the beliefs of Augustine, Dante, and Bunyan received from Scripture, but even the dubious verification that Franklin's idea of Reason received from the *consensus gentium.*

As far as Rousseau has moved away from those assumptions of personal typicality, spiritual reality, and objective truth which formed the original foundations of historical autobiography, he nevertheless maintains Augustine's essential belief in an absolute self or soul which transcends his experience. Although his experience provides the only available evidence for this unitary soul, and thus constitutes his only route of access to it, he remains convinced that he is ultimately something more than a collection of experiences, the product of his own isolated actions and reactions. We note, for example, that while his self-history begins, as Franklin's does, with an account of his forebears, Rousseau locates his true origin in what he calls "Nature"—that absolute, noumenal reality which occupies the place of God in the Enlightenment cosmos and manifests itself in whatever material or psychological phenomena (mountains, feelings) may be supposed to have escaped the corrupting touch of unnatural human society, or "culture." Impelled in one direction by his historical intention to trace through the succession of his experiences the evolution of his socially unique character, and in an exactly opposite direction by his philosophical desire to discover in the same experiences evidence of his transcendent "Natural" soul, Rousseau produces that mixture of candor and disingenuousness, of confident assertion and bewilderment, of sage serenity and jejune agitation that readers of

63

the *Confessions* have always found so maddening and fascinating at once.

Motivated initially by the conviction of his own complete individuality, Rousseau sets out to write a historical autobiography, to explain how he came to be the man he is by reviewing, in the light of his present situation, the train of events which led him to that situation. Rousseau's method here closely resembles Franklin's secularization of the historical form, interpreting the life solely in relation to its temporal outcome rather than in relation to some timeless, over-arching form of truth. Unlike Franklin, however, whose acknowledged success justified retroactively the actions, good and bad, that led up to it, Rousseau is a social pariah and a political exile. Consequently, although a review of his past life may explain how he came to be such a miserable scapegrace, it will not automatically reconcile him with the society upon whose good opinion his fame, his immortality depends. To justify himself in his reader's eyes, he must argue that his present troubles are due to circumstances beyond his own control and that his reputation does not accurately reflect his true character.

Rousseau therefore proposes to reveal the true self that lies hidden behind his often disgraceful behavior and thus to correct the misapprehensions of those who know him only from the outside—by reputation or through the slanderous reports of his enemies. In one sense, this intention differs markedly from Franklin's. Equating his reputation with the truth about himself, Franklin sought to align himself with society by portraying his life as an example of publicly acknowledged values. Rousseau, on the other hand, means to correct his reputation by persuading society to abandon its characteristic hard-heartedness and sympathize with him. In an equally important sense, of course, Rousseau's desire to remake society in his own image does not differ fundamentally from Franklin's hope of persuading society to imitate his own rise to success and Reason. It simply makes explicit the radical individualism that Franklin's acceptance by his public had enabled him to disguise as a lesson in social conformity. The point remains, however, that whereas Franklin could portray his experiences as having generated the true self which is also the basis for his good reputation, Rousseau must describe the experiences that produced his bad reputation as having somehow obscured his true, essentially worthy, self.

To prosecute this combined *apologia* and social indictment, Rousseau adopts the argument that the complete, true, and innocent soul he received from Nature at birth has been repeatedly violated and gradually dissipated by his confrontations with unnatural, unfeeling society. In effect, this interpretation of the life turns the historical form upside down. Instead of reviewing the process by which he came into possession of true being, Rousseau reviews the process through which his originally true being has been scattered among the times and places of his progressively unhappy life. His experiences, in other words, have taught him that experience is the enemy of truth and happiness. While this disparaging view of experience links Rousseau more closely to Augustine, who also distinguished sharply between the truth and the lessons of experience, than to Dante, Bunyan, and Franklin, who saw no necessary conflict between the truth and the experiences that revealed it to them, Rousseau stands apart from all his predecessors, including Augustine, in drawing a clear line between the truth and his narrator's acquired knowledge. In all those earlier works, the narrator stands simultaneously in true being and in a knowledge of it, whether that knowledge has come from revelation entirely, from experience alone, or from some combination of the two. In Rousseau's

Confessions, the narrator's knowledge comes entirely from the experiences that have perverted, destroyed, or at least obscured his true being. Consequently, his review of the experiences that taught him what he knows recapitulates the loss of his happiness, making the customarily happy task of historical recollection an occasion for mingled rancor and self pity.

As Rousseau reviews his long initiation into his present bitter knowledge, however, he finds that the recollection of the happier past does give him present pleasure by allowing him to return in imagination to the times when his original self was still intact. Indeed, the pleasures of remembrance are greater than those he felt at the time, when, unaware that his happiness would not last, he failed to appreciate it fully. Coupled with the pain of moving on to increasingly unhappy periods of his life and with the obligation he feels to omit nothing from his account, the pleasure he takes in revisiting the past makes him want to prolong the narrative indefinitely. Here again, Rousseau parts company with his predecessors. Whereas Augustine, Dante, Bunyan, and Franklin, having achieved complete being, tended to move briskly through the times of their incompleteness to the better times that lay ahead, and to linger over past events only to the extent that they participated in the present good, Rousseau proceeds reluctantly, unwilling to retravel the path that terminates in his present hateful condition, and goes ahead only because each successive remembrance generates some pleasure.

This conflict between Rousseau's wish to prolong his visit to the past and the necessity of moving ahead has a curious effect upon the structure of his narrative. Since each step forward in the protagonist's life removes him farther from the natal springs of his soul, each particularly memorable event seems to the narrator the point at which his original happiness ended and his present unhappiness began. At the same time, because any stage on the road to the narrator's unhappiness is necessarily happier than those to come, the supposed turning point in the protagonist's career keeps reappearing as the narrator brings his history closer to the present. No less than fifteen events in the protagonist's life, beginning with his birth and ending with his imprudent letter to de Choiseul, are designated the prime cause of the narrator's wretchedness. And in each case, the events that follow the supposed crisis prove far less unhappy than the narrator predicted upon announcing it. In effect, the narrative center moves continually, rearranging the pattern of the protagonist's life in order to prolong that pleasure of remembrance which has become the narrator's primary motive for rehearsing the loss of his happiness.

With the discovery that the feelings evoked by his memories rejoin him to his lost self and establish a ground upon which the reader can sympathize with him, while his review of the road he has traveled continually threatens to return him to his present unhappy isolation, the original public, historical aim of *The Confessions*, to explain the present by reflecting on past actions, gives way to a more personal, philosophical effort to recover the past by means of a present action. Denied access to the absolute through religious channels, he cannot attain true being by rising out of time, as Augustine did. And having located his true being in the past, rather than in the future, he cannot attain it by moving ahead, as Dante, Bunyan, and Franklin could. Nor, without some way to escape the temporal condition in which he is trapped, can he return to the past where his innocence lies buried. However, he does retain a link with his past self in the stream of feeling which issues from the pure fountains of his Natural being and runs beneath the broken terrain of his successive experiences. These feelings constitute the absolute, Natural ground of his conditional, social existence. Their succession constitues the life of his soul, gathering into a coherent, continuous whole the otherwise disconnected events of his hapless life. By re-experiencing in imagination the enthusiasms, hopes, ambitions, and pleasures of his youth, he can tap that undercurrent of feeling which binds together the near and distant ends of his temporal pilgrimage away from Nature and the truth.

Regarded as the noumenal reality behind the phenomenal circumstances of existence, feelings can be apprehended only through the medium of the conditional circumstances which evoke them and in which they manifest themselves. They cannot be contemplated directly. In order to recapture in the present the feelings which informed the past, therefore, the narrator must re-live the protagonist's life rather than simply reflect upon it from his present point of view. Although reflection is an appropriate and necessary instrument of self-knowledge, self-realization requires spontaneous expression—not mnemonic reflection but imaginative action. As a form of judgment, which, Rousseau says, is necessarily disinterested and passionless, reflective self-knowledge is susceptible to error. Self-realization, on the other hand, is divine. It causes the world to vanish, translating the time-bound consciousness, through feeling, onto an ecstatic plane of self-possession.

The problem is that this appetite for movement, the irresistible impulse to act, has been Rousseau's evil genius throughout his life, driving him relentlessly away from his original home in Nature and from every subsequent resting place along the route of his restless journey toward exile and homelessness. As a young man, he thought his true destiny awaited him in the future, down the avenue of experience projected by his ambitions for fame, success, and power. But now, having traveled that road to its inconclusive conclusion, he sees that his true being actually lay in his original innocence and that his search for happiness has led him into the country of death. Consequently, what he then saw as a series of opportunities for self-fulfillment, he now sees as a series of missed opportunities to retire from activity, to stop moving and take up the domestic life of contented resignation and circumscribed ambition.

Destructive and pointless as all his past wanderings have been, Rousseau finds that in order to realize himself in feeling he must become a traveler on an autobiographical journey. And since emotion, like all motion, takes time, it necessarily conveys him still farther from his original home in Nature, extending into the future the very path which has brought him to his present grief and which he has been so reluctant to retrace. Depending upon movement to evoke the feelings that verify his unconditioned soul, Rousseau can neither stop writing without losing contact with his true being nor go on without lengthening the train of actions that lie between him and his inexorably receding home.

This simultaneous inclination and disinclination to move leads Rousseau to de-emphasize the horizontal, temporal drift of his necessary movement and to emphasize the immediate, vertical relation of each isolated experience to the transcendent spirit of Nature through feeling. This quasi-allegorical rendition of experience closely resembles the method of Augustine's narrative of conversion, where historical events are treated primarily as emblems of an absolute truth beyond themselves rather than as links in a spiritually consequential chain of events. The difference is that Rousseau is attempting to recover through movement the still point of self-possession that Augustine attained by ceasing all movement. In this respect, Rousseau's method resembles even more closely that of parts two and three of Augustine's *Confessions*. Just as Augustine's meditations seek complete being through *faithful* action, Rousseau seeks it through *passionate* action. And yet there is a difference here, too. Because the subject of Augustine's meditations is the meditations themselves, his movement occurs entirely in the present, seeking a future goal in part two and an ever-present goal in part three. But Rousseau is still bound by his original historical intention to review the movement of his past life. The impassioned, youthful actions whose remembrance evokes present feelings of self are the very ones that have brought him to his present state of selflessness. While the moving events he remembers and the moving remembrance of them seem to lift him out of time, both movements also have temporal consequences. Sensation, he realizes, is at once the cause of those feelings which make the world vanish and a bond that ties him closer to the world. Experience is both the source of his virtue and its enemy, manifesting his otherwise ineffable, true nature and dissipating it in the process. As passion has been both the life and death of his soul, his autobiography cloaks his soul in the act of stripping it bare.

Rousseau's *Confessions* portray a consciousness trapped in time and dependent upon temporal action for its fleeting apprehensions of the absolute. Lacking an achieved self upon which to stand and see all past times laid out before it in a timeless design, the mind must move unceasingly among its memories of conditioned experience in search of their absolute ground. In this situation, biographical review, the method of historical autobiography, no longer serves its purpose of displaying the pattern which is described by past events and which assigns to each event its place and consequent meaning. With every movement of the self-seeking consciousness, the overall pattern, and hence the relative value of each event, changes. The value that historical autobiographers assigned to events on the basis of their place in the overall pattern of the life, Rousseau measures primarily by how much feeling a remembered event can elicit. And once feeling constitutes the primary standard of value, the truest autobiographical statements are those which bear the heaviest emotional freight, rather than those which conform to some generally accepted notion of historical accuracy, doctrinal orthodoxy, or public morality.

At this point, the distinction between fact and fiction, between autobiographical recollection and autobiographical invention, begins to blur. Not even lies or self-contradictions are untrue as long as they generate those ecstatic feelings which are the ground of true being and of sympathetic consanguinity. By the same token, a perfectly accurate recollection or an unexceptionable reflection which evokes no feeling, no conviction of self, can only exacerbate the autobiographer's estrangement from the truth and erect another barrier of individual peculiarity between him and his potentially sympathetic reader. Rousseau says that he became self-conscious upon learning to read, that his character was formed by what he read, and that his nature has found its proper theatre of action in writing and imagining fictions. Conversely, among the experiences in which his original being has deposited portions of itself over the years, the most important are his fictions, which, being still available in their original form, do not require the mediation of unstable memory but rather provide immediate access to the lost self that went into them. In very much the same sense that these fictions are autobiographical, *The Confessions* are fictional, resting their truthfulness less upon the accuracies of its depicted events or the acceptability of its judgments than upon the feelings it calls forth and expresses—the self that is realized through them, is preserved for posterity in them, and cannot be abstracted

from them. Rousseau's autobiography does not so much refer to the life he lived elsewhere as record the life he lived
in the act of composing it—the only life he could count on
to overcome time and achieve the immortality he sought.

Having begun his autobiography with the idea of telling
the truth about himself, Rousseau came to regard the book
as a way of finding out that truth and then as a way of living
truthfully, imaginatively, in the flickering light of that ineffable bliss which he had always considered his true destiny
but from which time and experience had exiled him. Although *The Confessions* retain the biographical content of
historical autobiography, and although Rousseau attempts
sporadically to maintain a stable perspective on the moving
past, his belief that his past experiences have divorced him
from true being and his conviction that passionate, imaginative action is truer than calm, rational judgment deny the
fundamental premises of the historical form and foreshadow the eventual abandonment of both biographical
data and a comprehending narrator by autobiographers in
the poetic mode. Rousseau's shift, in mid-passage, from historical explanation to philosophical inquiry is itself fore-
shadowed, far back, in the movement from part one to part
two of Augustine's *Confessions*. And like that movement,
Rousseau's points far ahead, to those modern writers who
turned from life to find themselves in autobiography.

The Prelude

Franklin and Rousseau may be thought of as standing at
a point where the evolutionary line described by Augustinian autobiography divides in two, one branch maintaining
the direction set by Franklin's secular redaction of Augustine's historical form, the other striking off with Rousseau in
the formal direction of Augustine's meditations and final
prayer, toward what Carlyle would call "philosophico-

poetic" autobiography. For those autobiographers who followed Franklin, the historical form would continue to explain the relation of an individual life to the shared beliefs of its stipulated audience, selecting events from the writer's own past life and arranging them in retrospect into a narrative pattern which simultaneously illustrates the writer's opinions and shows how he came to hold them. For those who followed Rousseau, however, autobiography was to serve a very different purpose. Instead of defining themselves exoterically, in relation to the consensual values of their audience—seeking complete being, as it were, through consanguinity—these philosophico-poetic autobiographers would pursue the opposite course and attempt to discover within themselves an absolute, spiritual ground for the erection of a true society—a "fixed point of sound humanity" as Wordsworth calls it.* Speaking more and more in those esoteric, fictive metaphors that Hawthorne called "the talk of secluded man with his own mind and heart," rather than in "the style of a man of society," Rousseau's followers would shun the foregone conclusions of retrospectively selected and arranged self-biography to prospect for the self through the organic formulations of philosophic inquiry and poetic expression.

Rousseau set out in his *Confessions* to explain himself and came in time to realize that he had lost the only self capable of explanation. Wordsworth began where Rousseau left off: beached alongside the Natural stream that flows in a vital tide from infinitude to infinitude, stranded somewhere between his original and ultimate home, and, unable either to rest where he is or to regain his proper course, "Unprofitably travelling toward the grave" (I, 267) in Augustine's country of death. Having been carried from home

* *The Prelude* (1850), ed. Carlos Baker (New York, 1954), VIII, 455. Subsequent references to this edition appear in parentheses in the text.

by the Natural flow of energy, passion, and ambition that governed his youth, and then deposited on this listless shore, he perceives a deep fissure between his past and present selves: the thoughtlessly active boy and the torpidly reflective man. In this intolerable situation, he considers it profitable to recall Nature's earliest dealings with him, to move ahead, as Bunyan did, by going back over the path he has traveled as a "sojourner on earth" (VI, 49). If he can return in memory to "fetch / Invigorating thoughts from former years" (I, 620–21), when Nature was still present to him, and then imaginatively re-create his life without allowing that energy to flag along the way, he can propel himself autobiographically through his present state of self-division to self-knowledge and the mature accomplishments, both spiritual and poetic, which depend upon that knowledge and for which he feels himself divinely ordained.

The Prelude is thus philosophical from the outset. Like the meditative Augustine of Books X through XII of the *Confessions*, Wordsworth forgoes explanation to "make rigorous inquisition" through himself (I, 147) in search of some ultimate wisdom, a universal truth that can inform the long philosophical poem to which his autobiography is a necessary prelude. No more able than Augustine was to "hold the mind and fix it firm" upon eternity, he, too, seeks to conquer time through time, to "rescue from decay the old / By timely interference" (I, 116–17), to ripen "dawn into steady morning" (I, 127). Like Augustine's meditations, Wordsworth's autobiography aims not to report what the writer's life has done but to do something the life has not done: convey him through inquisitive action to self-knowledge. Accordingly, Wordsworth employs Augustine's prospective method, allowing one subject to dictate the next, moving naturally from recollection to reflection to affective reaction to spontaneous expostulation and on to the next recollection, finding his way by going there. And, as in Augustine's case, the sole object of this autobiographical action is the attainment of rest, that union of the knower and the known which makes further movement unnecessary.

For Wordsworth, this reposeful condition amounts to a reconciliation of the vitally extravagant youth he once was with the torpidly restless adult he now is, a union of his passionate and reflective selves in a state of vital rest. Stated this way, Wordsworth's task is nothing less than to solve the implicit but unacknowledged problem of all those historical autobiographies that, departing from Augustine's model, had placed the narrator farther along the time-line of the protagonist's life rather than on a fixed point above it: how may the knowing and acting selves, dispersed in time, be brought together? Unable, and in any case disinclined, to swim back up the stream of history to Augustine's divinely revealed, eternal ground, Franklin and Rousseau had tried, in their separate ways, to reconcile these two *personae* on their own temporal ground: Franklin by turning the impulsive protagonist into the reasonable narrator, Rousseau by turning the reasonable narrator into the impulsive protagonist. But neither Franklin's Reason—being a product, rather than the governing form, of experience and hence merely a stage of ongoing experience—nor Rousseau's feeling—which is generated by experience and is itself a motion—will provide that ecstatic condition of ultimate self-possession and knowledge which Augustine had made the goal of autobiography. Moreover, in order to subordinate the protagonist to the narrator, Franklin had to deny the uniqueness of his own life; while Rousseau, in sinking the narrator in the protagonist, had to deny the representativeness of his. Neither strategy, in sum, could fulfill the aims of Augustinian autobiography: the reconciliation of protagonist and narrator, of unique experience and comprehensive knowledge, of true being and true consanguinity, of temporal action and eternal form.

Only a vantage-point like Augustine's could meet those strenuous demands, and the various avenues to that privileged eminence were all closed off. In this respect, Wordsworth's autobiographical problem is also the Romantic problem of knowledge. Augustine, Dante, and Bunyan had all derived self-knowledge, in some degree, from a prior, revealed knowledge of universal truths. Franklin and Rousseau had to take exactly the opposite course and derive universal truths from self-knowledge, elevating individual Reason and individual feeling to the status of eternal principles. For them and for Wordsworth, as for every other heir of the Enlightenment, all knowledge had to begin with individual experience. But, where the Enlightenment regarded experience primarily as a source of information to be accumulated, analyzed, and arranged until it finally produced a comprehensive picture of reality, the Romantics considered this presumptuous erection of data a tower of Babel, destined to produce only confusion. The quantity of data multiplied faster than the reason could gather and arrange it. Each new discovery seemed not only to reveal the existence of hitherto unsuspected worlds of fact but to discredit the very concepts that had led to the discovery. With each effort to exhaust its content and to encompass it rationally, reality seemed to expand and change its shape, necessitating a correlative shift in the point from which it could be comprehended.

In order to acknowledge this perception of an ever-expanding, ever-changing reality without either succumbing to utter relativism or withdrawing into some fancied realm of "medieval" or "oriental" absolutism, the

Romantics sought to locate the *center* of reality—the point where all things have their true, eternal being, where nothing is lost and everything can be truly known—in a place that was at once sufficiently mobile to keep pace with the changing shape of reality and sufficiently stabile to provide some assurance that a principle of continuity and purpose underlies all change. Augustine had located this point in the unmoving God who is the source and rectifying form of all movement. Dante identified it with Beatrice, who sits in the center with eternal Love even as she moves on the justified circumference of temporal desire. Bunyan placed the center in Christ, who sits at God's right hand and moves the sinner's heart toward redemption. Franklin located it Reason, which changing experience reveals to be the unchanging pattern of individual and collective history. And Rousseau had located it in Nature, the universal principle that manifests itself in the sub-rational stream of individual feeling. In every case, the center had anchored change to permanence, but in each successive case the abiding center of mutability had shifted farther along the radius that Augustine drew between God and the human heart, until that center came to rest deep within dark cavern of the individual psyche. Located there, it could be presumed to radiate, and hence to concentrate, whatever experiences might swirl about it, but it could be approached only through that unceasing swirl. For Rousseau, eternal Nature is indistinguishable from the temporal flow of his own passions.

These conditions—the need to locate the fixed personal center that lends pattern and value to unstable reality, and the necessity of approaching that center through one's own moving experiences—stipulate autobiography as the prime instrument of Romantic knowledge, and movement as its method. After considering several possible topics for his poem, Wordsworth settles upon that of his own youth and upbringing. The subject recommends itself on several counts. It tacitly acknowledges his present uncertainty about those permanent truths which a grander topic would require, and it offers an avenue to that internal point where such truths reside. That is, autobiography is not simply an alternative to a work "Of ampler and more varied argument / Where," he says, "I might be discomfited and lost" (II, 644–45). It is a means—the only one available—of fixing "the wavering balance" of his mind (I, 622) upon the enduring truths that underlie his experience and, hence, of occupying the eternal point from which an ampler argument may be conducted. Since he stands presently in doubt, furthermore, he must move to wisdom, and autobiography—"a theme / Single and of determined bounds" (I, 640–41)—identifies his proper direction. To sit at home with the truth may be the greatest bliss, but that state is "vouchsafed, / Alas! to few in this untoward world." For those who find themselves adrift in doubt, happiness comes only from "wandering . . . step by step . . . to wisdom" (XIII, 120–33). "The road lies plain before" him (I, 640), and he must become a traveler among the days of his youth, "A Traveller . . . / Whose only tale is of himself" (V, 198–99).

Since movement is unavoidable, Wordsworth must be sure to choose a mode of conveyance that, like Augustine's faithful action and Rousseau's feeling action, is consonant with the truth it aims to apprehend. For Wordsworth, as for all the Romantics, the cognitive vehicle most capable of carrying the questing soul to truth is poetry. In his mind, poetry is associated with both divinity and the knowledge of it. The poetic imagination is a higher power, creative, Godlike, equivalent to moral power and divinity. It speaks in a "living voice" that tells us "what is truth (VI, 112–14).

It reveals "our being's heart and home" in infinitude, and it puts the soul in possession of that blessed estate (VI, 592–616). Perfect poetry is also associated with true being. Just as our "immortal spirit grows / Like harmony in music" through the natural experiences which are the cause and adequate symbol of that growth, the soul may grow through the correlative objects of words to a state in which its "discordant elements" cohere in poetic harmony (I, 340–44). If the youthful self is passionate and the adult self is reflective, true poetry spans these poles; and when the soul is in possession of itself, "poetic numbers" come "to clothe in priestly robe / A renovated spirit" (I, 51–53).

Poetry is also akin to Nature. Those who have been conversant with "living nature" in their youth receive

> Knowledge and increase of enduring joy
> From the great Nature that exists in works
> Of mighty Poets.   [VII, 587, 593–95]

Accordingly, Wordsworth hopes that his poem,

> Proceeding from a source of untaught things,
> Creative and enduring, may become
> A power like one of Nature's.   [XIII, 310–12]

And since true being consists in the adjustment of self to Nature, whose "sister horns" are emotion and calmness, and whose gifts are the energy one needs to seek truth and the stillness of mind one needs to receive it, poetry is the divinely regulated action through which the discordant soul may achieve Natural harmony. By imitating the inscrutable workmanship of Nature, the poem can both move, as it must, and also achieve a final form of truth that will justify, redeem, its necessary movement.

The cognitive aim of *The Prelude* and its attendant method of inquiry are based on a set of closely related assumptions, which need to be made clear. First of all, Wordsworth assumes that although life is a temporal process, this "earthly progress" (II, 233) takes place within a larger, enduring frame of things called Nature, which precedes and directs his life and can be discerned through his life. Second, just as the justification for the processes of Nature and of life lies in their unchanging forms, the ultimate justification for the poetic process that imitates those of Nature and life resides in its end, that final form which, like theirs, is "marked out by Heaven" (II, 753). Third, since the point toward which poetry and life move when they are Natural is eternally designated, it exists apart from, unconditioned by, the processes that embody and reveal it. Consequently, once discovered, it can become a basis of future conduct, an authority for ampler argument in future poems. And finally, because the truth toward which all Natural process tends is divinely appointed, it will be reassuring, consoling, redemptive, harmonious, healing, and joyful, like Nature itself.

While Wordsworth sets his autobiography the task of discovering the true form of his life by projecting an unbroken line from its Natural beginning, through the cultural experiences that now divide past from present, and on ahead to reveal his divinely appointed destination, his assumption that the origin, course, and destination of this poetic movement will be Natural blocks his passage through the very experiences that have caused his problem in the first place. Determined from the outset to trace the flow of Nature's stream from his youth to the present, he tends to treat sympathetically those youthful foibles which seen Natural and to disparage or dismiss as insignificant those which seem in retrospect to foreshadow his present state of cultural exile. Unlike "the vulgar works of man," Nature's works are "enduring" (I, 408–09), and the soul that seeks immortality must shun the former to intertwine itself with the latter. Natural things nurture the "creative sensibility" (II, 360); cultural scenes thwart it. Just as true poetry is Natural, Natural subjects come fully formed for poetry, while cultural subjects are anti-poetic and must be smoothed by art. Because cultural things are equally worthless, any one will serve to represent the rest. But each Natural thing has a particular value as a cause and symbol of some stage in the soul's growth in grace.

Because the poetic that is Wordsworth's self-correcting instrument of inquiry, and the idea of true being that is the stipulated end of the inquiry, are both modeled on Nature, which is also the scene and condition of his boyhood, the poem cannot negotiate the necessary passage through that cultural barrier which divides the vital past from the torpid present. As long as the protagonist moves among Natural scenes, propelled and guided by the healing, elevating power of Nature, the poem moves purposively, melodiously, and can be allowed to take its own way. But when the young man leaves home, for Cambridge, London, or France, sensation assaults and stuns his powers of reflection. The purposive, eloquent flow of the poetic stream loses itself in marshlands, breaks up in rapids, or whirls like a maelstrom, and Wordsworth must direct its course back into the easier terrain of his past, or linger in some more placid bye-canal outside the mainstream, or rise, "as if on wings" to a level of generalization above the turbulence of anti-poetic details. "Loth to quit / Those recollected hours that have the charm / Of visionary things" (I, 630–32), his song attempts to move naturally through the cultural barrier, to see "the parts / As parts but with a feeling of the whole" (VII, 735–36), diffusing

> Through meagre lines and colors, and the press
> Of self-destroying, transitory things,
> Composure and ennobling Harmony.   [VII, 769–71]

Often, when the recusant details of agitated social life refuse to take a poetic shape, he tries ruralizing them. Although Cambridge puts the imagination to sleep, it is a "garden of great intellects" (III, 267). The events of the French Revolution overtax his powers of poetic assimilation, but when he was young the fife of war was "A blackbird's whistle in a budding grove" (VI, 760). And, while "There is no end" to the catalogue of lying sights and sounds of London, he regards them all summarily, as he would "daisies swarming through the fields of June" (VII, 583, 593). This tactic will not serve, however. Although Nature sustains him in the "City's turbulent world" (VII, 71), it will not carry him through, for society lacks the "substantial centre" by which Nature controls the thoughts it incites to motion (VIII, 430–32). Consequently, when the agitated cultural scene threatens to overwhelm him, he must break off and return to his rural solitude.

There, instead of ruralizing culture, he looks for rural counterparts of the problems that beset him in society. Still searching for that unbroken line that will lead him from "Love of Nature" to "Love of Man," he describes three situations in which the boundary between Nature and culture is somewhat indistinct: a social gathering of country folk at a fair, an alliance between Nature and Art in Gehol's gardens, and a mixture of Arcadian ideality and tragic reality in the life of an English shepherd. In all three cases, however, the brief sojourn in the middle-ground between Nature and culture leads him back to Nature rather than ahead in the direction his autobiography means to take. The people at the fair he treats very condescendingly, loving them mainly because they are powerless to change the direction of history. Gehol's gardens simply remind him how much he prefers the primitive Nature of his boyhood, and the shepherd's "vice and folly, wretchedness and fear" fail to sustain his imaginative interest (VIII, 291–92).

No better prepared and even less inclined now than previously to deal with anti-poetic society, Wordsworth sets out again to tackle the problem of London—to treat seriously, he says, the subject he only toyed with before. But he no sooner takes the matter up than he drops it. The narrator knows that London, not Nature, is the "Fount of my country's destiny" (VIII, 593) and hence his own. He knows that he must make sense of his life at Cambridge and that England's declaration of war upon France has opened a gulf between past and present that must be bridged. Nostalgic though he is, furthermore, he knows that the Natural vitality and passion for which he longs is the very energy that drove him out of Nature, attracted him to London, and set him up for disappointment by fostering revolutionary sympathies in him. At those crucial points where the poem seems most determined to pick out the thread that runs through his life, the narrator can even suggest that the experiences themselves, and not their transcendent Natural form, are "the ties / That bind the perishable hours of life / Each to the other" (VII, 461–63), and that the shapes which experiences lend to the soul are fatal, ineluctable. Still, whenever thronging sensation begins to produce fragmented catalogues instead of the harmonious verse that reconciles emotion with steady thought, he must cry, "Enough" (VII, 219), stop his serial rendition of the protagonist's experiences, and insist that his Naturally formed soul somehow managed to resist the imprint of social vice and folly.

Wordsworth's unwillingness, on the one hand, to abandon the youthful poetic soul that is his only source of virtue, and his inability, on the other hand, to convey that virtue intact through the dismembering experiences of his middle period send him back again and again to recover in imagination that youthful condition, which comes increasingly to seem not simply the vital counterpart to his present contemplativeness but something complete in itself, not an early stage in the evolution of his present self but a blessed state of innocent wholeness prior to, and separate from, the train of altering experiences that have led him to his present fallen estate. Much as he may desire to linger in that lost time, however, his chosen poetic method will not let him. Like Nature and the evolving soul, the poem is a stream whose feeding source is the creative imagination. "With intricate delay," it can turn and return,

> Even as a river—partly (it might seem)
> Yielding to old remembrances, and swayed
> In part by fear to shape a way direct,
> That would engulph him soon in the ravenous sea—
> Turns, and will measure back his course, far back,
> Seeking the very regions which he crossed
> In his first outset. [IX, 1–8]

But even though it turns back, each turn occurs farther downstream, closer to the "ravenous sea." With each turn, it becomes a different river, and with each return the revisited regions assume a different guise.

"Like one who rows, / Proud of his skill, to reach a chosen point / With an unswerving line" (I, 367–69), Wordsworth has attempted to regulate his forward movement by keeping his eye fixed upon a receding landmark behind him. In moving ahead, however, he has lost sight of his navigational point upon "The horizon's utmost boundary" (I, 371), and in turning back to relocate it, he has wandered from his true course and lost track of his chosen destination. After a great deal of such meandering, he finds himself in an uncertain place, unable to retrace the course that brought him here or to go ahead with any hope of reaching his original goal. To this difficult autobiographical problem, Wordsworth alternately offers and withdraws a number of mutually incompatible solutions. His life has a principle of continuity, a form and a purpose, he suggests, but it cannot be known. "We see but darkly / Even when we look behind us" (III, 482–83), and who can say that the most regrettable experiences have had no beneficial effects? Nature's movement in the soul "lies far hidden from the reach of words" (III, 188), and even forgotten experience "still works, though hidden from all search / Among the depths of time" (V, 196–97). In one such despairing moment, he calls a "written paper" that a blind beggar wears "to explain / His story, whence he came, and who he was," an "apt type / . . . of the utmost we can know, / Both of ourselves and of the universe" (VII, 641–46).

Since the object of the poem is healing self-knowledge, however, the narrator tends more often to deny the difficulties of knowing himself than to doubt the possibility of doing so. Having failed several times in Book Eight to discover some common, Natural ground beneath his rural and urban experiences, he simultaneously acknowledges the waywardness of his procedure and dismisses the very problems that his wandering reflect:

> Nor shall we not be tending towards that point
> Of sound humanity to which our Tale
> Leads, though by sinuous ways, if here I show
> How Fancy, in a season when she wove
> Those slender cords, to guide the unconscious Boy
> For the Man's sake, could feed at Nature's call
> Some pensive musings which might well beseem
> Maturer years.   [VII, 451–58]

The recollection that follows, moreover, images the separation of man and boy, rather than their spiritual identity, for it depicts the dying man standing at the unknown close of his "mortal course" and looking back across a dark valley, which "Is no where touched by one memorial gleam," to the "dear mountain-tops where first he rose" (VII, 469–75). This telling image is itself dismissed with the words, "Enough of humble arguments" (VII, 476), and there follows a quick recapitulation of the poet's life prior to his removal to London: his innocent boyhood, his departure from home, his time at Cambridge. Here again, the narrator interrupts his account, which seems to be making no more progress than heretofore, and simply asserts that, while "It might be told" how his Natural upbringing conducted him to truth, showed him what is good, and taught him to "love / The end of life, and everything we know," there is no need to "speak of things common to all" (VIII, 518–29). Little wonder that the renewed poetic assault on London which follows this inadequate preparation succeeds no better than his previous attempts. After another hundred lines fail to turn up something Natural in the City, he simply drops the matter, first with an assertion that London, like Nature, revealed to him "the unity of man, / One spirit over ignorance and vice / Predominant in good and evil hearts" (VIII, 668–70), and then with a suggestion that, far from having taught him anything, life in the City merely failed to overpower the soul he brought full-formed from Nature.

When the narrator is not suggesting that the problem is insoluble or that there is no problem to be solved, he is apt to profess that there was indeed a problem but that he has solved it. Instead of standing imaginatively on the youthful side of the gulf that divides past from present and trying to project the poem across it, the narrator takes up a retrospective station on the near side, as if he has in fact managed to traverse the dark vale, and explains how he did it. Although troubles have detained the poem, he says in the opening lines of Book Twelve, "Not with these began / Our song, and not with these our song must end" (XII, 7–8). Once again, he reviews his fall from Nature into the thralldom of "the bodily eye" (VIII, 128). But this time he assumes the posture, not of the groping protagonist who could find no sign of Nature in the cultural maelstrom, but of an all-seeing narrator who knows, as the converted Augustine did, that "We of our own accord fell" from our originally blessed estate and that "our home, which is [God's] eternity, does not fall down when we are away from it." "O Soul of Nature," Wordsworth's narrator says, "how feeble have I been / When thou wert in thy strength!" (XII, 93, 105–06). He could, he insists, "gladly" explain how Nature thwarted the tyranny of sense (XII, 131), but he finds it enough to say that "the degradation . . . was transient."

> I shook the habit off
> Entirely and for ever, and again
> In Nature's presence stood, as now I stand,
> A sensitive being, a *creative* soul. [XII, 194, 200, 204–07]

Having jumped, as it were, to the conclusion he could not arrive at by way of his poetic movement, he must deny that his autobiography was meant initially to discover something yet unfound and represent it as a "history . . . brought / To its appointed close," the point "(our guiding object from the first)" where his "knowledge" is sufficient, he says, "to make me capable / Of building up a Work that shall endure" (XIV, 302–11). The feeling remains that "much hath been omitted" (XIV, 312), that in following "this intricate and difficult path," he has failed to explain either how a soul formed from Natural experience managed to resist the malformations of cultural experience or, if it did not, how those cultural experiences fostered instead of thwarting his creative soul. Indeed, if his original object was to reconcile the passionate and reflective halves of himself, he admits that the goal has not been attained, for the mind, he says, "Learns from such timely exercise to keep / In wholesome separation the two natures, / The one that feels, the other that observes" (XIV, 344–47). Furthermore, even as he nears what he calls "the termination of my course," he cannot rest entirely content with his conclusion. In the "distraction and intense desire" of his original mood, he "said unto the life which I had lived, Where art thou?" And he now catches a note of reproach in the imagined response of his reader. To quiet this accusing voice, he again maintains that he has in fact arrived at a comprehensive view of his life:

> Anon I rose
> As if on wings, and saw beneath me stretched
> Vast prospect of the world which I had been
> And was.

Precisely what he sees from this ecstatic coign of vantage, we are not told—only that the poem, like the life, is "All gratulant, if rightly understood" (XIV, 379–87).

Different as they are, each of these proffered responses to the problem—that there is no solution, that there is no problem, that the problem has been solved—arises from Wordsworth's original assumption that the ultimate justification of both his life and his poem depends upon their achieving some final, comprehensible form, "a frame of things" akin to Nature, "Which, mid revolution in the hopes / And fears of men, doth still remain unchanged" (XIV, 451–52). There is suggested at various moments in *The Prelude*, however, a solution to the autobiographical problem which does not require prospective action to culminate in static comprehension and which thus reveals the inherent tendency of philosophical self-inquiry (already evident in Augustine's and Rousseau's confessions) to turn away from its stated goal of historical self-comprehension toward poetic self-realization. That solution is to find within the autobiographical action itself, rather than in its ultimate form, isolated, epiphanic moments when the temporally dispersed elements of passion and reflection, of movement and fixity, of protagonist and narrator, are reconciled in symbolic equipoise. Wordsworth offers, or rather considers, this rather surprising solution quite late in the poem. "There are in our existence," he says in Book Twelve,

> spots of time,
> That with distinct pre-eminence retain
> A renovating virtue, whence . . . our minds
> Are nourished and invisibly repaired.
> [XII, 208–15]

Although these "spots of time" occur amidst the concerted temporal flow of Nature, life, evolving soul, and poetic action, they exist apart from prior and next things, with a radiance and wholeness of their own. Although they are cast up by the narrative movement of action and reflection, their value lies almost entirely in themselves, in their delicate lyric adjustment of sensation and thought, experience and meaning, rather than in their contribution to the overall form of the poem. In these isolated, purely poetic instants, Wordsworth manages to glimpse and preserve that beatific state of true being that his narrative has been seeking all along.

It would be a mistake, however, to see these isolated lyric moments themselves as having been his "object from the first." Once they have been defined, to be sure, they can be found scattered throughout the earlier Books—passages in which "all / The terrors, pains, and early miseries, / Regrets, vexations, lassitudes interfused / Within my mind," as the narrator says, "have borne . . . / . . . a needful part in making up / the calm existence that is mine when I / Am worthy of myself!" (I, 344–50); moments when

> such a holy calm
> Would overspread my soul, that bodily eyes
> Were utterly forgotten, and what I saw
> Appeared like something in myself, a dream
> A prospect in the mind.   [II, 348–52]

But these earlier passages were set down to exemplify the protagonist's original kinship with Nature and thus to lay a solid foundation for the evolution of his soul to complete being in the present. It is only now, when the narrative movement shows no sign of reaching its divinely appointed end, that they begin to seem ends in themselves—limited, purely aesthetic mitigations of the temporal condition that philosophical inquiry has failed to overcome. Satisfying as these lyric spots of time may be to the twentieth-century reader, who has learned to expect from poetry something less than absolute knowledge, they clearly did not provide for Wordsworth a conclusion in which he could rest content. For he never stops insisting, in the face of all contrary evidence and of his own persistent doubts, that the narrative has in fact achieved its justifying form, its divinely appointed close, and that

> from its progress we have drawn
> Faith in life endless, the sustaining thought
> Of human Being, Eternity, and God. [XIV, 204–06]

To say that *The Prelude* fails to do autobiographically what Wordsworth wanted it to do and what he maintains it has done, is not to say, by any means, that it fails as a poem. The passages which re-enact the boy's Natural experience provide ample evidence that the man has indeed managed to retain or recover the poetic powers he attributes, rightly or wrongly, to the circumstances of his rearing. The point is that Wordsworth could fully realize those powers only by re-experiencing imaginatively the situations to which he ascribed them. He sought to fetch invigorating thoughts from the recollection of his early life, not for their own sake, but to run them poetically through his entire life to the present, where, validated by the life they had redeemed, they could provide a firm basis for some ampler argument. *The Prelude*, in other words, was intended to be a means to something beyond itself—a prelude to something else. Instead, it became a prelude to itself, and it did so in a very special, peculiarly Romantic sense. Augustine's story of his conversion is a prelude to itself: it recounts the genesis of the person who narrates it. Wordsworth's autobiography leads back into itself rather than on to something else because he never could complete it. The self he set out to discover philosophically, he ended up realizing poetically; it could not be abstracted from the words which are its cause and adequate symbol. What was to have been a prelude to his life's work, a work that would "endure" because its truth was timeless, became his life's work, one whose truth is inseparable from its enduring poetic action.

Confessions of an English Opium Eater

In Book Eleven of *The Prelude*, Wordsworth tacitly acknowledges the failure of his autobiography to account as fully for the cultural experiences that have brought him to his present state of bewilderment as for the earlier Natural ministrations that, he says, sustained him during his wanderings through the wilderness of time and change and delivered his immortal soul intact to its appointed resting place. "Share with me," he asks his reader,

> the wish
> That some dramatic tale, endued with shapes
> Livelier, and flinging out less guarded words
> Than suit the work we fashion, might set forth
> What then I learned, or think I learned of truth.
>
> [XI, 281–85]

The materials for such a poem are all present in *The Prelude*. There is Wordsworth's stated belief that the soul evolves through experience, a belief which implies that time and change are essential elements of reality rather than the accidental manifestations of an eternal, unchanging truth. There is his intuition that self-knowledge consists in a symbolic action rather than in static comprehension, and there is in his inclination to equate life and virtue with movement and to find the justification for movement in the aesthetic glory of motion itself rather than in its doctrinal teleology. To write that poem, however, Wordsworth would have had to abjure his belief in an eternal reality that precedes, conditions, and ultimately justifies all human action—a home, as Augustine put it, that does not fall down while we are away from it. Although we can see that this home lay far back in the unrecapturable history of belief, Wordsworth located it, as Rousseau had, in a childhood sanctified by loss. And so, for all his determination to "follow with no timid step" wherever his autobiographical inquisitions might lead him, he could not allow his poem to wander very far off the joyful ground of Natural childhood, into the undiscovered country of conditional existence, where human action is the only reality. Wordsworth had glimpsed that forbidding territory of suffering and unceasing change; its exploration required the recklessness of an autobiographer who had nothing to lose.

The composition of those autobiographical writings that De Quincey collected under the running title of his *Confessions* recapitulates the evolution of autobiographical form since Augustine and negotiates the transition to its final stage, poetic autobiography. In 1821, he completed and published serially his original *Confessions of an English Opium Eater*, which he supposed would be the last word on the subject but which subsequent events taught him to regard as merely the first installment of an autobiographical project that was to occupy his entire creative life. These "preliminary *Confessions*," as he came to call them, present a history of opium addiction from the point of view of the reformed addict, retracing the chain of events that led into addiction and then out of it to the narrator's conquest over his habit. As faith detaches the converted from the sinning Augustine, the cure gives De Quincey's narrator "a power of surveying his own case as a cool spectator and a degree of spirits for adequately describing it which would be inconsistent to suppose in any person speaking from the station of an actual sufferer."* Not since Augustine described his conversion, perhaps, had an autobiographer felt more keenly that division between the known and knowing selves upon which the historical form depends.

And yet there is something amiss with this supposedly detached narrative, a progressive blurring of the difference

---

* Thomas De Quincey, *Confessions of an English Opium Eater and Other Writings*, ed. Aileen Ward (New York, 1966), p. 103. Subsequent references to this edition appear in parentheses in the text.

between narrator and protagonist which reflects not only Augustine's problem of maintaining his narrator's distinctiveness as the protagonist draws closer in time to the moment of conversion, and not only the even greater problems of Dante, Bunyan, and Franklin, who attributed the narrator's wisdom wholly or in part to the protagonist's experiences, but also the tendency of Rousseau and Wordsworth to locate true being in the experiences of their protagonists rather than in the knowledge their narrators possess. No reader can proceed very far into the narrative before he begins to feel, as De Quincey himself is finally forced to admit, that "Not the opium-eater," which is to say the person who broke the habit and became the narrator, "but the opium," the thing renounced by the protagonist when he became the narrator, "is the true hero of the tale, and the legitimate center on which the interest revolves" (100).

And indeed the narrative does give to opium all the virtues which previous autobiographers had given to the still center of temporal change. Under the drug's spell, the addict stands "aloof from the uproar of life, as if the tumult, the fever, the strife were suspended, a respite granted from the secret burdens of the heart, a sabbath of repose. . . . Here were the hopes which blossom in the paths of life, reconciled with the peace which is in the grave; motions of the intellect as unwearied as the heavens, yet for all anxieties a halcyon calm; . . . infinite activities, infinite repose" (71). Placing the addict at that still center, opium "invigorates" his "self-possession," composing "what had been agitated" and concentrating "what had been distracted" (63), displaying before him, "as in a piece of arraswork, the whole of [his] past life—not as if recalled by an act of memory, but as if present and incarnated in music" (68). The drug is nothing less than the truth, the ground of the addict's true being, and the *Confessions* are its scripture.

Given this hyperbolic praise of a vice purportedly abandoned, the reader is not altogether surprised to learn, from the "Appendix" De Quincey added to his narrative a year later, that the author is once again sunk in addiction. Whether De Quincey really thought he was cured when he wrote the original *Confessions*, as he protests, or whether he merely assumed that pose in deference to a reading public that expected all specimens of vice to be exhibited in stout cages of virtue, is moot. The "Appendix" transforms the earlier narrative from a history of conquered addiction into an event in the addict's life—one of those exercises in self-deception to which all addicts are prone. As an addict, moreover, the narrator of the "Appendix" cannot be certain that he is not now equally deceived in his views. Unable to escape his illness, he cannot see it whole from the relatively fixed, external vantage-point of health. He must view it from the moving, internal point of addiction itself. In this situation, each apparent statement about addiction is in fact a symptom of addiction, and while any statement may be in error, every one will truthfully express the addict's condition. Consequently, no statement, however erroneous, need be corrected. Although the narrator of the *Confessions* thinks he has conquered his habit, when that document is re-read in the light shed upon it by the "Appendix," every word proves perfectly consistent with the now revealed "literal truth" of his addiction (104). By the same token, no statement, however erroneous, *can* be corrected. Because each statement is an expression of addiction, any statement— including the correction of a previous one—merely adds to the errors it tries to rectify. If nothing in the addictive life is altogether untrue, neither is anything finally true. As long as De Quincey remains an addict, he must go on acting out a condition he cannot comprehend.

Addiction, in sum, stands as a metaphor for conditional existence, that temporal succession of individual experiences whose eternal form had been divinely revealed to Augustine, Dante, and Bunyan, rationally inferred by Franklin, and philosophically sought after by Rousseau and Wordsworth. For De Quincey, as for Franklin, the shared opinions of society provide the only ground outside his own experience upon which he might stand to see himself. But, like Rousseau and Wordsworth, he finds that ground at once too unstable and too flinty to support the luxuriant growth of his exotic inner life. Finding it inaccessible as well, by reason of his addiction, he must search within his own conditional experience for the unconditioned, absolute ground of his true being and his kinship with the rest of humanity. In the original *Confessions*, De Quincey had tried to reconcile the conflicting demands of public opinion and private experience by simultaneously assuming the guise of a cured addict who shares the public view that opium is a low vice and portraying the drug as a divinely vouchsafed medium of beatific ecstasy. Far from reconciling the conflict, however, this strategy does not even manage to equivocate the private and public terms, leaving him still no choice between publicly denying the worth of his own life and hoping privately that his readers will heed the scripture and join him in the true church of opium, of which he is as yet "the only member" (64). Upon hearing that his readers have not been persuaded of his cure, but are in fact demanding a more just account of the drug's evil effects, then, he drops the pose and confronts the public, and himself, in the "Appendix" as an unregenerate addict.

The question arises, why does he come before the public at all? His return to the drug prevents him from fulfilling his reader's wishes at the same time that it excuses him from the obligation to disparage further the habit that constitutes his individuality. He said in the *Confessions* that whereas opium had given him "the keys of Paradise" (71), his release from addiction exiled him from Eden (102) into the fallen, temporal world of healthy public life, where one must sweat for his bread by stringing together words that only obscure further the lost bliss they seek to recapture. Why, then, does he not return to his blessed quietude, where the truth is silence and words are unnecessary, instead of continuing to address a society to which he can no longer even pretend to belong? The biographical answer is obvious: De Quincey's true church of opium depended on tithes from the false world of commerce. He wrote to support his habit. The autobiographical answer, although not altogether different, is at once less obvious and more to the point. Opium, it seems, is no more the "alpha and omega" (64) of his temporal existence than was the cure, no more the *telos* and final form of his life than was Augustine's conversion. If opium arose from and justified his prior suffering, it also leads to even greater suffering in the form of addiction. And while opium may seem a terminus, addiction is a fatal, unretraceable downward course whose "gates of ingress" (116) close behind him the moment he embarks upon it.

As part two of Augustine's *Confessions* takes up the subject of the writer's faithful life after conversion, the third installment of De Quincey's autobiography essays the topic of his addictive life following the regression announced in the "Appendix." In 1845, he published in *Blackwood's Magazine* the first version of *Suspiria de Profundis*, a work that he would revise many times in the years to come. Here, the cooly detached, judging narrator of the original *Confessions*, having gone the way of the unforgiving Augustine who narrates the story of conversion, is replaced by a narrator who suffers the same afflictions that the protagonist does and who seeks in the agitations of his own spirit that rounding grace and still center which Augustine had pursued through the meditative actions of his own inquiring soul. No less convinced than was Augustine that "in parts and fractions eternal creations are carried on," De Quincey's philosophical narrator, too, finds that "the nexus is wanting, and life and the central principles which should bind together all the parts at the center, with all its radiations to the circumference, are wanting" (viii). That the addictive life, like the autobiography which simultaneously enacts and records it, is an eternal creation, De Quincey does not doubt. Cast out as they are into the temporal darkness, however, these correlative actions are condemned to describe unconsciously "parts and fractions" of an eternal figure whose complete design they cannot know.

When opium proves not the alpha and omega of his suffering but, like his cure, simply another arc on its outrunning curve, De Quincey takes up an idea that had occurred momentarily to Wordsworth when innocent joy seemed incapable of justifying his own patently joyless experiences: the idea that suffering is the constant element in human existence and hence a more likely medium than bliss for perceiving the absolute. De Quincey has already said, in the original *Confessions*, that while time breaks up the self into shards of impermanent, unrecapturable feeling, suffering creates a bond between the child and the man (57); and in the "Appendix" suffering unites the narrator and protagonist, healing the breach that the cure had opened between present and past. Now he begins to develop these earlier suggestions regarding "the hieroglyphic meaning of human sufferings" (44), attributing to grief those divine qualities which he previously ascribed to opium. Only suffering, that *"primary* formation of the human system," is sufficiently sensitive to move the soul along the eternally circular course through which "the *primary* convulsions of nature . . . come round and round again by reverberating shocks" (154–55). Because suffering participates in both the conditional and the absolute realms, it is humbling yet exalting, agitating yet calming, debilitating yet healing (136). Although suffering is a movement, and not a stillness, it lends a purpose to motion, "creating the intellect" (187), enabling "profound natures" to express and thus to know themselves (190), expanding the soul (201). As the agency through which the individual soul arrives at true being, furthermore, it is also the common lot of humanity, "diffused amongst all creatures that breathe" (147). With the passing of the true church of opium, "profound grief" has come to answer the need for "profound religion" (139).

If suffering, like Augustine's faith and Wordsworth's joy, is the evidence of things unseen, it is not itself those unseen things. When experience alone provides information about the eternal purposes of experience, it must be rendered in a form, a language, that is sufficiently translucent to let those hidden purposes shine through. Having stood successively upon his impermanent cure, the fleeting pleasures of opium, and the endless sufferings of addiction in the attempt to discern the pattern of his life, De Quincey changes his vantage-point once again to view his disordered experiences in the perspective of his dreams. Seen from this new thematic station, the relentless and wayward progress of his career begins to assume a more promising shape. His early sufferings caused him to take opium, which made him dream. His dreams recalled forgotten events from his childhood, the earliest being a dream of "terrific grandeur" (123). Thus closing the circle of his temporal existence, binding up all its dispersed fragments "in unity" (164), showing the hidden connection between "the nearer and more distant stages of life" (185), awakening past experiences that lie sleeping in the palimpsest of the brain, and presenting them "not as a succession but as parts of a coexistence" (170), dreams reveal the absolute. The dreaming faculty ". . . is the one great tube through which man communicates with the shadowy" and "the magnificent apparatus which forces the infinite into the chambers of the human brain" (114).

As dreams unify the life, so also do they organize the "parts and fragments" of the autobiography in which that life is at once enacted and recorded. The original *Confessions*, which became a testimony to continuing addiction when seen from the "Appendix," now become primarily a treatise on the "grandeur which belongs . . . to human dreams" (113) and a study of opium addiction only by the way. In the *Confessions*, the narrator had reported his dreams because they were "the immediate and proximate cause" (89) of the sufferings he had escaped. But now his sufferings are important mainly insofar as they cause and help to explain his dreams. Instead of following and rehearsing remembered events from the waking life, his dreams recall past experiences that would have otherwise been forgotten, and the content of his dreams takes over from biographical chronology the authority for determining which remembered events shall be included and the order of their appearance in the narrative. Indeed, the dream of Levanna is said in a footnote to be the structural model for the entire *Confessions*, "in that it rehearses or prefigures their course" (178–79). Originally De Quincey's secondary theme and then his primary one, dreaming becomes with this announcement not just a subject, or even the subject, of the *Confessions* but their presentational mode. In something more than a metaphorical sense, he is now dreaming his autobiography.

The implications of this autobiographical mode will bear some investigation. On the one hand, dreaming seems to be a source of information about things unseen, a radius extending directly from the circumference of temporal experience to that eternal center which lies, ambiguously, above or beneath conscious understanding. Considered in this light, dreams are a fit topic for autobiography in that they reveal the absolute, unconditioned ground of the writer's conditional existence, the way Dante's dreams reveal the central point of divine love which justifies the arc of his erotic desires. The problem here is that whatever dreams reveal they reveal in dream language, and whereas Dante's sacred writings gave him the key to this cryptography, De Quincey has only the undecipherable text and the feeling that it means something once known but long since forgotten. "I have been struck," he says, "with the important truth that far more of our deepest thoughts and feelings pass to us through perplexed combinations of *concrete* objects, pass to us . . . in compound experiences incapable of being disentangled, than ever reach us *directly* in their own abstract shapes" (130). In this sense, dreaming is not so much a source of information about experience as it is an especially intense way of experiencing things, a way of making experience suggest unknowable meanings beyond itself.

As dreaming ceases either to explain the meaning of life or to supply data through which that meaning may be discovered and becomes a mode of conduct, moreover, it also relinquishes the duty of representing actual experiences, or even actual dreams, and becomes free to invent its own materials. As a child, De Quincey recalls, he often made up dreams, which then recurred to him in sleep. Opium reawakened this creative propensity, and the paradigmatic dream of Levanna had its origin not in some noumenal realm but in a legend, "most of which," he confesses, "I had myself silently written or sculptured in my daylight reveries" (178). Even his actual dreams are an inseparable blend of representational and inventive elements. Possessing "a power not contented with reproduction, but which absolutely creates or transforms" what they seem to reveal (183), his dreams are "far less like a lake reflecting the heavens than like the pencil of some mighty artist . . . that cannot copy in simplicity, but comments in freedom . . ." (185). "The unsearchable depths of man's nature" that dreams reveal are not a still point, it seems, but a creative power (189), not a final form but an unfolding shape which alters with each effort to realize itself. The dream discovers, reveals, what the dreaming power invents (225) and is therefore less obedient to some higher, absolute law than "a law to itself" (224).

Throughout De Quincey's *Confessions*, as in Augustine's, writing is associated with the temporal life and distinguished from the eternal truth, which is silence. Regarding his cure as a banishment from paradise into time, the narrator of the original *Confessions* is forced to write about a state of narcotic quietude which would require no utterance if he were still in it. Once the cure fails, however, and becomes, along with the pleasures of opium, simply a turn in the meandering course of addiction, writing detaches itself from the cure and becomes a symptom of addiction. The narrator of the "Appendix" says that his withdrawal from the drug prevented him from writing (109), while his relapse has enabled him to resume his composition. As the reconfirmed addict must now find the justification for his condition in addiction itself, the writer must discover the formal design of his autobiography in the endless succession of words which express his addiction. After searching "the abysses" of his childhood sufferings with no conclusion but "some wandering thoughts unintelligible to myself," the narrator of the *Suspiria* outlines an overall plan for "the movement of these *Confessions*." The downward sweep of his inquiries into his sufferings, he says, was to have been counterbalanced by a "whole arch of ascending visions." Unfortunately, "accidents of the press have made it impossible to accomplish this purpose," and so he "jury rigs" a conclusion in the form of the Oxford dream which reconciles all his sufferings in an ecstatic vision of unity (162).

Like all the preceding conclusions, however, this one soon proves inconclusive, for in the very next section the narrator explains that the Oxford dream, is to be viewed "together with the succeeding dreams [i.e. "Levanna and Our Ladies of Sorrow" and "The Apparation of the Brocken"] . . . as in the nature of choruses winding up the overture contained" in the preceding section (171). Hard upon the completion of the overture there follows a "Finale: Savanna-la-Mar," which concludes that suffering is no doubt necessary to God's inscrutable purposes and which is itself followed by "A Vision of Life." Here the narrator says that all the Oxford visions together were "but anticipations necessary to illustrate" how opium dreams opened up the childhood he will now explore for its relations with the present. After doing so, however, he can only conclude that if he could have seen as a child what awaited him in maturity he would have recoiled from its purposelessness. That is, he would have so recoiled had he been able to understand such a prospective vision, which is altogether unlikely since our view of life changes as we proceed through it.

And so the "exploring voyage of inquest into hidden scenes . . . of human life" (218) that started with the relapse

into addiction has ended up no closer to its projected destination than it began. Instead of completing the autobiography, each attempted conclusion has merely altered its
shape, moving its center and necessitating yet another turn
to close its spiraling course. De Quincey worked on the
Confessions for the rest of his life, adding new sections,
revising already published sections in the light of new
ones, excising passages that subsequent ones seemed to
contradict, sketching plans for elaborate structures that
would unite all the parts and fragments in a comprehensive
design. But addiction repeatedly thwarted the aims that addiction set itself. In the prefatory note to "The Daughter of
Lebanon," which he added to the *Suspiria* when the *Revised Confessions* were published in 1856, De Quincey explains that the entire narrative was to have concluded with
"a crowning grace . . . reserved for the final pages." Unfortunately, the manuscript containing this "succession of
some twenty or twenty-five dreams and noonday visions
which had arisen under the latter stages of opium
influence" was destroyed in fire, also set "under the latter
stages of opium influence" (191). Each goal the addict en-
visioned was an expression of his addiction, and hence not
a fixed destination but a step in that "endless pilgrimage of
woe" (133). The plight of addict and autobiography alike is
that of inescapable, unredeemable conditionality, aptly described in the addict's most compelling dream: "I, in spirit,
rose as if on billows . . . ; and the billows seemed to pursue
the throne of God; but *that* also . . . fled away continually.
The flight and the pursuit seemed to go on forever and
ever" (132).

Although De Quincey never stopped trying to discover
in his *Confessions* the underlying principle that would dictate their final form and logical conclusion, he appears to
have stumbled on that unifying principle when he decided,

after the fact, that "The English Mail Coach" was really a part of his autobiography. The sketch appeared without any reference to the *Confessions* in 1849, some time before he included it in one of his grandiose and never-realized schemes for the complete autobiography, and five years before he announced publicly that the piece had always been intended to be part of the *Confessions*. Whether or not it was so intended, De Quincey's decision to include it was in effect a decision that any written enactment of his addiction in the dreaming mode of the *Suspiria*, whatever its subject, would be a chapter in his ever-changing, never-ending autobiography. He clearly did not consider "The English Mail Coach" autobiographical because it originated in an actual event from his life. The germinal event is altogether inconsequential biographically and is important only in that it produced the sketch, which does not really report or interpret the event but rather "radiates as a natural expansion from it" (224). Nor does the essay recapitulate the process by which it arose from the event. According to De Quincey's prefatory note, the event triggered certain powerful feelings which led to "a rolling succession of dreams" (224), and these dreams led in turn to reflections upon the role played by the British Mail Service in spreading the news of Waterloo. But the essay begins with the historical reflections, proceeds to the personal experience and then dramatizes the consequent feelings in a single composite dream which also contains the theme of Waterloo. De Quincey's explanation of this reshaping defies analysis and is probably not to be taken seriously in any case, since he concludes it with the remark that "If anything is amiss, . . . the dream"—which is to say the sketch itself—"is the responsible party," and "the dream is a law to itself" (224–25). The very obscurity of his explanation makes his main point perfectly clear, however: with the inclusion of imagined dream-visions like "The English Mail Coach," "The Daughter of Lebanon," "Who is this Woman . . . ?" and "The Dark Interpreter," the *Confessions* had stopped trying either to explain the addictive life histori- cally or to discover its meaning philosophically and had be- gun to enact it poetically.

De Quincey had already shown an inclination to or- ganize his proliferating materials artistically, rather than biographically or logically, when the researches of the *Suspiria* refused to yield their desired conclusions. The decision to counterbalance the downward sweep of his "nursery afflictions" with an "arch of ascending visions" was made, he says, "according to the principles of *art* which govern the movement of these *Confessions*" (162). Throughout the *Confessions*, De Quincey suggests that the model for this aesthetic organization of otherwise disparate materials is music. At one time or another, each of its suc- cessively proposed central themes is dignified by an asso- ciation with music. The comprehensive vision granted by opium in the original *Confessions* is "a chorus . . . of elabo- rate harmony" (68). When opium leads to addiction, the narrator of the *Suspiria* announces that the true subject of the *Opium Confessions* is "not the naked physiological theme . . . but those wandering musical variations on the theme . . ." (120). In the ensuing analysis of grief, the "tears and lamentations" of infant suffering are said to "run through a gamut that is an inexhaustible as the cremona of Paganini," and although these cries are as "different as a chorus of Beethoven from a chorus of Mozart," all are "yet finally harmonizing" (190–91). Finally, when suffering proves interminable, his dreams reveal the great truth that "the rapture of life does not arise, unless as perfect music arises, music of Mozart or Beethoven, by the confluence of the mighty and terrific discords with the subtle concords" (200).

With the modulation from dreaming as the autobiographical subject to dreaming as the autobiographical mode in the "Dream Fugue" that closes "The English Mail Coach" and in the later additions to the *Suspiria*, the *Confessions* abandon the hope of achieving musical closure in a reconciling coda or finale and begin to extemporize on random themes in the hope of striking accidentally "a right key" on the "dreadful organ" of eternity (187). In this serial form, each successive movement redefines the structure of all foregoing passages and thus suggests a line of development for passages to come. Instead of moving about a fixed harmonic point within a fixed form, the composition creates its own, endlessly changing structure as it proceeds. Because this music is composed *ex tempore*, on the spur of the moment, no future passage exists until it is played, and each note is no sooner played than it vanishes into the past, where it can be neither recaptured, redeemed, nor expunged. Because each movement arises from and reshapes everything that has gone before, however, and sets the conditions for what is to come, all past and future movements are contained in each present one. When time rather than the eternal is the ground of reality, the ever-moving, never-vanishing present becomes the alpha and omega, the point upon which all times concentrate and from which all times radiate.

While this time-centered aesthetic is clearly implied in "The English Mail Coach," De Quincey could no more rest secure upon that point of eternal movement than could Rousseau or Wordsworth. "The present," he says, "which only man possesses, offers less capacity for his footing than the slenderest film that ever spider twisted from her womb. . . . All is finite in the present, and even that finite is infinite in its velocity of flight toward death. But in God there is nothing finite, . . . nothing transitory, . . . nothing that tends to death. Therefore it follows that for God there can be no present" (199). The art of the *Confessions* suggests again and again the idea that true being is contingent upon, nor prior to, human action. The idea is implicit in the modulation of the work's representative mode from biographical metaphors that reflect the self, to fictive metaphors that express the self, to fictive metaphors that create the self they reveal. The same idea appears in De Quincey's sometimes baffling tendency to confound the order of temporal causality and make later events the cause as well as the effect of earlier ones; and again in his readiness to make the narrator an active presence in remembered scenes and a fully dramatized, autonomous character in the dream of "The Dark Interpreter," rather than simply a spokesman for the author's present reflections. But nowhere is this notion made clearer than in the statement that the autobiography is responsible for its own shape and content and is not governed by a life or a truth outside it. Nevertheless, De Quincey held firm to that belief in the absolute, substantial self which is the necessary condition of Augustinian autobiography. "The fleeting accidents of a man's life and its external shows may indeed be irrelate and incongruous," he says, "but the organizing principles which fuse into harmony and gather about fixed predetermined centers whatever heterogeneous elements life may have accumulated from without will not permit the grandeur of human unity greatly to be violated or its ultimate repose to be troubled . . ." (169–70).

If De Quincey's readers have agreed with him in nothing else, they have largely concurred in his judgment that opium was responsible for his failure to complete the *Confessions*. Nor can we doubt that his inability to escape the interminable and seemingly pointless sufferings of addiction prevented him from formulating some final, clear opinion about the shape and meaning of his life. And yet,

De Quincey's problems were by no means unique. He was not the only Romantic who saw in "the gathering agitation of our present . . . life" a threat against the inviolate self, the last stronghold of the absolute. "Already in this year 1845," he wrote in the *Suspiria*, "what by the procession through fifty years of mighty revolutions amongst the kingdoms of the earth, what by continual development of vast physical agencies . . . the eye of the calmest observer is troubled; . . . and it becomes too evident that unless this colossal pace of advance . . . can be met by counter forces . . . in the direction of religion or profound philosophy, that shall radiate centrifugally against this storm of life so perilously centripetal towards the vortex of the merely human, . . . this fierce condition of eternal hurry . . . is likely to defeat the grandeur which is latent in all men . . ." (113–14). Nor was he the only Romantic who spent his entire life trying to bring his autobiography abreast of an ever-moving present and of changes caused by the autobiography itself. It is probably more accurate to say, therefore, that addiction simply made painfully clear to De Quincey what every deep-thinking autobiographer since Franklin had suspected: autobiography is not a reflection of the life but something added to it, not a picture but an action, which can neither stand still long enough to see the life whole nor pursue its own movement to a point of certain rest. Unable to escape the conditions of the addictive life that was his subject, De Quincey could neither explain nor discover its final form. He could only go on enacting it endlessly in a language that might, by its sheer intensity, strike an occasional, accidental harmony with the eternal, celestial music he had to believe in but could not hear.

4

Poetic Autobiography

Sartor Resartus

Sartor Resartus is at once a commentary on, and an example of, the kind of autobiography dictated by the situation in which the Romantics found themselves. "Who am I," Teufelsdröckh asks; "What is this me? . . . Sure enough, I am; and lately was not: but Whence? How? Whereto? . . . We sit as in a boundless Phantasmagoria and Dream-Grotto; . . . but Him, the Unslumbering, whose work both Dream and Dreamer are, we see not. . . ."* God is absent; "no Pillar of cloud by day, and no Pillar of Fire by night, any longer guides the Pilgrim. . . . The whole world is . . . sold to unbelief; . . . and men ask now: Where is the Godhead; our eyes never saw him?" (161). Fled from the external world, God exists only in the heart, and there only in the form of an objectless longing, "a certain inarticulate Self-consciousness" (162). Time is the only reality. "Our whole terrestial being is based on Time, and built of Time; it is wholly a Movement" (127). Timeless innocence is a dream, from which the infant is awakened by the devil Time into the realization that "Time will not stop" and that he, too, a Son of Time, "must enact that stern Monodrama, *No Object*

* Thomas Carlyle, *Sartor Resartus: The Life and Opinions of Herr Teufelsdröckh*, ed. C. F. Harrold (New York, 1937), p. 53. Subsequent references to this edition appear in parentheses in the text.

and no Rest; must front its successive destinies, work through to its catastrophe, and deduce therefrom what moral he can" (121). Since "man lives in Time, has his whole earthly being, endeavor and destiny shaped for him by Time" (112), his "spiritual nature" is continually changing, "for how can the 'Son of Time,' in any case, stand still?" (157). He can therefore know himself only in time, in motion, through a mind that is also in motion, for "only in the transitory Time-Symbol is the ever-motionless Eternity we stand on made manifest" (112).

In such an age, "it happens that, for your nobler minds, the publishing of [autobiography], in one or the other dialect, becomes almost a necessity," a means by which the spirit can free itself and the time-imprisoned writer become a man (156). The question is, what form is this autobiography to take? In what dialect should it be published? Obviously, it must reveal the heart's center, God's last domain in a Godless world. But, "How paint to the sensual eye . . . what passes in Holy-of-Holies of Man's Soul; in what words, known to these profane times, speak even afar-off of the unspeakable?" (185). "Only our works can render articulate and decisively discernible" the spirit within; they are "the mirror wherein the spirit first sees its natural lineaments. Hence . . . the folly of that impossible Precept, *Know thyself*; till it be translated into this partially possible one, *Know what thou canst work at*" (162–63). While it is not certain what specific form this self-apprehending action must take, it is at least clear that "outward Biography" (204) will not do. "In a psychological point of view, it is perhaps questionable whether from birth and genealogy, how closely scrutinized soever, much insight is to be gained" (81). Nor can the living career reveal anything essential. In the first place, every life is unique. At each stage in his life, "the new man is in a new time, under new conditions; his course can be the *fac-simile* of no prior one, but is by its nature original" (119). Because each experience is unique, moreover, each is equally important. "The simplest record" of a life, "were clear record possible, would fill volumes. Hopeless is the obscurity, unspeakable the confusion" (152). "What are your historical Facts," Teufelsdröckh asks, "still more your biographical? Wilt thou know a Man . . . by stringing together beadrolls of what thou namest Facts? The Man is the spirit he worked in; not what he did, but what he became" (203).

Although the naked self remains invisible to "memory and conjecture" (11), it will reveal itself in symbolic garments woven by the creative imagination. These garments may be words as well as deeds. As the temporal world is "the Time-vesture of the Eternal" (74), and man's terrestial life is "a Clothing or visible Garment of [the] divine ME" (73), speech is the finite manifestation of infinite silence (219), and "Language is the Flesh-Garment, the Body, of Thought" (73). These garments may also be either material or altogether imaginary, for anything "in any way conceived as Visible, . . . is . . . but a Garment . . . of the higher, celestial Invisible" (67). What matter, then, whether the "stuff" in which the spirit works "be of this sort or that, so the Form be . . . poetic?" (197). Clothing is an art, in which "every snip of the Scissors has been regulated and prescribed by ever-active Influences" (36), an art that reveals in its symbolic creations its own creative principles. "In the Symbol there is concealment yet revelation: . . . Silence and . . . Speech acting together. . . . [T]he Infinite is made to blend itself with the Finite, to stand visible, and *as it were*, attainable there" (219–20, italics mine). Instead of facts, therefore, the autobiography will offer "Nothing but innuendoes, figurative crochets: a typical Shadow, fitfully wavering, prophetico-satiric; no clear logical Picture" (185).

The autobiographer himself will be "not once named" in it. It will contain "Dreams, authentic or not, while the circumjacent waking Actions are omitted." There may appear in it "long purely Autobiographical delineations; yet without connexion, without recognisable coherence . . ." (78). "Philosophico-poetically written," such a "remarkable volume" must be "philosophico-poetically read" if we are to see that although the author's "Life, Fortunes, and Bodily Presence, are as yet hidden. . . . his Soul [lies] enclosed," and thus revealed, in its pages (27).

The effect of such an autobiography will be not to inform the reader but to transform him. By participating in the symbolic actions through which the writer realizes "that divine ME of his" (73), the reader comes to share the autobiographer's achieved state of being and view of the world. As the words of the text are the cause and adequate symbol of the writer's spiritual evolution, so are they the correlative objects of an analogous development in the reader's soul. And since the truth of the writing consists less in what it says about things the reader might learn through other means—through personal observation or received opinion—than in its symbolic evocation of things otherwise unknowable, the writer's words become the reader's reality. Willy-nilly, he finds himself "somewhat infected" by the autobiographer's "mode of utterance" (269), and "Even as the smaller whirlpool is sucked into the larger, and made to whirl along with it," the reader's mind becomes a portion of the writer's and, "like it, see[s] all things figuratively" (293). In providing a fund of symbolic experience in which the reader may participate, moreover, rather than just a record of the writer's own unique experience, the autobiography counteracts both the anarchic effects of individual existence and the totalitarian effects of social organization. If the autobiography is a true "Work of Art," letting "the God-like manifest itself to Sense. . . . Then is it fit that men unite there; and worship together before such Symbol" (223). In an unbelieving age, when "mutual devotedness to the Good and True" is impossible "except as Armed Neutrality or hollow Commercial League," such an autobiography may be "an enormous Pitchpan," which the writer "in his lone watchtower had kindled, that it might flame far and wide through the Night, and many a disconsolately wandering spirit be guided thither to a Brother's bosom!" (295).

The autobiographical conditions and aspirations thus described in *Sartor Resartus* are dramatized in its structure. Since time is inescapable, narrator and protagonist find themselves in the same boat, adrift on the same temporal stream, which flows from an unknown source to an obscure destination. As Wordsworth's narrator had been not only an observer of the historical action but a participant in the poetic action, a traveler among the scenes of his youth; and as De Quincey's narrator had taken on the shifting forms of the phantom of the Brocken and the Dark Interpreter when biography gave way to dreams; Carlyle's narrator appears as a fully dramatized character who is *contemporary* with the protagonist. Portrayed as distinct characters to represent the division between the knower and the object of his knowledge, they converge in the final pages of the autobiography as the Editor finds himself engulfed in the whirlpool of Teufelsdröckh's metaphorical style. There is even a suggestion that the Editor and Teufelsdröckh are one person from the beginning. A footnote, written by Carlyle and spuriously attributed to his publisher, says that the Editor has always communicated with *Fraser's Magazine* "in some sort of mask, or muffler . . . under a feigned name" (13). Whether this means that the Editor is really Teufelsdröckh in a disguise calculated to allay the xenophobic suspicions of his English readers, or that the Editor is really Carlyle, the implication remains the same, since the essential ingredients of Teufelsdröckh's biography are based on Carlyle's own life.

The main significance of these two dramatized *personae*, however, lies in their close kinship with the narrators and protagonists of previous autobiographies. Together, they reflect both the tendency of autobiographers after Franklin to divide their narrators and protagonists along primarily psychological rather than ontological lines, and also the shift of authority from narrator to protagonist that marks the evolution of autobiographical form since the Renaissance. Both of these developments accompany the removal of the absolute ground from Augustine's God, whose eternal form embraces temporal change like a celestial sphere, to ever deeper recesses within the Romantic psyche, at the still center of surrounding change. Whereas Augustine's narrator and protagonist represent the ontological realms of eternity and time, the two *personae* stand in Franklin's *Autobiography* for the psychological faculties of reason and impulse, in Rousseau's *Confessions* for thought and feeling, in *The Prelude* for reflection and imagination, and in De Quincey's *Confessions* for waking and dreaming. Although Franklin's universal Reason retains the authority of Augustine's eternal faith, its only perceivable source is the protagonist's impulsive actions. From then on, the center of narrative gravity shifts steadily from narrator to protagonist and the faculty he represents, until it comes to rest entirely in Teufelsdröckh, whose higher reason Carlyle locates in the deepest psychic recess of all—the realm of *unconsciousness*.

With the protagonist in full possession of what the narrator seeks to know, and the narrator in hot pursuit of this elusive quarry, the narrative becomes an action, rather than the report of an action. Like Rousseau, Carlyle's narrator sets out to explain his protagonist to an antipathetic audience but soon finds that he lacks sufficient information for the task and begins to inquire philosophically into his subject. If his original intention was to bridge the gulf between German transcendentalism and English empiricism— which is to say, between the unhealthily dissociated inner and outer realms of the private imagination and public common sense—by conveying Teufelsdröckh to England, he now reverses his course and seeks to transport his reader into those unmapped territories where Teufelsdröckh roams. And while his ultimate object remains the noble work of "transplanting foreign Thought into the barren domestic soil," he must voyage far abroad to capture the prize. "Forward with us, courageous reader," (80), he cries, in the manner of an adventurer drumming up a crew for a particularly risky expedition. True, Teufelsdröckh's philosophy is, like Nature itself, "a mighty maze, yet as faith whispers, not without a plan." And whenever the reader grows timid in the face of danger, the ever-sanguine Editor is there to encourage him with the prospect of a landfall, "a promise of new Fortunate Islands, perhaps whole undiscovered Americas, for such as have canvas to sail thither" (52).

But the object of this quest, being a Son of Time, will not stand still to be apprehended. "He glides from country to country, from condition to condition; vanishing and reappearing, no man can calculate how or where" (152). As an avatar of the truth, he is a law to himself; unpredictable in his movements and knowable only through his movements, he ranges over a territory whose boundaries, the Editor ruefully notes, "lie quite beyond our horizon" (36). Moreover, because the Editor himself is in motion amidst territories that grow larger and more complex the farther he penetrates into them, he finds his own ideas—about the object of his quest and about himself—changing constantly. Instead of circumnavigating the truth or driving to its still center, the expedition seems merely to enlarge and complicate what must be comprehended, projecting the destination farther and farther ahead. While the Editor continues to hope that his narrative voyage will reach its appointed end, that "for all the fantastic Dream-Grottoes through which, as is our lot with Teufelsdröckh, [the reader] must wander," there will appear "between whiles some twinkling of a steady Polar Star" (206), it soon becomes clear that the Editor and Teufelsdröckh, being at once the causes and effects of changing motions in each other, can never converge but must circle about each other endlessly in empty, relative space, "their stillness . . . but the rest of infinite motion . . ." (16).

The Editor has appreciated from the outset the risks involved in this expedition. Even when dragooning readers to accompany him, he warned them that it might lead to failure as well as success and that they would share no less in the latter than in the former. When he saw the New World of Teufelsdröckh's philosophy "unfolding itself into new boundless expansions, of a cloudcapt, almost chimerical aspect, yet not without azure loomings in the far distance, and streaks of an Elysian brightness," he could also see its lurking ambiguity and ask, "Is that a real Elysian brightness, . . . or the reflex of Pandemonian lava? Is it of a truth leading us unto beatific Asphodel meadows, or the yellow burning marl of a Hell-on-Earth?" (70). He has always been unsure whether Teufelsdröckh is an angel or a devil, whether the imagination that both weaves the visible world and sees through it "into the infinite deeps of the Invisible" (218) is the gate to heaven or a byway to the pit, a straight path along which the "Living Spirit" may travel to its "celestial Home" (209) or an unretraceable, winding way to an endless succession of places that the soul creates by going there. Having left the snug harbor of complacent opinion to voyage in imagination toward a "nobler Era, in Universal History" (80), ever hopeful of tracking the vagrant soul to its "still Home" (265), yet ever aware that "his whole Faculty and Self [were] like to be swallowed up" in the voyage (80), he finally realizes Teufelsdröckh's truth: "nothing is completed, but ever completing" (247). " 'Your America is here or nowhere.' . . . Yes here, in this poor, miserable, hampered, despicable Actual, wherein thou even now standest . . ." (196).

That is to say, the absolute self, the "divine ME," for which the autobiography has been imaginatively seeking lies in the autobiography itself, created in the act of searching for it. To what end the soul creates itself, "Sense knows not; Faith knows not; only that it is through Mystery to Mystery, from God and to God. 'We *are such stuff* / As dreams are made of . . .' " (267), the stuff of the imagination. "We stand in a region of conjectures, where substance has melted into shadow," the real into the imagined, "and one can not be distinguished from the other" (297). In this region, where the soul creates its own reality, the imagination "is King over us" (222); the poet is "something of a . . . Divinity" (289); and "LITERATURE" is the true scripture (253). Because every book is made in time, none is ever complete. And yet, true books confront and conquer the "Time-prince" (293) by transmuting his own weaponry of temporal things into symbols of the eternal. Of all such redeeming, liberating books the noblest are the "Lives of heroic god-inspired Men; for what other Work of Art is so divine?" (224). Recognizing that *The end of Man is an Action, and not a Thought*" (155), these "Lives" will be "hieroglyphically" rather than "literally authentic," but nonetheless true for their "so-called Facts" being "little better than a Fiction" (202).

David Copperfield

Those who call *David Copperfield* an "autobiographical" novel usually mean that portions of David's history closely resemble what we know about Dickens's own early experiences. While this rough and ready terminology may serve the presumably, but not self-evidently, useful purpose of identifying novels that contain biographical information about their authors, it fails to explain how such novels are necessarily more autobiographical than those which do not. The fictional detail we can trace back to some documented event in the writer's prior life is not more autobiographical than one whose source we cannot discover because the germinal experience was either too deeply personal to admit of documentation or too common to be noticed. For that matter, unless we take a writer's "life" to include only those situations, actions, and experiences for which we have some independent evidence (even if that evidence, as in Dickens's case, is supplied by the writer himself), everything a novelist puts into his fiction has a source somewhere in his "life." Where else could it come from? Indeed, Dickens's use of events from his own past life does not even constitute sufficient evidence that *David Copperfield* is an autobiography in any essential sense. As Augustine's concluding prayer, portions of *Suspiria de Profundis*, and most of *Sartor Resartus* indicate, biographical facts are not necessary to autobiography. Consequently, the definitive traits of the genre must lie elsewhere.

If autobiography does not require the presence of biographical facts and requires something more than that its materials originate in the writer's own experience, in what does it consist? The evolution of autobiographical form from Augustine's *Confessions* to *Sartor Resartus* shows that, along with the chronological arrangement of biographical facts, autobiography can do without a consistent point of view in the present, the assignment of the author's name to the narrator and protagonist of the action, and even the assignment of the same name to these two *personae*. In showing what is not necessary, this formal evolution also suggests certain elements that remain constant in, and thus perhaps essential to, the genre. First of all, each of the autobiographies we have examined has been grounded in the assumption of an absolute, unconditioned self or soul that transcends and hence justifies all conditioned experience. Second, each of these autobiographies has as its central concern the realization of that absolute self, either by explaining it, or by discovering it, or by enacting it symbolically. But, whatever means are employed, the autobiographer seeks to possess the self consciously, on the assumption that self-consciousness is the consciousness of universal principles. And third, we have seen in each of these autobiographies the deployment of certain narrative *personae* who represent—in various ways, depending on whether the autobiographer seeks to explain, to explore, or to express himself—on the one hand, the self he knows or wishes to know, and on the other hand, the self that knows or seeks to know.

To these three recurring elements of autobiography, I would add a fourth: a language that can only be called *allegorical* in that whatever the explicit, sensible referent of any linguistic figure may be, its ultimate and principal referent is always the otherwise ungraspable self. The language of autobiography has been allegorical in this sense from the beginning—the biographical metaphors of Dante, Bunyan, and Franklin no less so than the fictive metaphors of De Quincey and Carlyle. None of these historical autobiographers thought that the truth about his life lay in its historical events. They simply considered these events an adequate medium for the apprehension and transmission of a truth beyond the facts, while De Quincey and Carlyle found fictive metaphors better suited to the same allegorical purpose. It is perfectly true that the allegorical tenor of autobiographical language becomes more noticeable when self becomes a mystery to "memory and conjecture" and available only to the imagination, when autobiography gives up trying to explain the self historically or to discover it philosophically and attempts to reveal the self in fictive metaphors whose explicit referents are not events from the writer's own past life. Nevertheless, this change from biographical to fictive metaphor should not be taken as a change either in the ultimate purposes of autobiography or in the linguistic means of achieving those ends.

While this allegorical language remains constant amidst the several alterations that mark the evolution of autobiography, the relation between the figures used and the *allos*, the "other" thing to which they refer, changes perceptibly with the modulation from historical, to philosophical, to poetic form. For Dante, as for medieval writers generally, allegory was not a way of disguising something known and expressible in its own terms, but a way of revealing something otherwise unknowable to the fallen intelligence. His poetic figures are the verbal analogues of that mundane speculum through which men try to discern the truth. For Franklin, on the contrary, allegory was a means of taking what human reason knows and dressing it in a figurative garb calculated to arrest the attention and move the hearts of less enlightened men. Having replaced providential revelation with human reason, the enlightened man took over God's function of instructing the lower orders through allegory, which ceased to be a way of knowing something ineffable and became a way of making concrete something abstract.

In their deep dismay over the pretensions of human reason and its effects upon what we call the quality of life, the Romantics sought to recover the cognitive function of medieval allegory by restoring to verbal figures the power of revealing otherwise ungraspable truths. The difference is that whereas Dante's allegories had participated in a widely shared system of belief, presided over by the Scriptures (the grandest allegory of all), Romantic allegory operated in an ideological vacuum, with no fund of consensually validated figures upon which to draw and no widespread agreement about the *allos* to which its figures should refer. As a result, the "otherness" of allegory becomes effectually indistinguishable from, and to that extent conditioned by, the allegory itself. While Carlyle retains the necessary belief in an absolute self, in the eternal, "divine ME" that his autobiographical time-symbols reveal, his inability to define that self in any terms except those of the time-symbol unavoidably implies that the "divine ME" is whatever the autobiography reveals, that self-revelation is in fact self-creation, and that the autobiography is not just a manifestation of the self but its very embodiment. As the self becomes identified with autobiography, moreover, the autobiography becomes the subject of its own allegory; the autobiography becomes a work about itself.

David Copperfield, then, is autobiographical only to the extent that it expresses through the deployment of conventional narrative *personae* and through the allegorical tenor of its language Dickens's over-riding concern with the realization of his self, the achievement of true being. By this measure, only the first fourteen chapters of the novel have any serious claim to membership in the genre. Although the remaining three quarters of the book contain fictional treatments of documented events from Dickens's own prior life, these later chapters really tell an altogether different story with an altogether different subject—one, I might add, in which Dickens seems only indifferently engaged. The protagonist who makes "Another Beginning" in Chapter Fifteen, in new clothes, with a "new name, and with everything new about" him, seems to have no connection, even in memory, with the earlier protagonist, the remembrance of whose life "is fraught with so much pain" to the narrator, "with so much suffering and want of hope" that he gladly drops the curtain upon it.* Nor is it altogether surprising that the novel should make "Another Beginning" at this point. For, the first fourteen chapters are structurally complete in themselves, both novelistically, in that the action negotiates the conventional cycle from home through a period of domestic exile to the achievement of a perfect domicile and the just distribution of rewards and punishments among the characters; and autobiographically, in that, as we shall see, the protagonist and the narrator meet on a common ground at its conclusion.

The concern with self that permeates autobiography is evident throughout these first fourteen chapters in Dickens's apparent need to write about a period of his life that was so distasteful, even vaguely shameful, to him; to confess himself publicly, as it were, and to redeem his past by giving it that domestic form by which the English novel, from its very beginnings, had represented the middle-class ideal of virtue and justice, if not the real state of the world. In Dickens's case, as in that of every autobiographer who preceded him, the autobiographical impulse arose from a feeling that the connections between his past and present lives were not clear, and hence that his public character

---

* *The Centenary Edition of the Works of Charles Dickens* (London, 1911) 19:257. Subsequent references to this edition appear in parentheses in the text.

was at odds with his own vision of himself. When Dickens regarded his boyhood historically, which is to say from an external point in the present, that painful early period appeared to comprise a small portion of his life and to have had a happy issue in his present success. When he viewed those painful experiences imaginatively, from their own ground, however, they seemed interminable, hopeless —not a part of some larger happier story at all, but, like De Quincey's addiction, a powerful image of despair. In this recusant form, those past experiences were still present to him, unredeemed by his new station in the world and so detached from his actual circumstances, like some recurring nightmare of a near-fatal accident. To redeem this past but ever-present time, Dickens had to square not only its disgraceful appearances with his present success but its private vision of hopelessness with his publicly avowed belief in moral justice. In order to prove that the despair he experienced then was not a real picture of the world but only the imperfect vision of a frightened, lonely boy who could not foresee the happy outcome of his sufferings, he had to discover for himself and explain to his readers how those sufferings participated in the larger truth of his reassuringly fortunate destiny.

In *David Copperfield*, as in all the autobiographies we have examined thus far, the relation between the writer's past and present selves appears as a problem in narrative form. If Dickens had understood the connection between his damned youth and his present redemption, he could have assumed the role of Augustine's converted narrator and explained the process by which the protagonist became him. Since he did not know the true ground on which these two apparently disparate selves were really one, however, he had two alternatives. He could stand his ground in the narrative present, as Franklin had, and edit the past in the light of the present, or he could adopt his protagonist's point of view, as Wordsworth did, and re-live the past imaginatively in the hope of arriving by this course back at his present faith in the world's providential design. Although Dickens did not know what the value of that terrible past was, he believed that it did have value, that it was truer in some inexpressible sense than his present situation and therefore worthy of a full accounting. Indeed, it is that feeling which lies behind his obsession with this inexplicable and yet unforgettable period of his life. For these reasons, Dickens elects Wordsworth's autobiographical strategy and becomes a traveler amidst the scenes of his youth. Instead of standing his ground in the present and looking back over past times, the narrator remarks repeatedly that he is re-living them.

This narrative technique serves both Dickens's novelistic and autobiographical purposes at once. By concentrating his attention on the immediate experiences of the protagonist, who does not know how things will turn out, he effectually suppressed information that the retrospective narrator might be supposed to know and thus creates suspense in the face of presumably foregone conclusions. The mere presence of the narrator and the fact that he is looking back on his troubles from a point outside them assures the reader that David's domestic exile will end happily. The novel reader can thus attend to the moving action with pleasurable anxiety and wait for the denouement that the narrator could supposedly reveal now, if he chose. For the philosophico-poetic reader of philosophico-poetically written autobiography, however, this withholding of information creates another kind of suspense. By concentrating his attention upon the protagonist, Dickens veils the situation and even the character of his narrator. While the narrator is always present as a disembodied voice, hinting at a satisfactory conclusion in the manner of the elder Dante or at least hoping for one in the manner of Carlyle's Editor, the autobiographical reader is anxious to see him finally appear on the fictive stage, as a character in the novel rather than as a voice outside it, when David's adventures arrive at their conclusion in the narrative present.

When David's adult self does step upon the fictive stage, the novel reader will doubtless not recognize him, for he makes his appearance long before the novel is finished. And even the philosophico-poetic reader of autobiography will be much amazed, for the character who represents the consequences of David's experiences bears no immediate resemblance either to the narrator whose voice has presided over the action so far or to the protagonist whose adventures have led up to the convergence of these autobiographical *personae*. Nevertheless, the account of their strange meeting has that allegorical tenor which is essential to autobiography. Standing outside Aunt Betsey's cottage, David says, "I lifted up my eyes to the window above . . . , where I saw a florid, pleasant-looking gentleman, with a grey head, who shut up one eye in a grotesque manner, nodded his head at me several times, shook it at me as often, and went away" (228). Inexplicable in purely novelistic terms, except as one among many examples of Mr. Dick's relentlessly odd manner, "this unexpected behaviour" and David's resulting discomposure constitute a significant event in the history of autobiography: the first meeting of past and present selves *facie ad faciem* as fully dramatized characters in the action.

Although Mr. Dick seems to resemble neither the young David nor the older narrator who has been telling the story, his autobiographical relation to these two *personae* becomes clear enough when the description of his foibles is philosophico-poetically read. In the first place, Dick bears an allegorical relation to Dickens that complements David's different but equally allegorical kinship with his author. Without wishing to underscore the obvious, or to translate the allegory too literally (and thus effectually to deny the autobiographer's need to write allegorically in the first place), I feel obliged to point out some of the more striking resemblances between Mr. Dick and Charles Dickens, and especially between the former's literary project and the one in which that strange opus is described. When David remarks upon the shortness of Dick's name, Aunt Betsey, who seems to know everything about everyone, assures the boy that Dick has a longer name "if he chose to use it," but "Dick is his name here, and everywhere else now—if he ever went anywhere else, which he don't" (241).— Mr. Dick is also a prolific writer, at work upon a memorial which Aunt Betsey says is about "his own history" and then immediately says is about someone else, one of those famous people "who are paid to *be* memorialized." Whatever its subject, the work proceeds slowly, for the oppressive memory of the author's own youthful unhappiness keeps intruding itself in the form of allusions to "Charles the First," whose headful of troubles have unaccountably found their way into Dick's own muddled brain.

These references to "King Charles," Aunt Betsey explains, are Dick's "allegorical way of expressing" his "great disturbance and agitation" over the ill-treatment he received as a child. They are "the figure, or the simile, or whatever it's called, which he chooses to use. And why shouldn't he, if he thinks proper?" Still, "It's not a business-like way of speaking . . . nor a worldly way . . ." (245), so instead of publishing the memorial through the usual channels, Dick inscribes his facts on a kite "with plenty of string . . . ; and when it flies high, it takes the facts a long way. That's my manner of diffusing them," Dick explains in his customary tone of mingled seriousness and jest. "I don't know where they may come down. It's according to circumstances, and the wind, and so forth; but I take my chance of that" (243). Whether or not the recipients of these airborne missives over the years have detected in the memorial the presence of "King Charles," that intrusive yet shadowy figure has been "constantly getting into it; and was there now" (246).

If Dickens's memories of his past life may be discerned through the more or less transparent biographical allegory of David's adventures, his view of himself as the author of *David Copperfield* shines through the translucent fictive allegory of Mr. Dick. The problem is that while both of these characters bear some autobiographical relation to their author, they seem to relate to each other only as characters in the same novel, which is to say fictively and not autobiographically at all. And yet, there are fictive resemblances between them that bear directly on the autobiographical problem Dickens gave his novel to solve. For example, upon first meeting Mr. Dick, David notices that the older man's head is "curiously bowed," like "one of Mr. Creakle's boys' heads after a beating" (231–32). Dick also appears to feel for David a mysterious kinship, whose ground can only lie outside the novel, and he repeatedly signals this secret bond in nods and winks, which he endeavors to hide from Aunt Betsey. But, as in all poetic autobiographies, the most important relation among the *personae* in whom the author has invested irreconcilable aspects of himself is the fictive one. And the stunted personality of Mr. Dick, the child-man, represents, far more persuasively than does either the Charles Dickens of public repute or the David Copperfield who appears in later chapters, the consequences of a childhood like David's, blighted by cruelty and devoid of any prospects for improvement.

This is not to say that Mr. Dick is a full-length self-portrait by the mature Dickens. Most obviously, he lacks that comprehensive and penetrating moral indignation that suffuses the narrator's treatment of the Murdstones. To fill out the autobiographical portrait, in which all the temporally and psychologically fragmented aspects of the author's self are united in a single significant design, we need a character who possesses the powers of vision and control that we have seen in the narrator and will also perform the narrator's requisite duty of distributing rewards and punishments according to the deserts of the several characters. Except insofar as she dresses like a man, Aunt Betsey bears no physical resemblance to the mental picture that a reader is likely to have formed of the narrator. Nevertheless, like that disembodied *persona*, she was present at the protagonist's birth, and although she looks at David as if he "were an immense way off" (239) in temporal and psychological distance, she knows all the important details of his life and neither requires any information from the Murdstones on this subject nor is fooled by their misrepresentations. Furthermore, she is fully responsible for Mr. Dick, who came under her protection at the very hour of David's birth and whose character she values highly enough to make public when others in his family would have "shut him up for life" (244). Prone to candid statement herself, of course, she vaguely distrusts Dick's unbusinesslike way of writing his memorial and insists that "there shan't be a word" of allegory in it. And, while she insists that "nobody knows what that man's mind is except myself" (245), she rather uncharacteristically withholds her knowledge on this interesting topic. In fact, when she tells David about her association with Dick, she seems not so much to be revealing something she has always known as to be reflecting upon this odd relationship for the first time, very much as if the meeting of David and Dick had raised a hitherto unanticipated question. When the Murdstones appear, however, Aunt Betsey's ruminations give way to action as she performs the domestic narrator's righteous office of unmasking David's tormentors and installing the exiled hero in a perfect domicile under the mutual guardianship of herself and Mr. Dick.

With the closing of this domestic circle Dickens resolves the basic autobiographical problem in entirely poetic terms. Irreconcilable historically or philosophically, Dickens's several past and present selves assume the guise of characters in a domestic novel and commune among themselves in that invented world. Like Rousseau, Dickens saw in his past experiences not the tangled root-system of a single self but the seeds of many separate selves, all of whom had some ineffable kinship with each other but could be brought together only upon a fictive stage. In writing the first part of *David Copperfield*, he seems to have come to the conclusion that the experiences he gave to David had produced an aspect of himself which his narrator did not represent and consequently had to be embodied in the altogether different character of Mr. Dick. Since Mr. Dick, being a character in a novel, never goes "anywhere else," the narrator can take up a proper relationship with him and with David only by abandoning the conventional intermediary position of autobiographical narrators, between the inner world of the text and the outer worlds of author and audience, and becoming a character in the fictive action. It is a highly significant move. Although the narrators of *The Prelude*, *Suspiria de Profundis*, and *Sartor Resartus* had entered into those autobiographical actions as more or less dramatized characters, they had all done so in the hope of eventually returning from their interior voyages with some form of self-knowledge that could be conveyed to the outside world in generally understandable—that is, non-allegorical—terms. In setting his narrator firmly upon the interior fictive stage, however, Dickens indicated as clearly as might be that the self could know itself only in the enigmatic mirror of allegory, that true being could be realized only in autobiography.

The union of Dickens's past self with his present selves, public and private, in their allegorical home concludes the autobiographical portion of *David Copperfield*. The chapters to come will contain characters named Copperfield, Aunt Betsey, and Mr. Dick, but these characters will bear only a superficial resemblance to their namesakes in the first fourteen chapters. The new David, being an innocent, will come under the sway of Steerforth, whereas the old David would have been far too worldly wise not to see through that smooth dissembler. And even though David's later adventures will contain thinly disguised details from Dickens's own life, that story will engage the author's attention so sporadically that he will doubt at last whether David is really its "hero" (1). This new David, of course, will grow up to be nothing like Mr. Dick. On the contrary, although these two begin the second part of the novel as "the best of friends," flying "the great kite" together (258), they will move steadily apart as David grows up. Indeed, the Mr. Dick of the autobiography will remain present less in his dramatized figure than in that often lamented tendency of the author to portray the world as a moral contest between heartless adults and warm-hearted children of all ages. While these later chapters will not be an autobiography written in a form of a domestic novel, but rather a domestic novel posing as an autobiography—not an autobiographical fiction but a fictional autobiography—the persistent spirit of Mr. Dick will serve to confirm the accuracy of Dickens's autobiographical discovery. Whatever experiences may have produced the Aunt Betsey in him, the terrors he gave to David had produced the Mr. Dick in him: that ineradicable conviction that the real world is hopelessly corrupt and that true being and the true society are possible only in the admittedly unbusinesslike, unworldly, even childish realms of the poetic imagination.

The Scarlet Letter

Sartor Resartus and *David Copperfield* help us to trace the formal evolution of autobiography through its final, most problematic stage: the abandonment of all reference to biographical event and the adoption of of totally fictive materials. Although both of these works cloak themselves in the garb of fiction, both maintain a connection, however tenuous, with historical and philosophical autobiography through those details in the lives of their protagonists which repeat their author's own extra-literary experiences. At the same time, these two works take us very close to purely poetic form in that their autobiographical import lies less in these fictionally encoded biographical data than in the symbolic uses to which the fictional metaphors themselves are put. What makes *Sartor Resartus* and *David Copperfield* autobiographies, in other words, is not their inclusion of biographical materials but their efforts to discover, through a fictive action, some ground upon which conflicting aspects of the writer's own nature might be reconciled in complete being.

The intellectual situation that necessitated this non-biographical program for autobiography may be sketched in the words of Emerson, whose thought connects, as his life did, the worlds of Carlyle and Hawthorne. Borrowing from Coleridge a statement that was made in one form or another by virtually all of Kant's followers, Emerson said, "The problem of philosophy is, for all that exists conditionally, to find a ground unconditioned and absolute." But when the mind has no immediate access to the absolute, when we have no way, as Augustine said, to "so hold the mind of man that it may stand and see . . . eternity, which stands still," then how is the mind to overcome its own conditionality and take hold of the unconditioned? Emerson's contemporary, Orestes Brownson, put the question and its answer this way: "How shall we place ourselves in the Absolute as our point of observation? We must attain the summit by a slow and toilsome ascent from the valley, where is our starting-point, not by dropping from the heavens." Emerson reiterates the idea that the absolute must be sought by way of the conditional and suggests its connection with autobiographical procedure when he says, in *Nature*, that "Every man's condition is a solution in hieroglyphic to those inquiries he would put" to the order of things. "He acts it as life before he apprehends it as truth." That is, conditioned individual action writes the hieroglyphic language that, once deciphered, discloses what Emerson elsewhere called "the aboriginal Self, on which a universal reliance may be grounded." Now, of the many possible forms that this hieroglyphic action may take, verbal action is the most significant. For, while "Words and deeds," according to Emerson, "are quite indifferent modes of the divine energy"—words being "also actions" —yet the vision of the absolute is "clearest and most permanent in words." It follows, then, that for those whose inquiry to the creation is, "Who am I?" autobiography will comprise a series of verbal actions in which the answer to that question may be hieroglyphically read. And having moved through this process of poetic self-enaction to full self-possession, the autobiographer will experience the ecstasy that Emerson described as the effect of true poetry: "And now my chains are to be broken; I shall mount above these clouds and opaque airs in which I live—opaque, though they seem transparent—and from the heaven of truth I shall see and comprehend my relations" and "know what I am doing."*

These theories regarding the identity of the self and the absolute, the possibility of knowing the absolute through conditioned individual experience, and the essential similarity between verbal and non-verbal experience as modes of symbolic action remove any necessity for an autobiography to reflect the writer's extra-literary experience. An autobiography written under the aegis of these ideas could dispense with biographical data altogether, even in a fictional guise. It need only assume that a substantial, unitary self or soul exists independent of the actions of the poetic imagination and may be discerned through them. The question is whether this faith in the absolute self, and hence the traditional idea of autobiography as a genre addressed to that subject, could survive this virtual identification of the self with the conditional, poetic actions performed in the hope of realizing it.

The Scarlet Letter is Hawthorne's definitive formulation of the autobiographical problem that informed his entire literary career: his abiding sense of himself as two quite distinct and unrelated persons, one public and typical, the other private and unique. "I have a mind," he wrote to Sophia Peabody on New Year's Day in 1840, "to send my dearest a journal of . . . my whole external life, from the time

---

* *The Collected Works of Ralph Waldo Emerson*, ed. R. E. Spiller and A. R. Ferguson 1 (Cambridge, Mass., 1971):33. *The Confessions of St. Augustine*, p. 265. Orestes Brownson, "Victor Cousin," *The Christian Examiner* 21 (1836) :40. *The Collected Works of Ralph Waldo Emerson*, 1:7. *The Complete Works of Ralph Waldo Emerson*, ed. E. W. Emerson (Cambridge, Mass., 1903), 2:63, 3:8. *The Collected Works*, 1:84. *The Complete Works*, 3:17.

I wake at dawn, till I close my eyes at night. . . . But then, apart from this, I would write another journal of my inward life throughout the self-same day. . . . Nobody would think that the same man could live two such different lives simultaneously."*

This problem was not Hawthorne's alone, of course. The relation between individual and collective existence, between true being and the true society, had been a matter of deep concern to autobiographers ever since Augustine wrote his *Confessions*. And it had been the decisive question of autobiography since Franklin and Rousseau had demonstrated that, without the assistance of such divine revelations as had enabled Dante and Bunyan to unite the individual and society upon a higher common ground, the gulf between private and public truth was unbridgeable. From that time on, reflective autobiographers had been forced to locate the truth on one or the other side of this chasm and either deny the individual self to find true being in social conformity or else withdraw from society to seek true being within the uncompromised self.

What set Hawthorne apart from most of his contemporaries who shared this characteristically modern problem was his constitutional inability to place his faith entirely in either of these contestant selves. The interior, imaginative life might offer a spiritual haven from soul-less collective existence, but it could also be a private hell, from which only public contact could rescue him. Worse yet, if he could not finally decide which of these incompatible selves was the true one, neither could he accept any resolution of the conflict that depended upon some unstable intermixture of the two. The only thing he hated worse than over-sim-

---

* *The Love Letters of Nathaniel Hawthorne, 1839–41* (Chicago, 1907), p. 122.

plification was ambiguity. Unwilling to live entirely in Franklin's public world or in Rousseau's private one, and unable to live in both at once, Hawthorne wanted nothing less than to rediscover the absolute ground of all things that exist conditionally, in both the haunted mind and the daylight of common sense. Rather than deny his individuality, as Franklin had, or his common humanity, as had Rousseau, he would find the golden principle beneath these baser elements of existence, unveiling "the light that is to reveal all secrets, and . . . unite all who belong to one another."*

This spiritual problem presented itself to Hawthorne in a preponderantly literary form. Like Rousseau's progeny, he associated the private self with symbolic action, those unpremeditated expressions of the creative imagination that he called "the heart's native language." He did not compose obscure allegories out of any "love for mystery," he wrote to Sophia on May 19, 1840, but because plain words are useful "merely for explaining outward acts, and all sorts of external things, leaving the soul's life and action to explain itself in its own way."† To his mind, no less than to Carlyle's, the public language of self-biography had no access to these secrets of the individual life. When a writer indulges in "a little preliminary talk about his external habits, his abode, his casual associates, and other matters entirely on the surface," Hawthorne wrote in the preface to *The Snow Image and Other Twice-Told Tales*, he reveals nothing peculiar to himself. On the contrary, "these things hide the man instead of displaying him" (XI, 4). After expatiating upon his past and present circumstances in "The Old Manse," Hawthorne advises his reader that, for

* *The Centenary Edition of the Works of Nathaniel Hawthorne*, ed. W. Charvat et al. (Columbus, Ohio, 62–77), I, 154. All subsequent references to this edition appear in parentheses in the text.
† *The Love Letters of Nathaniel Hawthorne*, p. 193.

all these seeming confidences, "So far as I am a man of really individual attributes, I veil my face" (X, 33). And, preparatory to discussing his public life in the Salem custom house, he reiterates the point: "We may prate of the circumstances that lie around us, and even of ourself, but still keep the inmost Me behind the veil" (I, 4). Only symbolic expression can catch and display the writer's unique, private nature. "In order to detect any of his essential traits," Hawthorne contends, "you must make another kind of inquest, and look through the whole range of his fictitious characters, good and evil . . ." (XI, 4).

If the story of David Copperfield's "new life" suggests that biographical information is not sufficient to autobiography, and Carlyle insists that such data are not even necessary to the genre, Hawthorne's statements appear to argue that self-biography is essentially non-autobiographical, that fiction is the only true autobiography. The matter is not so simple, however. As a descendant of Rousseau, Hawthorne did subscribe to that Romantic cosmology which located Augustine's heaven of truth within the individual heart, where it speaks to the mind through the medium of symbolic action. But he was also a direct descendant of that Franklin who located true being in a collective reality to which the mind has access through its own native language of rational, public discourse. While his autobiography could not simply describe his public self, therefore, neither could it simply express the private self. It would have to display the private self in symbols that common sense could comprehend. At the same time, it would have to make the public self receptive to the heart's secret truths, no matter how unpalatable they might seem. This is to say that, for Hawthorne, the achievement of complete being was synonymous with, and contingent upon, the creation of a complete work of art, one that would have, for himself and for his audience, the healing effect that Augustine, Dante, and Bunyan had ascribed to God's revealed word. Not until the heart's secret flame and the communal sun were shown to derive their light from a single source could the divided self truly become one.

This autobiographical program accounts for the peculiar self-reflexiveness of Hawthorne's fictions, which may be described as attempts to comprehend their own, often extravagant, symbolic actions within a framework of moral values that Hawthorne shared with his audience. Typically, these actions turn upon the efforts of one or more characters to discover the meanings behind their own and each other's appearance, the motivating principles of their behavior, and the true basis of their relationships to each other. Invariably, Hawthorne's narrators participate in this investigation of meanings and motives, asking questions, proposing answers, changing their minds in response to events which seem to arise unexpectedly. As the characters strike emblematic poses and carry on vaguely portentous conversations, they seem to be acting out an idea that the narrator cannot quite grasp. And since the narrator is the source, the creator, of the symbolic actions he is trying to understand, their ungraspable meaning seems to be the secret of his own true being. As the narrator of "Monsieur du Miroir" puts it, upon begging his reflection to break the silence between them, "A few words, perhaps, might satisfy the feverish yearning of my soul for some master thought that should guide me through the labyrinth of life, teaching wherefore I was born, and how to do my task on earth, and what is death" (X, 171).

Among the self-expressive metaphors that reappear again and again in Hawthorne's fiction, one in particular seems to have held for him what T. S. Eliot called the undefinable symbolic value of images which "come to represent the depths of feeling into which we cannot peer." On June 1, 1842, Hawthorne wrote in his notebook:

> The human heart to be allegorized as a cavern—at the entrance there is sunshine and flowers growing about it. You step within, but a short distance, and begin to find yourself surrounded with a terrible gloom, and monsters of diverse kinds; it seems like Hell itself. You are bewildered, and wander long without hope. At last a light strikes upon you. You peep towards it, and find yourself in a region that seems, in some sort, to reproduce the flowers and sunny beauty of the entrance, but all perfect. These are the depths of the heart, or of human nature; bright and peaceful; the gloom and terror may lie deep; but deeper still is the eternal beauty. [VIII, 237]

This complex figure relates to Hawthorne's life-long autobiographical project in a number of ways. First of all, it diagrams the autobiographical problem he gave his fiction to solve. The setting represents, among other things, the contrast between the sunny, exterior world of communal existence and the dark interior of the secret life. And the implied action proposes a solution to the conflict between these two realms: by proceeding inward, away from the pleasant but imperfect exterior, and by confronting the horrible but ultimately insubstantial terrors of the buried life, one can discover the absolute self, which is also the exterior world made perfect. Second, the figure of the cavern served Hawthorne's metaphor for the difference between reflectively discursive and symbolically expressive autobiography. Denying that his circumstantial remarks in "The Old Manse" have any real bearing on his "individual attributes," he asks, "Has the reader gone wandering, hand in hand with me, through the inner passages of my being? . . .

Not so, we have been standing on the greensward, but just within the cavern's mouth, where the sunshine is free to penetrate, and where every footstep is therefore free to come. I have appealed to no sentiment or sensibilities save such as are diffused among us all" (X, 32–33). And he employs elements of the same figure in the preface to *The Snow Image* . . . to make the same distinction between those autobiographical statements which serve "to pave the reader's way into the interior edifice of a book" and the fictions themselves, which record the author's "burrowing . . . into the depths of our common nature" and "his researches in that dusky region" (XI, 3, 4).

Standing in Hawthorne's mind both for the autobiographical problem he set his fiction and for those fictions themselves, this figure also provided a structural and thematic model for some of his richest and most puzzling works. In "My Kinsman, Major Molineux," "Young Goodman Brown," "The Man of Adamant," and "Peter Goldthwaite's Treasure," to cite only a few examples, a protagonist withdraws from a sunlit social world into a dark interior space in search of some symbolic object that will reveal both his own true being and the principle of his common humanity, and so justify all the guilt, anxiety, suffering, and moral risks incurred by his social defection. "With an emblematical divining-rod," Hawthorne wrote in his notebook, "to seek for emblematical gold, that is for Truth—for what of Heaven is left on earth" (VIII, 240).

In every case, however, the protagonist's discovery proves unacceptable to the narrator who has been following the action with great interest to see where it will lead. "A man seeks for something excellent," another notebook entry reads, "but seeks it in the wrong way, and in a wrong spirit, and finds something horrible—as for instance, he seeks for treasure, . . . and brings to light his accumulated sins" (VIII, 242–43). Unable to reconcile the apparent meaning of the discovered symbol with the moral principles he shares with his audience, the narrator then construes the foregoing action as an example of some avoidable error—pride, presumption, unholy curiosity, lack of human sympathy, secretiveness, or whatever. The effect of this often repeated pattern is that each of the tales Hawthorne called his "Allegories of the Heart" describes the complete process of its own composition—from the author's motivating desire to discover his true self, through his withdrawal from the daylight realm of social discourse into the interior space of imaginative action, to some discovery about the private self which the public self cannot accept, and finally to a repudiation the entire experiment in the name of public morality.

Much as these tales may please the present-day taste for moral ambiguity, they certainly did not satisfy Hawthorne. "I am possessed," says the narrator of one of his more transparently autobiographical sketches, "with the thought that I have never yet discovered the real secret of my powers; that there has been a mighty treasure within my reach; a mine of gold beneath my feet, worthless because I have never known how to seek for it . . ." (XI, 315). For twelve years, he wandered imaginatively through what he called "the inner passages of my being," groping "into all its chambers," examining "their treasures or their rubbish" (X, 32), without finding what he sought—the priceless gem of that truth in which individual uniqueness and common nature have "the oneness of their being" and "live immortally together" (I, 207). Then, sometime late in 1849, a tale he was writing grew to an inordinate size—too long to be considered a tale, too short to be a proper "romance." Whatever it was, *The Scarlet Letter* had somehow managed to overstep the obstacles that had blocked the self-seeking actions of his previous works, quite unexpectedly fulfilling a prophecy he had written in his notebook years earlier: "A person to be writing a tale, and to find that it shapes itself against his intentions; that the characters act otherwise than he thought; that unforeseen events occur; and a catastrophe comes which he strives in vain to avert. It might shadow forth his own fate,—he having made himself one of the personages" (VIII, 16).

Among the several artistic decisions which appear in retrospect to have contributed to this unforeseen development, the most important for our purposes are those regarding the work's narrative mode, for these also have the effect of making *The Scarlet Letter* a true poetic autobiography. Although Hawthorne's tales resemble *Sartor Resartus* and the first part of *David Copperfield* in displaying the self through fictive rather than biographical metaphors, the tales remain formally philosophical by virtue of their undramatized narrators, who, like their counterpart in *The Prelude*, strive to comprehend the justifying design of an imaginative action that expresses the wayward but vital actions of the buried self. In a sketch called "Sunday at Home"—one of Hawthorne's many experimental presentations of himself as two persons—the narrator dramatizes his "mind," or moral reason, and his "heart," or poetic imagination, as "colleague pastors—colleagues but often disputants." "The former," he says, "pretends to be a scholar and perplexes me with doctrinal points; the latter takes me on the score of feeling." Now, insofar as the narrator represents the consciousness of this division within himself, he is an essential part of the complete self depicted in the passage. Furthermore, when he goes on to say, "I, their sole auditor, cannot always understand them" (IX, 24), he admits his dependence upon their dialogue for whatever knowledge he may have about himself. Nevertheless, his location outside the action identifies him less with these *dramatis personae* than with the author, who wrote the tale and is therefore publicly responsible for its moral import. Because Hawthorne felt this responsibility so keenly, whenever the symbolic action of a tale threatened to express something that he could not justify to his audience, or to that part of himself that he identified with it, he had his narrator cut off the action with a reassuring moral, which, however ambiguous it might prove on closer inspection, at least appears to construe the action as an improving lesson.

There is, however, one instance in Hawthorne's tales where this ostensibly disengaged narrator formally reveals his lack of control over the symbolic action and his very deep involvement in it. Toward the end of "My Kinsman, Major Molineux," the narrator abandons his external vantage-point and enters the story to witness its outcome. To be sure, this strangely disembodied figure retains certain traits of his recently relinquished authority. He is the only character in the tale who is not very precisely described. He is the only one whose impressions of Robin are reported to the reader. He addresses Robin in the same language of ironic condescension that the narrator has been using all along, and he recites the putative lesson of the tale at its conclusion. At the same time, his removal from the cavern's mouth, between the public greensward and the private interior, to the dark labyrinths of the symbolic action signals the fundamental change in Hawthorne's autobiographical method that would lead to the surprising growth of *The Scarlet Letter*. The appearance of this hitherto authorial *persona* onstage as a character capable of conversing with those whose mutual relations he seeks to understand tacitly acknowledges the essential kinship between self-consciousness and the problematic self of which it is aware, as well as the interaction of these two psychic activities—self-reflection and self-expression—in the process of self-realization. Whereas the voice of inquisitive self-consciousness in "Sunday at Home" remained inaudible to the disputant mind and heart—precisely as the voice of Carlyle's Editor had remained inaudible to Teufelsdröckh—the conversation between narrator and protagonist in "Major Molineux" simultaneously recalls the meeting of David, Mr. Dick, and Aunt Betsey in *David Copperfield* and foreshadows the dramatic interaction of Hester, Dimmesdale, and Chillingworth in *The Scarlet Letter*. Their three-way conversation would constitute an affirmative answer to the question posed by the *quondam* narrator at the end of "Major Molineux": "May not a man have several voices . . . as well as two complexions?" (XI, 226).

The narrator of *The Scarlet Letter* presents himself, not as its author, who would be responsible for its meanings, but merely as its editor, one who entertains no more hope than did his counterpart in *Sartor Resartus* of finally solving the riddle of the "mystic symbol" that speaks to his sensibilities but "evades the analysis of his mind" (I, 31). Meanwhile, the ambiguous role of inquiring interpreter played by the narrators of the tales is assumed by a fully dramatized character in the action, one who—being "not a spectator only but a chief actor in the poor minister's interior world" (I, 140)—is both responsible for, and deeply affected by, the events of the story. Alongside the scarlet woman and the pale minister, Chillingworth appears as the Black Man. An avatar of all those artistic alchemists who seek the golden truth through the manipulation of symbolic matter in the tales, Hester's husband is also a type of the coldly inquisitive spirit that Hawthorne detected in his own artistic methods and personified in the autobiographical sketch "Sights from a Steeple" as Paul Pry, the unfeeling voyeur who lives entirely through other people. Arising from, and empowered by, the conflicts between passionate Hester and moral Dimmesdale, with whom he is also necessarily at odds, Chillingworth seeks the truth that connects them, "probing everything with a cautious touch, like a treasure-seeker in a dark cavern," "like a miner searching for gold" or "a jewel"—if "only for the art's sake" (I, 124, 129, 138).

The two characters whose obscure relation to each other occupies Chillingworth's attention and whose separation from each other constitutes his *raison d'être* reenact the conflict between the passional and moral selves that Hawthorne had dramatized in so many of his tales. In addition, like Chillingworth, each of these two figures typifies one of the conflicting ideas Hawthorne held about the purposes of art in general and about himself as an artist in particular. Although Hester has sometimes been adjudged one of the few satisfactory portraits of a woman by a male author, it is probably more accurate to say that she is merely a projection of certain traits in her male creator—his intuitive, "poetic" nature—that Victorian sexual mythology labeled "feminine." Whatever the case, many people who knew Hawthorne felt, as Bronson Alcott put it, that there was "some damsel imprisoned in [his] manly form, pleading alway for release."* Hawthorne seems to have entertained the same fancy, for the autobiographical protagonists of "The Village Uncle" and "The Vision of the Fountain" both see in their own reflections the women who are to become their "better halves." Indeed, the emblematic bits that form the mosaic of Hester's character can be found scattered throughout the tales, which record Hawthorne's increasing identification with the seductive but tainted

* *Concord Days* (Boston, 1972), p. 194.

woman who came gradually to represent the Romantic side
of his artistic life. Arrayed with all the symbolic regalia that
had stood in the tales for subversive energy—exotic garb,
"antique gentility," skill with the needle, contagious infec-
tion, the devil's flaming brand—Hester embodies those artistic impulses, at once vital and morally formless, that
Hawthorne located in the heart and called the imagination,
a faculty "imparting vividness to all ideas, without the
power of selecting or controlling them" (IX, 306).

If Hester expresses the secretly anarchic energies that
move the incendiary artist of "The Devil in Manuscript,"
Dimmesdale portrays the artist in his public role, as a minister to the spiritual needs of his audience. An artist-priest
like Adam in "A Shaker Bridal" and the autobiographical
narrator of "The Old Manse," he objectifies both Hawthorne's idea of the true artist as a moral preceptor, whose
duty is to render faithfully the common beliefs and familiar
experiences of his audience, and also the ministerial half of
himself that Hawthorne describes in "Sunday at Home"
and "Passages from a Relinquished Work." Against
Hester's lawless fecundity Dimmesdale poses the principle
of moral form, lifeless in itself and yet necessary to
significant human action. Whereas Hester's creativity is
unconsciously impulsive, his proper works are, like Owen
Warland's butterfly, altogether intentional, expressing a
lust for spiritual perfection and a detestation of things carnal that might clog the pure flame of his "spiritual lamp" (I,
120). And yet, he is somehow a partner in the creation of
Hester's morally ambiguous offspring, a fact which he
finds as difficult to admit to himself as Hawthorne often
did the responsibility for his own offspring, both human
and literary. Consequently, Dimmesdale must remain an
anonymous parent—a type of "Oberon" or "Aubepine"
—suffering the same "unmerited praise" for aetherial pu-
rity that tortured his secretly guilty creator.

The occasion for Chillingworth's speculations regarding a possible connection between Hester and Dimmesdale is the birth of Pearl, who therefore becomes a primary object of this "philosopher's research" into the vexing problem of her paternity. While it is perhaps impossible for any reader not to know from the outset that Dimmesdale is Pearl's father, we must remember that this fact is not divulged —which is to say, not a fact—until half-way through the action, when the family mounts the scaffold together at midnight. Moreover, until Chillingworth, to his "wonder, joy, and horror" (I, 138), discovers upon Dimmesdale's breast the fiery token of animal passion and divine eloquence combined, Pearl bears no evident resemblance to the pale, heaven-aspiring minister but seems rather to be solely her "mother's child," as she herself tells the Governor (I, 110). Sumptuously ornamented by Hester's needlework, she is the product of her mother's imagination in "full play" (I, 90) and like all such creations, she has no "discoverable principle of being . . . save the freedom of a broken law" (I, 134). The elements of that being are "perhaps beautiful and brilliant, but all in disorder; or with an order peculiar to themselves," without "reference or adaptation to the world in which she was born" (I, 91).

For all her uncontrollable energy, however, Pearl appears to want a regular father who can grant her something like normal status in the community by acknowledging her as his own. And when she makes up to Dimmesdale at the Governor's mansion, she seems less to be intuiting a natural fact—which is not yet established—than to be expressing a spiritual need for public acceptance. In this respect, Pearl's desire to discover her father—a desire shared in some way by everyone else in the work—simultaneously represents and furthers the aim of the symbolic action, of which she is at once the cause and the living emblem, to discover the moral principle of its own beautiful but disordered being.

The purpose of the symbolic action, in other words, is not to reveal something known—that Dimmesdale is Pearl's father—but rather to find out how his moral reason can embrace the uncontrollable offspring of Hester's imagination without either discrediting itself or smothering the secret springs of Pearl's magical vitality. Where is the treasure to be found, the Truth that is both symbolically expressive and morally comprehensible, creative and intelligible, hidden in the secret heart and revealed to the world?

If Hester, Dimmesdale, and Chillingworth represent the three conflicting elements into which Hawthorne felt himself to be divided, and if Pearl—whose "one baby-voice seemed a multitude of imaginary personages, old and young, to talk withal" (I, 95)—represents the imaginative creation which has caused this conflict and must eventually resolve it, the Boston community bears a striking resemblance to Hawthorne's notions, voiced in his discursively autobiographical prefaces, regarding his own audience. Just as the reading public described there is less an accurate portrait of Hawthorne's actual audience, about which he seems to have known very little, than a projection of his own moral reservations about his works, the townspeople of Boston are less an imitation of the New England Puritans than a dramatized set of moral reactions to the spectacle of the scarlet letter. Like the audience that Hawthorne imagined for his own creations, the crowd that beholds Hester's symbol—"so artistically done, and with so much fertility and gorgeous luxuriance of fancy" (I, 53)—is almost uniformly hostile, the one exception being a silently sympathetic woman, who fills the office of the single unknown friend Hawthorne addressed in the prefaces.

Remembering that Hawthorne was ever of two minds about his audience, however, we must resist the temptation to condemn them more, or to place less faith in them, than he did. True, the New England character is changing for the worse, evolving from an Elizabethan gentility and earthiness, like Hester's, toward Dimmesdale's pale spirituality and Chillingworth's skeptical materialism. For this reason, the townspeople consider Hester a damned soul, Dimmesdale a spotless angel, Pearl an imp of Satan, and Chillingworth a spokesman for their interests. On the other hand, they do not condemn Hester's lawlessness more severely than Hawthorne, or indeed Hester herself, does, and they remain the only agency short of death that can free the self-imprisoned individual from the haunted dungeon of a lonely heart, either by dispelling its phantoms in the common sunshine or by admitting that these demons are common to all mortals. Collectively secure but secretly troubled, "the great heart of humanity" is in fact a macrocosm of the individual heart, with its sunny portal and dark interior. Without this belief that his plight was representative, Hawthorne could never have brought himself to be so true, to show so freely to the world, and to himself, a symbol by which the worst in him might be inferred and, he hoped, redeemed by an understanding public.

The mental stage upon which this knot of characters acts out the relations among them recapitulates Hawthorne's paradigmatic allegory of the heart in a uniquely complex form. Whereas the tales had tended to posit the sunlit exterior world only to withdraw immediately into the "dismal maze" of the secret heart, leaving collective reality uninvolved in, and therefore unaffected by, the action, *The Scarlet Letter* includes the communal realm in the allegory by making it the mirror-image of the heart. The resulting figure is a set of concentric, alternately light and dark spheres, which represent the analogous moral conditions of individual and collective existence. At the center of this figure lies the dungeon from which Hester emerges bearing her ambiguous treasure, the flaming letter whose bloody hue she has defiantly highlighted with the gold of essential truth. Surrounding this dark enclosure and its central point of light is the sunlit town, the moral clearing in which the Puritan community pursues its ideal of living by God's commandments. As the sunny greensward is only the threshold of the individual heart, however, the town is only the surface of the communal life, for it is encircled by the dark forest, the demonic realm to which the community has banished its inadmissible desires and fears, in which Hester's living symbol was conceived, and from which Chillingworth arrives to assist in the communal work of dragging sin into the sunshine. Outside the entire design, finally, lies the sphere of God's holy sunlight, which is at once the heavenly goal of Dimmesdale's spiritual aspirations, the model of the civic order, the marriage altar where Hester hopes her sinful love will be redeemed, and the universal counterpart of the golden truth at the center of the individual heart.

The cumulative effect of Hawthorne's decisions regarding the narrative mode, characterization, and symbolic setting of *The Scarlet Letter* is a total identification of the autobiography and the life that is its subject. With all the customary elements of autobiography—fictive protagonist, interpreting narrator, the audience, and the work itself—all located in the autobiography, the distance that the historical and philosophical forms place between the work and the life disappears entirely. The autobiography becomes, not a history or a philosophical analysis of a life lived elsewhere, but a series of actions performed in the composition of it, a record of those actions, and an interpretation of them, all at once—a book about its own origins, processes, and consequences. As the scarlet letter stands for a word that is also a deed, *The Scarlet Letter* comprises verbal deeds which simultaneously enact, record, and interpret a fictive confrontation among the several aspects of himself that Hawthorne felt to be in conflict and which he placed upon his "mental stage, as actors in a drama" (III, 156), to work out, through the "dark necessity" of their own fictive logic, their true relationships to each other and, in so doing, to tell him who he was.

The drama enacted by Hawthorne's characters upon his allegorized mental stage is determined by the situation in which these characters find themselves in the opening scene. When the curtain rises, each character is in conflict with each of the others as a direct result of Pearl's birth. Given this situation and the autobiographical problem it represents, the action must try to reconcile all of these conflicts and bring the estranged parties together on a common ground. Insofar as their mutual estrangement arises from the appearance of Pearl and the scarlet letter, their reconciliation depends upon their coming to some agreement about the meaning and value of that symbol. That agreement depends, in turn, upon the letter's being transformed, "in some sort," into something all parties can accept on the same terms. And since the symbol derives its meaning from the world in which it was born, its revaluation will require a significant change in that world—which is to say, both in the moral structure of the allegorical landscape and in the form of the work itself.

The symbolic action that issues from this initial situation is best described as a movement by Hester and Dimmesdale between the poles of public and private reality, as these are represented in the setting, in search of the one true place where her individual, passional energies and his communal, moral structures can be united in complete being. Unlike so many of the tales, which begin by withdrawing from the public world to seek the truth within, *The*

Scarlet Letter opens in the sunshine of communal reality, with the publication of the symbol that Hester has so artfully embroidered during her solitary imprisonment. Whatever she may have been thinking when she conceived her child in the dark forest and when she decorated her badge in the dark dungeon, here in the sunshine of public scrutiny these twinned offspring of her passion bespeak evil to her as clearly as they do to the townspeople, who read them as signs of an unrepentant defiance of divine and social law alike. Indeed, there is almost complete agreement on this matter. Dimmesdale fully accepts the townspeople's idea of the letter as a sign of damnation and therefore cannot bring himself to participate in Hester's shame. Chillingworth similarly refuses to acknowledge Hester publicly and shares the community's desire to discover Pearl's father. And Hester places her public, legal obligations to Chillingworth so far above her secret, affectionate ties to Dimmesdale that she disobeys her own heart and agrees to keep Chillingworth's identity a secret.

In the beginning, then, all of the characters, Hester among them, stand together on the public ground of their inability to see in Hester's symbol any virtue that would permit them to associate themselves with it. While Hester shares the general opinion that her letter signifies only evil, however, her defiant embroidery of it expresses, in the heart's native language, something her reason cannot admit: that her fallen state is the truth, not a deviation from it, and that any assuagement of her condition will depend upon her remaining faithful to the hard truth symbolized by her letter. Guided by this as yet unspeakable intuition, she elects to live on the outskirts of town after her banishment instead of either returning to the England of her vanished innocence or fleeing to "the dark, inscrutable forest" (I, 79), the abode of those whom the community considers ir-

revocably damned. Lying halfway between the repress-
ively legalistic town and the licentious forest, this spot perfectly reflects Hester's divided reasons for choosing it. On
the one hand, it answers her publicly acceptable intention
to do penance at the "scene of her guilt" (I, 80). But it also
fulfills the desire, which she cannot admit even to herself,
to be near her secret lover.

Had Hester been allowed to remain in town or inclined
to live in the forest, her attitude toward her letter would
never have changed, since the forest simply shelters the
evil that the town condemns. Like the Old Manse in its
"near retirement and accessible seclusion" (X, 4), however,
Hester's home on the peninsula enables her to look upon
town and forest with an equal eye and thus to discern in
Pearl's disordered nature an element of creative vitality
that is inseparable from her lawlessness. This intuition, un-
certain though it is, allows Hester to think less despairingly
of Pearl, of herself as Pearl's mother, and of the impulse that
led her, first, to stray into the forest and then to remain near
the town that harbors her lover. This altered position,
which is both geographical and moral, also changes her attitude toward Boston authority and encourages her to resist
the Governor's plan to take Pearl away. With the help of
Dimmesdale, who speaks in a language that simultaneously
reveals and hides his relation to Hester and Pearl, she succeeds in formulating the complex meaning which her symbol has acquired in the years since Pearl's birth. The child
is "meant for a blessing" as well as "for a retribution" and
"a torture," a "boon . . . to preserve her from blacker depths
of sin into which Satan might else have sought to plunge
her" (I, 114). Once this compound meaning is expressed,
moreover, Hester can act upon it, offering Pearl as her excuse for refusing Mistress Hibbins's invitation to the
witches' sabbath.

Up to this point in the action, the scarlet letter may be said to have "done its office." Whereas all the characters were once united in their public disparagement of the scarlet letter and its living surrogate, they are conjoined now in the opinion that Pearl's nature may be "divine" as well as "infernal." Like all such "lurid intermixtures" (X, 105), however, this ambiguous light merely obscures what it should reveal, making truth and error, reality and illusion, even less distinguishable than they were in the clear sunlight of the marketplace. Worse yet, this "intermingled gloom and brightness" is Chillingworth's proper element. Once he perceives the "divine" aspect of Pearl's dual character, he sees the possibility of discovering in that character the identity of the child's father. Empowered by Hester's promise not to reveal his identity, by Dimmesdale's fear of appearing too suspiciously secretive, and by the community's tacit support of his designs, Chillingworth assumes control over Dimmesdale and begins his "philosopher's research" into the dark cavern of the minister's troubled heart. Although Chillingworth starts from humane motives, seeking the knowledge that will enable him to cure his patient's obscure malady, the desire for knowledge quickly assumes a malignant life of its own. And when that desire is frustrated, it becomes a wish to torment the object of its original solicitude, exactly as the initially humane inquiries of Hawthorne's narrators in the tales so often culminate in the moral chastisement of their most deeply troubled characters.

Clearly, the equilibration of the worst and best aspects of Hester's love, which results from, and is symbolized by, her removal to the middle-ground between town and forest, cannot reconcile the several dislocations that have precipitated the action. This momentary equipoise is merely a labile ambiguity, inseparable from the action that produced it, and not the sort of abiding truth that might be taken to be the unconditioned ground of all human actions. Although Chillingworth's inquisitions drive Dimmesdale to his secret reunion with Hester and Pearl on the midnight scaffold, this mock revelation only reconfirms the minister's determination to hide his connection with them. And when Hester sees the terrible consequences of her early promise to Chillingworth, her loyalties shift even further from the town, where her public, marital duties reside, to the forest, the exterior counterpart of that secret place in her heart where her love for Dimmesdale lies hidden. Publicly separated from each other and from themselves in the communal sunshine, then ambiguously conjoined in the moral half-light of the peninsula, and then secretly reunited in the darkness, Hester, Dimmesdale, and Pearl are moving inexorably to their forest reunion.

This inward, secretive drift of the action carries the lovers and their child beyond the reach of Chillingworth's loveless intellect, into a symbolic realm which is Pearl's native habitat. All the while that Chillingworth's cruelty has been lowering Hester's opinion of the town, Pearl's emerging traits of "unflinching courage . . . uncontrollable will . . . sturdy pride" (I, 180) and truthfulness have been altering her mother's estimation of the lawless passion from which the child sprang. This moral transition is by no means easy for Hester, who cannot altogether dispel her long-held belief that the scarlet letter stands for something evil and that to value or trust it is to embrace her own damnation. When, determined to assist her lover, she begs Chillingworth to release her from her promise, she characterizes their common situation as a "dismal maze" (I, 173) from which there is no escape; and despite her growing trust in Pearl, she still cannot bring herself to tell the child what the scarlet letter betokens. Nevertheless, by the time she has met Dimmesdale in the forest and revealed her complicity in his suffering, she can finally admit to herself that she loves him and that, whereas Chillingworth's publicly approved ministrations are unforgivable, their secret love has "a consecration of its own" (I, 195).

With this admission, Hester negotiates the last turning in that "moral wilderness," so "intricate and shadowy," where she has been wandering ever since her banishment (I, 183). Here at the center of the dark forest and her own dark heart, the scarlet letter can at last "speak a different purport" (I, 169) and stand for *amor*, her secret and sustaining love, instead of adultery, her public shame. And yet, there remains in the letter something untransmutable. Just as the badge of her public sin contained one intransigent element of her secret love, so the symbol of her now consecrated love retains an obdurate residue of her shame. To rid herself of that painful memory, so out of keeping with the secret place to which she has come, she repudiates her badge and throws it away, denying for the first time the truth that she has heretofore ascribed to it and forgetting for a brief, ecstatic moment that the scarlet letter was itself her "passport" into this otherwise forbidden region (I, 199).

When Hester casts off the last tie that binds her to the town, the movement from publicity to privacy is complete. The action that began in the public denial of the heart's secret truth has brought Hester and Dimmesdale to a heartfelt rejection of communal values. It is "the point whither their pathway had so long been tending, and darkening ever, as it stole along" (I, 195). Suddenly the dark forest of the guilty heart is bathed in sunshine, which comes not from without but from a love that fills "the heart so full of radiance, that it overflows upon the outward world" (I, 203). And with this displacement of the sun from the collective sky to the center of the individual heart, the world is reborn in a new form. As the sunlit marketplace has gradually darkened under Chillingworth's shadow into the midnight scene of Dimmesdale's vigil, the once dark forest of Mistress Hibbins's unholy revels has steadily brightened in the dawning of the heart's emerging truth.

Alluring as it is, however, this "wild, heathen" light, unillumined by a "higher truth" (I, 203), is no less partial than the sunshine of the marketplace, for both deny some essential element in the scarlet letter's complex meaning. If one half of Pearl's nature defies the town's authority, the other half insists that Dimmesdale acknowledge her before the townspeople. In refusing to recognize her mother without the badge or her father unless he will take her hand in the marketplace, Pearl says, as plainly as the heart's native language can, that there is no life for them or for her anywhere but in the human community. She is "the oneness of their being," but her ability to hold them together depends entirely on their willingness to rescue her from airy spritehood and grant her normal status by revealing her to the world as their common offspring. Pearl has been from the beginning both the cause of her parents' public separation and the "living hieroglyphic" (I, 207) of the secret bond between them. Having led them to the private place where they can value that bond, she will now lead them back to the town, where that value must be publicly confirmed.

The events which follow immediately upon their return to town demonstrate both the virtue and the incompleteness of the truth revealed to Hester and Dimmesdale in the forest. The submergence of Dimmesdale's moral reason in Hester's passion has made him a stronger, truer man, but it has left him to wander in a moral maze, exactly as Hester's earlier denial of her heart had drawn her into a labyrinth of speculation. In this respect, he is no better off than when his character was submerged in the community. And while his reunion with Hester has given him the energy to decline Chillingworth's assistance and write his Election Day sermon in the heat of rekindled passion, Hester soon discovers that the Black Man cannot be evaded so easily. Neither in her own lawless forest nor in Dimmesdale's tradition-ridden Europe can they hope to escape Chillingworth's vengeful prying, for he is at home in both places, having come to Boston from Europe by way of the wilderness. His power—indeed, his very existence—stems from the breach between Hester and Dimmesdale, and since that dissociation, although repaired in the heart of the forest, still exists in the mind of the community, he will retain his power over them until they accede to Pearl's demands and stand together before the townspeople.

Dimmesdale's newfound energy carries him, with unwonted vigor, through the delivery of his Election sermon and then flags, leaving him weak and pale as before but once again in possession of his moral reason. Then, in a tableau that recalls the union of power and will in Augustine's conversion, Dimmesdale takes Hester's hand and, supported by her strength, guides her to the scaffold, where they stand together with their child, "the character of flame" (I, 207), in the communal sunlight. Now, surely, the scarlet letter has "done its office." Having led Hester and Dimmesdale from the marketplace where they were untrue to each other, to the forest where they could be true to each other only by being false to the world, it has brought them back to town, prepared to be true to themselves by being true to the world. And, indeed, we are told that when Dimmesdale reveals the scarlet letter burning on his own breast, his "burden was removed"; that when he kisses Pearl, "A spell was broken"; and that when he utters his dying words, "The multitude, silent till then, broke out in a strange, deep voice of awe and wonder, which could not as yet find utterance, save in the murmur that rolled so heavily after the departed spirit" (I, 254–55). Apparently, *The Scarlet Letter* has done its office, too, revealing through the fictive logic of its own action the firm ground upon which the extraordinary private imagination and ordinary public mind can unite in the mutually sustaining harmony of complete being.

The magic moment of atonement no sooner comes, however, than it passes, swept away by the very tide of symbolic action that has brought it into being. "The gaze of the horror-stricken multitude," we are told, "was concentred on the ghastly miracle" of Dimmesdale's red stigma only "for an instant" (I, 255). Immediately thereafter, the union breaks up. Dimmesdale dies after quashing Hester's hope that their brief reunion on the scaffold might be made eternal in heaven. The momentary concentration of the townspeople upon the scarlet letter disintegrates into a dispute about its meaning and even its existence. Pearl leaves the community into which the minister's kiss has symbolically ushered her and takes up permanent residence somewhere in the Old World. After long absence, Hester returns once again to her home on the peninsula, where she resumes the drab attire of her public office as an angel of mercy and counsels troubled women of the town in the moral inefficacy of passions like her own and the virtues of spotless love. Not even in the grave do Hester and Dimmesdale find the union that has been denied them on earth and in heaven, for even their graves are separated, "as if the dust of the two sleepers had no right to mingle" (I, 264). If *The Scarlet Letter* was to have disclosed the source of that light which illuminates both the deepest chamber of the private heart and the broad day of the exterior, public world, all the evidence now suggests that it has failed.

"Yet," the final paragraph informs us, "one tombstone served for both"—a monument inscribed with a device which "the curious investigator may still discern, and perplex himself with the purport" and which might also "serve for a motto and brief description" of the whole work: "ON A FIELD, SABLE, THE LETTER A, GULES" (I, 264). This motto, written "in a tongue native to the human heart" (I, 242) has the effect of turning the purport of *The Scarlet Letter* away from the independent, external truth for which it has been searching, back upon itself. Like the lamp of the imagination, which provides the only light in the dark prison of the heart and in the impenetrable night of the external world, the scarlet A is the only point of light in the surrounding blackness—a character of fire upon an infinite gloom, itself the "beacon-light of humanity," attracting all the otherwise divided world to "one centre" (X, 143). Although Hawthorne appears to have hoped that *The Scarlet Letter* would point beyond itself to the unconditioned ground of his fragmented existence, "the tale shaped itself against his intentions," revealing itself to be the only place where his several selves could come together and be one. In this work, and there alone, "was visible the tie that united them." "All written in this symbol,—all plainly manifest,—had there been a prophet or magician skilled to read the character of flame . . . was the oneness of their being . . . at once the material union, and the spiritual idea, in whom they met and were to dwell immortally together" (I, 206–07).

Considered in terms of autobiographical form, this removal of the locus of complete being from some place outside the autobiography to the autobiography itself amounts to a transference of responsibility for the work's meanings from the narrator, who possesses the meanings of the protagonist's actions in historical autobiography and seeks the

meanings of the protagonist's actions in philosophical autobiography, to the protagonist, the fictive *persona* who enacts the meanings known or sought for by historical and
philosophical narrators but has become, in *The Scarlet Letter*, the cause, the adequate symbol, and the final repository of its own meanings. Appropriately, *The Scarlet Letter*
dramatizes this transference of responsibility as a gradual
shift of authority from Chillingworth, the compulsive
knower, to Pearl, the symbolic actor. Chillingworth derives
his power from the separation of Hester and Dimmesdale
and from his alliance with the community's desire to know
the secret relation between them. But this relation is visible
only in Pearl, and, while he has power over her parents, he
cannot "catch" her (I, 134) any more than the narrator of
"The Custom House" can recover the "now forgotten art"
of the scarlet letter by "picking out the threads" (I, 31). As
long as Hester and Dimmesdale refuse to see themselves
reflected in Pearl and thus to see her as the only place
where they can "dwell immortally together" in the "oneness of their being," Chillingworth will retain his power
over them. But when they acknowledge the truth of the
scarlet letter by acceding to Pearl's demand that this truth
be directly revealed to the community, Chillingworth loses
his place as the intermediary between the symbolic action
and the audience that wants to understand it, and his power
vanishes. " 'Thou hast escaped me!' he repeated more than
once. 'Thou has escaped me!' " (I, 256).

As much as Chillingworth's final words may sound like
the foot-stamping of a frustrated villain, it is impossible not
to hear in them an undertone of relief, even of triumph.
True, the tale has shaped "itself against his intentions," and
"the characters" have acted "otherwise than he thought."
He has struggled "in vain to avert" the "catastrophe" precipitated by these "unforeseen events," admonishing Dim-

mesdale to "Wave back that woman! Cast off this child!" rather than "bring infamy" on his "sacred profession" by linking his fate to theirs (I, 252). Nevertheless, this catastrophic revelation seems to fulfill Chillingworth's designs as much as to frustrate them. When he tells Dimmesdale that only on the scaffold "couldst thou have escaped me," and the minister answers, "Thanks be to Him who hath led me hither" (I, 253), we are immediately reminded of Mistress Hibbins's remark to Hester that "the Black Man . . . hath a way of ordering matters so that [his] mark shall be disclosed in open daylight to the eyes of all the world" (I, 242). Chillingworth's actions have been motivated all along by a "lurid intermixture" of love and hate, those apparently opposite feelings which may be "the same thing at bottom" (I, 260). Knowing that, while Dimmesdale's life rests upon his spotless reputation, the minister's redemption depends on the revelation of his secret, Chillingworth wants both to save his patient by maintaining the secret that is killing him and to destroy his victim by revealing the truth that alone can save him. Insofar as Chillingworth's own survival depends on the preservation of Dimmesdale's good name, moreover, he cannot fulfill his original aim to discover and reveal Dimmesdale's relations with Hester without destroying himself. In other words, Chillingworth cannot both reveal the meaning of the scarlet letter and preserve its essential secrecy at the same time. Only the living symbol itself, the child whose "garb was all of one idea with her nature" (I, 228), can reconcile the conflicting demands of privacy and publicity, hiding what she reveals. And so, while Chillingworth resists Pearl's usurpation of his power over her parents' fate, we detect a sign of acquiescence, however begrudging, in his bequeathing to her, "by his last will and testament, . . . a very considerable amount of property, both here and in England" (I, 261).

Because *The Scarlet Letter* did not reveal to Hawthorne an absolute ground beneath his public and private selves, as he hoped it would, but rather proved itself to be the only place where "the Actual and the Imaginary" could "meet, and each imbue itself with the nature of the other" (I, 36), the work left him even more hopelessly divided against himself than before. On the one hand, the absolutist temperament that informed both his Enlightenment and Romantic views of the truth prevented him from accepting *The Scarlet Letter* as being itself "the treasure" he hoped it would bring to light (I, 29). From this angle, it appeared to him a "positively a hell fired story," altogether bereft of "sunshine." On the other hand, there was in him an artist who believed first of all in his art. Employing a figure that recalls the petrified hearts of Digby and Ethan Brand, this artist could say of *The Scarlet Letter*, "I think I have never overcome my adamant in any other instance." And so, the self-division that had been poetically healed in the autobiography persisted in the autobiographer, who would spend the rest of his life searching for an immortal self that he could neither fully believe in any longer nor relinquish to the realm of art.

This search is recorded in *The House of the Seven Gables*, *The Blithedale Romance*, and *The Marble Faun*, whose styles, forms, settings, characters, plots, and emblems reflect the enduring problem of Hawthorne's self-conflict and whose increasingly despairing conclusions reveal the hopelessness of his ever evading the fate that was shadowed forth when he made himself the personages of *The Scarlet Letter*. These works merely confirmed what *The Scarlet Letter* had said "in a tongue native to the human heart": that he had no self beyond the one created in his autobiography. Nearing the end of this fruitless quest, when he could no longer find his way, he let one of his characters express his feeling of selflessness:

> I assure you that the current of my life runs darkly
> on, & I would be glad of any light on its future, or
> even its present course. . . . I sprang out of mystery,
> akin to none, a thing concocted out of the ele-
> ments, without visible agency— . . . all through my
> boyhood, I was alone; . . . I grew up without a root,
> yet continually longing for one—longing to feel
> myself connected with somebody—and never feel-
> ing myself so. . . . I cannot overcome this natural
> horror of being a creature floating in the air, at-
> tached to nothing; ever this feeling that there is no
> reality in the life and fortunes, good or bad, of a be-
> ing so unconnected. There is not even a grave, not
> a heap of dry bones, not a pinch of dust, with which
> I can claim connection. . . . [XII, 257–58]

The removal of Hawthorne's golden treasure from the
heart's cavern to *The Scarlet Letter* and his consequent inability ever to find it again made him unwilling to continue
the "philosopher's researches" that had directed his creative life. Concerning *The Dolliver Romance*, he wrote to
his publisher: "There is something preternatural about my
reluctance to begin. I linger at the threshold, and have a
perception of very disagreeable phantoms if I enter."
Ironically—perhaps necessarily—this unwillingness to enter the heart's cavern coincided with a conscious awareness
of what he had been doing all along. Faced with a particularly difficult problem in the composition of *Doctor
Grimshawe's Secret*, he wrote,

> There is—or there was now many years ago,
> and a few years also, it was still extant—a chamber,
> which when I think of it, seems to me like entering
> a deep recess of my own consciousness, a deep
> cave of my nature; so much have I thought of it and
> its inmate, through a considerable period of my
> life. . . . After I had seen it long in fancy, then I saw

it in reality, with my waking eyes; and questioned with myself whether I was really awake.

The chamber, however, was now empty. "Compare it," Hawthorne suggests, "to Spenser's Cave of Despair. Put instruments of suicide there" (XII, 335–36). Turning to the *Faerie Queene*, we can see what remained of the heart after its "eternal beauty" had been transferred to *The Scarlet Letter*:

> Dark, doleful, dreary like a greedy grave,
> That still for carion carcasses doth crave:
> On top whereof aye dwelt the ghastly owl,
> Shrieking his ghastly note which ever drove
> Far from that haunt all other cheerful fowl;
> And all about it wandering ghosts did wail and
> howl.

And yet, no reader who takes up the work in the "twilight atmosphere in which it was written" (IX, 5) can help but feel that, although Hawthorne himself only half knew it, he did find his true being, his true society, and his immortality in *The Scarlet Letter*, that "complaint of a human heart, sorrow-laden, perchance guilty; telling its secret, whether of guilt or sorrow, to the great heart of mankind; beseeching its sympathy or forgiveness,—at every moment,—in each accent,—and never in vain!" (I, 243–44).

Afterword

Insofar as *The Scarlet Letter* is the *allos* of its own allegory, it is fitting that the critical reception of the work has imitated the public reception of the scarlet letter in the work. Just as some of the townspeople take Dimmesdale's brand to betoken a spiritual victory, while others see in it only the consequences of a guilty passion, some critics have taken *The Scarlet Letter* to be a case against radical individualism on behalf of collective morality, while others have read it as an indictment of the repressive society in favor of rebellious passion. To be sure, these conflicting interpretations have a precedent in Hawthorne's own divided opinion of his masterpiece. At the same time, their common assumption that the meaning of the work lies outside it, in some moral proposition which it merely illustrates, betrays a lingering reluctance, very much like that of both the townspeople and Hawthorne himself, to locate reality in human action rather than in some ideal realm, above or ahead, to which those actions point. Hawthorne performed the symbolic actions recorded in *The Scarlet Letter* in the hope of discovering just such an unconditioned ground beneath the conflicting elements of his conditional life. But his autobiography came to the conclusion that no such timeless ground exists and that the conflict within him could be reconciled only in the temporal, verbal action precipitated by that conflict.

With this discovery, *The Scarlet Letter* dismisses the assumption that a substantial self or soul precedes and governs individual experience and may be discerned through that experience. This assumption had enabled historical autobiographers to explain, philosophical autobiographers to search for, and poetic autobiographers to express, the absolute self behind their conditioned actions. Those autobiographers who have managed to maintain Augustine's belief in unconditioned selfhood have continued to write about themselves in the three forms he erected upon that belief. But, for those who have accepted Hawthorne's conclusion, that the self is continually reshaped by efforts to explain, discover, or express it, autobiography in the Augustinian sense is no longer possible.

In this situation, every individual action is artistic. "This self of which we take possession," Régis Michaud has argued, "is a veritable psychic creation. It is a character we spend our life in designing. . . . [E]very one of us is an artist and spends our life in drawing an original portrait of himself. Our actions write our autobiography, which is, of course a fiction." The corollary of this proposition is that every fiction is, willy-nilly, a self-portrait. "A man sets himself the task of portraying the world," Jorge Luis Borges writes. "Through the years he peoples a space with images of provinces, kingdoms, mountains, bays, ships, islands, fishes, rooms, instruments, stars, horses, and people. Shortly before his death, he discovers that that patient labyrinth of lines traces the image of his face." Beyond these symbolic actions, which create the self they reveal, no self exists to be explained, discovered, or expressed. "In the mid-twentieth century," Harold Rosenberg has observed, "the artist is obliged to invent the self that will paint his pictures—and . . . constitute their subject matter." The resulting autobiographies do not refer to someone who exists prior to them. "It is a very fact," Keats maintained, "that not one word I ever utter can be taken for granted as an opinion growing out of my identical nature—how can it, when I have no Nature?" On the contrary, the person referred to is the product of autobiographical reference—the creator of the work is in fact its creation. Necessarily, then, in these symbolic acts of self-creation, "the creator," as T. S. Eliot put it, "is everywhere present, and everywhere hidden."*

Statements of this sort, ubiquitous in the writings of modern artists and their critics, have the effect of making autobiography seem both impossible and unavoidable. Without a self, one cannot write about it, but whatever one writes will be about the self it constructs. Autobiography thus becomes synonymous with symbolic action in any form, and the word ceases to designate a particular kind of writing. To call any modernist work "autobiographical" is merely to utter a tautology. And yet, this situation can be understood only in relation to autobiography—which is to say, the succession of forms through which the genre evolved during the centuries that lie between Augustine's Confessions and *The Scarlet Letter*. Borrowing the termi-

---

* Régis Michaud's words are taken from *The American Novel Today* (Boston, 1931), p. 28; Borges's from his *Dreamtigers* [trans. Mildred Boyer and Harold Moreland (Austin, Texas, 1964), p. 93]; Harold Rosenberg's from *Saul Steinberg* (New York, 1978), p. 10; Keats's from *Letters of John Keats, 1814–1821*, 1:387, and T. S. Eliot's from "The Three Voices of Poetry" (1953) [in *T. S. Eliot on Poetry and Poets* (New York, 1961), p. 112].

nology of Wallace Stevens—a modernist for whom the absolute became the "supreme fiction" once the old "mythology of self" was "blotched out beyond unblotching"
—we may describe this evolution as having begun with
the efforts of historical autobiographers "To say more than
human things with human voice," proceeded through the
attempts of philosophical autobiographers "to say human
things with more than human voice," and ended with the
continuing struggle of poetic autobiographers "To speak
humanly from the height or from the depth / Of human
things. . . ."

The Study of Autobiography:
A Bibliographical Essay

This essay aims to answer the need, long felt by students of autobiography, for a review of the available scholarship and criticism and to dispel the notion, too often entertained by those same students, that nothing much has been written on the subject. As the survey below indicates, the published commentary is in fact both extensive and richly various—so much so that in order to complete my task I have had to omit many titles of potential value. For the most part, the list includes only studies that deal directly with the subject of autobiography and excludes works in the following categories:

1. Studies of such ancillary topics as—
    a. the theory of personality, identity, role-playing, self-consciousness, etc., although some works in this area have been written by experts in autobiography [e.g., Georges Gusdorf, *La Découverte de soi* (Paris, 1948)], and some use the word metaphorically [e.g., William Earle, *The Autobiographical Consciousness* (Chicago, 1972)];
    b. the nature of narrative and the relations between fiction and non-fiction, although recent studies of these topics have contributed significantly to the criticism of autobiography (for a sprinkling of titles see the section on *Sartor Resartus* below);

c. the theory of creativity, although a number of works on this subject [e.g., Jerome S. Bruner, "The Conditions of Creativity," in his *On Knowing: Essays for the Left Hand* (Cambridge, Mass., 1962), pp. 17–30] bear directly on the problems of modern autobiography;

d. the psychoanalytic interpretation of literature, although a work like Freud's "Creative Writers and Day-Dreaming" [in *The Complete Psychological Works of Sigmund Freud* 9 (London, 1959): 141–54] is obligatory reading for any student of autobiography;

e. the biographical interpretation of literature [see the checklist in René Wellek and Austin Warren, *Theory of Literature* (New York, 1956), pp. 317–18];

2. Studies of such closely related literary types as—

a. first-person narratives of travel, captivity, etc. [but, for a discussion of their relations with autobiography, see W. C. Spengemann, "Eternal Maps and Temporal Voyages," *Exploration* 2 (1974): 1–7];

b. first-person novels [see Michal Glowinski, "On the First-Personal Novel," *New Literary History* 9 (1977): 103–14, for references to a number of pertinent studies] and the "non-fiction novel";

c. letters, diaries, journals, *journaux intimes*, etc., although I do not wish to imply that such serial forms should be excluded from the study of autobiography;

d. lyric poetry, although this is perhaps the most ancient form of self-presentation;

3. Highly specialized studies (e.g., on German autobiography) that already appear on readily available lists

devoted to these special topics (the lists themselves are noted in the appropriate place below);

4. Scholarly reviews of the major monographs listed, although these sometimes define theoretical problems that the books themselves do not recognize;

5. Studies of individual autobiographies not treated in my own chapters—unless they contribute to the theory of the genre or seem to me models of analysis; and

6. Unpublished dissertations [for a list of over one hundred titles see Xerox University Microfilms, *Comprehensive Dissertation Index, 1861–1972* 29 (Ann Arbor, Mich., 1973): 105–06, and the subsequent annual indexes to *Dissertation Abstracts International*].

The works dealt with in this review are arranged in seven main sections: bibliographies, primary collections, journalism and early scholarship forming the historical backgrounds of the contemporary interest in autobiography, studies representing recent critical trends and problems, studies of autobiography as a source of information, studies of autobiography as a literary form, and studies of the autobiographies discussed in this book, arranged by chapter.

I. BIBLIOGRAPHIES

Since primary bibliographies normally concentrate on works written in particular times or places or by particular classes of persons, they are listed in the appropriate sections below. One attempt at a comprehensive list is Max

Arnim's *Internationale Personalbibliographie, 1800–1943*, 3 vols. (Leipzig, 1952), which includes biographical documents of all kinds.

The only separately published checklist of secondary materials is the accurately titled "Writings About the Autobiography: A Selective Bibliography," by Mary Sue Carlock [*Bulletin of Bibliography* 26 (1969): 1–2]. Otherwise, one must turn to monographs on the subject. But not even these can be counted on to list the available scholarship and criticism. The rule seems to be that as more and more gets written about autobiography the writers become less and less careful about acknowledging their predecessors. In the early 1950s, Wayne Shumaker [*English Autobiography: Its Emergence, Materials, and Form* (Berkeley and Los Angeles, 1954), pp. 253–55] listed most of the relatively few studies then in print. Two decades later, James Olney [*Metaphors of Self: The Meaning of Autobiography* (Princeton, N.J., 1972), p. ix] mentioned only a handful of the scores of books and articles that were available at the time. And in the very midst of the recent critical downpour, Jeffrey Mehlman [*A Structural Study of Autobiography: Proust, Sartre, Leiris, Lévi-Strauss* (Ithaca, N.Y., 1974)] and Elizabeth Bruss [*Autobiographical Acts: The Changing Situation of a Literary Genre* (Baltimore, Md., 1976)] listed almost nothing.

Three notable exceptions to this rule have been immensely useful to me in the preparation of this survey. Roy Pascal's *Die Autobiographie: Gehalt und Gestalt* (Stuttgart, 1965), pp. 239–40, and Philippe Lejeune's *Le Pacte autobiographique* (Paris, 1975), pp. 345–54, include good selections of twentieth-century studies printed on the Continent. Lejeune's list is especially strong in works on the relations between autobiography and fiction. And Karl J. Weintraub's extensive bibliography in *The Value of the Individual: Self and Circumstance in Autobiography* (Chicago, 1978), pp. 403–29, although more comprehensive in its coverage of intellectual historiography, contains many general studies of the genre and even more works on particular autobiographies. All three of these lists should be consulted for titles that are excluded from this survey by the restrictions of its plan.

II. COLLECTIONS

Earlier collections of autobiographical writings were published as commercial ventures, to capitalize on the complex demands of the reading public for agreeable instruction in the difficult business of getting on in modern society. The size of that market may be deduced from the appearance in London, between 1826 and 1832, of thirty-three very inexpensive volumes under the title, *Autobiography: A Collection of the Most Instructive and Amusing Lives Ever Published, Written by the Parties Themselves.* Many copies of this little library are still extant, providing access to some documents that are otherwise unavailable. Early in the present century, George Iles compiled the less ambitious but equally popular *Little Masterpieces of Autobiography*, 6 vols. (New York, 1908), the fourth volume of which is devoted to "Writers" of the nineteenth century. In the 1930s, the "Modern Anthologies" series, under the general editorship of Richard Wilson, issued *An Anthology of Modern Memoirs*, ed. F. W. Tickner (London, 1936); and Doubleday, Doran and Company congratulated itself by publishing *A Book of Great Autobiography* (New York, 1934), containing selections from autobiographies (by

Whitman, Conrad, Christopher Morley, and others) that had made money for the company over the years.

The translation of autobiography from the marts of trade to the groves of academe in England was marked by the publication of E. Stuart Bates's *Inside Out: An Introduction to Autobiography*, 2 vols. (Oxford, 1936; New York, 1937), which summarizes and excerpts nearly three hundred works by way of recommending the genre to the attention of scholars. Since that time two scholarly collections have appeared: Saul K. Padover's *Confessions and Self-Portraits: 4600 Years of Autobiography* (New York, 1957), which follows the historical plan of Georg Misch's *History of Autobiography in Antiquity*, trans. E. W. Dickes (London, 1950; Cambridge, Mass., 1951); and Margaret Bottrall's *Personal Records: A Gallery of Self-Portraits* (London, 1961), a by-product of her study of seventeenth-century English autobiography, *Every Man a Phoenix: Studies in Seventeenth-Century Autobiography* (London, 1958).

A number of collections of autobiographies of special types are listed under the appropriate subheadings below. Still others may be found in the *Bibliographical Supplement* to Donald Stauffer's *The Art of Biography in Eighteenth-Century England* (Princeton, N.J., 1941), pp. 279–83.

III. THE RISE OF AUTOBIOGRAPHY AS A SCHOLARLY TOPIC

The present critical interest in autobiography has its source in three rather distinct but, I believe, fundamentally related occurrences in the later nineteenth century: a sudden boom in the popular market for autobiographical writings of all sorts, an equally sharp rise in the number of essays on autobiography appearing in the literary journals, and the publication of Wilhelm Dilthey's proposals for a study of human history based on the reading of autobiographical documents. [Unaccountably, neither R. D. Altick's *The English Common Reader* (New York, 1957) nor James D. Hart's *The Popular Book* (New York, 1950) mentions the rising popularity of autobiography in the nineteenth century. For an excellent survey of the journalistic interest, see Keith Rinehart's "The Victorian Approach to Autobiography," *Modern Philology* 51 (1954): 177–86. Two items should be added to Rinehart's list of contemporary articles and reviews: A. O. Prickard, *Autobiography: An Essay* (London, 1866), and the anonymous "Links With the Past," *Living Age* 223 (1899): 775–86. For the scholarly interest, see Dilthey's *Ein Einleitung in die Geisteswissenschaften* (Leipzig, 1883) and Werner Flach, "Die wissenschaftstheoretische Einschätzung der Selbstbiographie bei Dilthey," *Archiv für Philosophie* 52 (1970): 173–86.]

What ties these three events together is their common subscription to the modern idea that human life does not reflect history, it *makes* it: each individual life contributes something to the endlessly evolving history of mankind and is therefore of interest to the one who lives it and, at least potentially, to everyone else. To be sure, neither the idea that individual existence is real and valuable nor the writing of autobiography originates in the nineteenth century. Both of these phenomena have been traced, by various modern scholars, to the Renaissance, to the dawn of Christianity, to Classical Antiquity and beyond. The word "autobiography" itself is two hundred years old [see Jacques Voisine, "Naissance et évolution du terme littéraire 'autobiographie'," in *La Littérature Comparée en Europe Orientale* (Budapest, 1963)], and the intellectual foundations for the genre as we know it were fully laid at least by the end of the seventeenth century [see the documents in *Biography as an Art*, ed. James L. Clifford (New York, 1962), pp. 35–36, 44–45, 61, 143]. Nevertheless, it was only in the closing decades of the nineteenth century that the idea of individuality and the writing of autobiography became sufficiently widespread to generate the kind, if not the degree, of popular, critical, and scholarly interest that we take for granted today.

Throughout the years between the turn of the century and the First World War, these interests grew apace. As more and more autobiographies appeared on the market, increasing numbers of book-reviewers took notice—gradually defining as they did so most of the critical issues that still preoccupy students of the genre today:

the motives for writing and reading autobiography ["The Vogue of Reminiscences," *Living Age* 225 (1900): 846–48; "Letters and Reminiscences of the Last Century," *The Critic* 41 (1902): 314–18; and three installments of "The Editor's Easy Chair" in *Harper's* by William Dean Howells: "Autobiography," 108 (1904): 478–82; "Autobiography: A New Form of Literature," 119 (1909): 795–98; and "The Tale Which Every Man Lives," 121 (1911): 795–98];

the distinction between private and public autobiography ["The Charm of Autobiography," *Munsey's* 22 (1900): 613–14; "Of Autobiographies," *Atlantic* 98 (1906): 863–65; and W. A. Gill, "The Nude in Autobiography," *Atlantic* 99 (1907): 71–79];

the value of autobiography as truth and as art ["Famous Autobiographies," *Edinburgh Review* 214 (1911): 331–56;

and "Musing Without Method: Commonplace Memoirs,"
Blackwood's 190 (1911): 840–51];

and the distinctions among various autobiographical
forms ["Decline of the Memoir," *Living Age* 225 (1900):
651–54].

The first decade of the twentieth century also saw the
publication of the first two scholarly books on autobiography: the landmark *Geschichte der Autobiographie* [2 vols.
(Leipzig and Berlin, 1907)], by Dilthey's pupil (and future
son-in-law) Georg Misch, and Anna Robeson Burr's far less
imposing but probably no less influential *The Autobiography: A Critical and Comparative Study* (Boston and New
York, 1909). Misch's imaginative and learned survey of autobiographical writing, from the tomb-inscriptions of ancient Egypt through the *Confessions* of St. Augustine, was
offered as the first of three planned installments—the second and third were to be forthcoming "shortly"—in a complete history of the genre down to "the present." Unfortunately, "the present" was to proceed more rapidly than
Misch's work; the last two volumes would not be published
until four years after his death, in 1969. Burr, on the other
hand, produced a second volume before the War: *Religious
Confessions and Confessants* (Boston and New York, 1914),
thereby establishing alongside Misch's teutonic rigor a
chatty, impressionistic approach to autobiography that
would remain the norm in English studies for at least fifty
years.

After the War, the production of autobiographies soared,
and the journalists resorted to omnibus reviews in order to
keep up [Grant M. Overton, "They Have Only Themselves
to Blame," in his *When Winter Comes to Main Street* (New
York, 1922): 118–32; "Ah, Did You Once See Shelley
Plain?" in his *American Nights' Entertainment* (New York,

1923): 139–56; and "Lest They Forget," in his *Cargoes for Crusoes* (New York, 1924): 197–211; Robert Cantwell, "The Autobiographers," *New Republic* 94 (1938): 354–56; and Eric Gillett, "Autobiography and Reminiscence," *Fortnightly* 150 n.s. (1941): 455–63, and 157 (1942): 57–66]. Many reviewers lamented the unseemliness of all this self-advertisement [Ben Ray Redman, "Autobiography," *Harper's* 142 (1921): 395–96; Robert C. Holliday, "This Communicative World," *Bookman* 56 (1923): 598–602; "The Age of Confession," *Saturday Review of Literature* 3 (1927): 509–10; Henry W. Taft, "Formal Autobiographies and Informal Exploitations," in his *Opinions, Literary and Otherwise* (New York, 1934), pp. 31–60; and G. K. Chesterton, "About Widows," in his *As I Was Saying* (New York, 1936), pp. 133–38], and some spoofed it [Don Marquis, "Autobiographies," *Saturday Evening Post* 202 (1930): 42, 58; Geoffrey T. Hellman, "How to Write Your Autobiography," *The New Yorker* 18 (1942): 18–19].

But, one way or another, every literary journalist responded to the outpouring of autobiographies, and in doing so asked the standard questions. Why do people write them? [Agnes Repplier, "The Happiness of Writing an Autobiography," in her *Under Dispute* (Boston, 1924), pp. 88–118; William R. Inge, "Autobiographies," in his *A Pacifist in Trouble* (London, 1939), pp. 285–89]. Why do people read them? [Dorothea L. Mann, "Butterflies on a Pin," in *Modern Essays of Various Types*, ed. C. A. Cockayne (New York, 1927), pp. 233–34; Storm Jameson, "Autobiography and the Novel," *Bookman* 72 (1931): 557–65; Joseph Collins, "Fictional Biography and Autobiography," in his *Idling in Italy* (New York, 1933), pp. 148–58]. Are they better when personal or when anecdotal? [Ludwig Lewisohn, "Culture and Barbarism," *Harper's* 153 (1926): 729–33; Augustine Birrell, "A Few Warning Words to Would-be Auto-biographers," in his *Et Cetera* (London, 1930), pp. 3–10; John N. Wheeler, "They Never Tell All," *American Magazine* 112 (1931): 36–38, 80; Hilaire Belloc, "Autobiography," in his *A Conversation with a Cat and Others* (New York, 1931), pp. 47–52]. Are they primarily factual or literary? [Augustine Birrell, "A Rogue's Memoirs," in his *Collected Essays and Addresses* . . . , *1880–1920* 2 (London, 1922): 319–29; Benjamin Crémieux, "Sincérité et imagination," *Nouvelle Revue Française* 12 (1924): 528–48; Arthur S. McDowall, "Autobiography as Art," in his *Ruminations* (Boston, 1925), pp. 162–80; Ian Z. Malcolm, "Memoirs and Biographies," in his *Pursuits of Leisure and Other Essays* (New York, 1929), pp. 41–52; and Irmengarde Eberle, "New Confessional," *New Republic* 63 (1930): 68–70]. And, what forms may they take? [William R. Inge, "On Books and Writers," in *The Wit and Wisdom of Dean Inge*, ed. Sir James Marchant (London, 1927), pp. 119–20].

Scholarship made headway in this period only in Germany, where Misch's continuing influence, reinforced by the reprinting of his *Autobiographie* in 1931, helped to generate a number of learned studies. In the English-speaking world, Arthur Melville Clark [*Autobiography: Its Genesis and Phases* (Edinburgh, 1935)] retrod the ground laid out by Burr, and one academic review attempted rather half-heartedly to define some alternative approaches to the form [Henry Trace, "Autobiography, Discursive and Analytical," *Yale Review* 22 (1933): 619–22].

After 1945, the spate of personal histories generated by the War and the continuing popularity of autobiographies of every sort got the usual responses from the literary reviews [Elizabeth Bowen, "Autobiography as an Art," *Saturday Review of Literature* 34 (1951): 9–10; E. P. Monroe et al.,

"Private Lives Make Lively Reading," *Saturday Review* 39 (1956): 16–17; A. Pryce-Jones, "The Personal Story," in *The Craft of Letters in England: A Symposium*, ed. John Lehmann (Boston, 1957), pp. 26–45; Raymond Walters, Jr., "The Confessions of Practically Everybody," *New York Times Magazine* 11 Sept. 1960: 54, 60, 62, 64; and "The Whole Man," in *The British Imagination: A Critical Survey from the Times Literary Supplement* (New York, 1961), pp. 1–7], while the more scholarly writers continued in Burr's tracks [Herbert N. Wethered, *The Curious Art of Autobiography from Benvenuto Cellini to Rudyard Kipling* (London, 1956)].

But there were also clear signs of a growing seriousness in England and America regarding the genre that had come to dominate their literary markets over the previous fifty years. Reviewing Wethered's book for *The New Statesman* ["All About Ourselves," n.s., 51 (1956): 601–02], V. S. Pritchett was unable to disguise his contempt for the author's utter lack of system, and in a rather belated notice Lane Cooper attacked Burr's useless categories, faulty scholarship, and inflated prose ["Anna Robeson Burr: The Autobiography," in his *Late Harvest: Literary Essays* (Ithaca, N.Y., 1952), pp. 139–44]. Far more significant, however, was the translation into English of Misch's *Autobiographie* in a revised and expanded edition: *The History of Autobiography in Antiquity*. British and American scholars were ready, it seems, to undertake the sort of theoretical and historical work that their German colleagues had been doing for years. In the next decade, there appeared Wayne Shumaker's *English Autobiography*, the first work in English to study that subject apart from biography; Margaret Bottrall's *Every Man a Phoenix*, the first English study to examine the genre closely in a particular period setting; and Roy Pascal's *Design and Truth in Autobiography* (London, 1960), the first extended theoretical work in the language. (A professor of German literature himself, Pascal partially repaid the debt to Misch in 1965 by translating this book into German.)

During the years when Misch's early volumes were setting a new standard for English scholarship, additional installments in his own comprehensive history, projected a half-century earlier, began to appear. In 1949, the revised and expanded version of his 1907 study came out under the title *Geschichte der Autobiographie, Band I: Das Altertum* (Frankfurt). Between 1955 and 1962, he published *Band II: Das Mittelalter: Die Früzeit* (Frankfurt, 1955) and *Band III* in two parts, both called *Das Hochmittelalter im Anfang* (Frankfurt, 1959 and 1962). At the time of his death, in 1965, he was writing yet another volume on the Middle Ages, which appeared posthumously as *Das Hochmittelalter in der Vollendung*, ed. Leo Delfoss (Frankfurt, 1967). This was followed by a final half-volume *Von der Renaissance bis zu den autobiographischen Hauptwerken des 18. und 19. Jahrhunderts*, ed. Bernd Neumann (Frankfurt, 1969), printed from a typescript that Misch had completed in 1904 but had never managed to get back to in a lifetime of trying.

In its final form Misch's work ironically resembles the herculean efforts of nineteenth-century autobiographers to bring an ever-expanding past abreast of an ever-moving present. Ironically, too, the study he published in 1907—although it deals with the least "autobiographical" era in Western history—has had a far greater influence than all the work he did subsequently. Nevertheless, the influence of his attitudes, his ideas, and his methods has been tremendous, and one can hardly imagine the time when his analyses of individual texts will no longer serve as models for anyone who seeks to understand and explain the actual complexity of what was once thought to be the most self-evident of literary forms.

IV. THE PRESENT CRITICAL INTEREST AND THE PROBLEMS OF DEFINITION

Autobiography may be said to have arrived at its present critical status with the publication of Francis R. Hart's very business-like and unpretentious essay "Notes for an Anatomy of Modern Autobiography" [*New Literary History* 1 (1970): 485–511]. Although a great deal of important work had already been done, both in America and in Europe, by the time Hart's essay appeared, most of it remained unknown even to those who were writing on the subject, let alone to literary critics in general. Throughout the later 1960s, one article after another had pleaded for the recognition of autobiography as literature [Vera Brittain, "Literary Testaments," *Essays by Divers Hands* n.s., 34 (1966): 19–35] or scolded the literary critics for neglecting it [Stephen A. Shapiro, "The Dark Continent of Literature: Autobiography," *Comparative Literature Studies* 5 (1968): 421–54]. Even in 1973, one critic could say, "There are very few critical works which, on the one hand, treat autobiography as a theoretical problem or, on the other hand, transcend a given national literature" [Christie Vance, Introduction (to a large collection of essays which also acknowledge practically no previous studies), *Genre* 6 (1973): iii]. Nevertheless, in its methodical presentation of the old journalistic questions about the motives, artistry, and formal variety of autobiography, Hart's essay reflected a general acceptance of the genre by literary critics as a form worthy of systematic analysis.

Hart also raised anew the problem of defining the genre. Although attentive students of autobiography had always recognized the difficulties of this problem [see, for example, Wayne Shumaker, *English Autobiography*, pp. 1–30], most critics were able to take the matter for granted, until so many people began writing about autobiography from so many different angles that the old unanimity seemed suddenly to evaporate. Reviewing the wide variety of meanings that had been attached to the word "autobiography" in recent publications, Mary Sue Carlock ["Humpty Dumpty and the Autobiography," *Genre* 3 (1970): 340–50] called on the critics to decide once and for all what autobiography is in fact, so that all their statements would refer to the same thing.

Although somewhat naive in its assumption that "autobiography" is a thing in nature rather than an idea that changes with every new statement about it, Carlock's essay fairly describes the apparent confusion that reigned at the time and persists today. In the last decade, the word autobiography has been used to designate everything from a "Récit rétrospectif en prose qu'une personne réelle fait sa propre existence, lorsqu'elle met l'accent sur sa vie individuelle, en particulier sur l'histoire de sa personnalité" [Philippe Lejeune, *Le Pacte autobiographique*, p. 14] to any "lifework" arising from "the vital impulse to order that has always caused man to create and that, in the end, determines both the nature and the form of what he creates" [James Olney, *Metaphors of Self*, p. 3]. [The problems of definition are discussed at length, in relation to theories of genres and of literary history, in two essays in the *Revue d'histoire littéraire de la France* 75 (1975): Philippe Lejeune's "Autobiographie et histoire littéraire" (pp. 903–30) and Georges Gusdorf's "De l'autobiographie initiatique á l'autobiographie genre littéraire" (pp. 957–94). The concluding paragraphs of Gusdorf's essay could serve nicely as an introduction to this book.]

Widely various as the available definitions of autobiography are, they appear to have several things in common. In the first place, they are generally stipulative: the definition in any case is not derived from an examination of all texts which might conceivably be about the person who wrote them; it is formulated *a priori* and used to select the texts that will be examined. In other words, while these definitions usually purport to be statements of fact, they are really explanations of how the word "autobiography" will be used in particular instances. As a result, the only arguable definition of autobiography would be a full account of all the ways in which the word has been used.

Second, the definition stipulated in each case is primarily a function of the use to be made of the works it designates. People who make lists of autobiographies, for example, tend to restrict the definition quite severely, for purely practical reasons. Those who wish to extract from autobiography information about the writer's life and times will regard the genre as comprising only works that contain this sort of information, while those who feel that our essential being is unconscious usually extend the definition to cover many forms of symbolic expression. Similarly, those who wish to demonstrate the artistry of autobiography have no difficulty including poems and novels in the genre. And, of course, those who maintain that writing refers primarily or solely to itself will find all writing to be autobiographical by definition.

Third, however autobiography is defined in any instance, that definition is normally assumed to hold true for autobiographical writing in all periods. Indeed, the recent proliferation of definitions is at least partly attributable to this static character. Since definitions of autobiography —like those of poetry and fiction—normally arise from contemporary practice in the genre, and since the tendency in criticism, as György Lukács once put it, is for each "new manifestation of literature [to be] immediately and uncritically raised into a criterion which is binding on all literature" [*The Historical Novel*, trans. Hannah and Stanley Mitchell (London, 1962), p. 301], the genre as a whole must be redefined every time someone writes an autobiography in a new way. [For a rare example of what I would call a truly historical view of autobiography, see Burton Pike, "Time in Autobiography," *Comparative Literature* 28 (1976): 326–42. Pike attributes the absence of autobiography before 1700, its flowering in the nineteenth century, and its impracticability in the modern era to specific ideological and literary conditions in those periods.]

When these similarly stipulative, utilitarian, and ahistorical definitions are arranged chronologically, they reveal yet another significant pattern: an increasing acceptance of the idea that autobiography may employ symbolic as well as biographical materials. Not that the idea itself is a recent development: Dilthey and Misch assumed a very catholic attitude toward the possible modes and forms in which the individual soul might reveal itself in different eras [see Misch, *The History of Autobiography in Antiq-uity* 1:4], and E. Stuart Bates wanted to open the genre to poetry and fiction nearly fifty years ago [*Inside Out: An Introduction to Autobiography*, 1:4–9]. Nor has the crite-rion of biographicality altogether disappeared from contem-porary definitions, as the passage from Lejeune, quoted above, demonstrates. Nevertheless, one can discern in the criticism written over the past fifty years or so a shift of em-phasis from the biographical and historical facts recorded in autobiography, to the psychological states expressed in the text, to the workings of the text itself; and at each stage in this general development the definitions stated or im-plied in the criticism can be seen to embrace a wider vari-ety of literary forms.

Before the 1930s, virtually everyone except a few jour-nalists and German scholars considered autobiography a subcategory of biography [see, for example, André Maurois, *Aspects of Biography*, pp. 131–60]. On the other hand, the earliest English studies of autobiography as a distinct genre—Anna Burr's *The Autobiography* (1909) and *Reli-gious Confessions and Confessants* (1914)—had justified separate treatment of this literature on primarily psycholog-ical grounds, and a large share of credit for the subsequent growth of critical interest in the genre belongs to English translations of Freud's work—especially *An Autobiograph-ical Study* (New York, 1927). Insofar as these psychological interpretations of autobiography emphasized its deep struc-tures and the author's unconscious self-revelations, they di-rected attention to the text and, simultaneously, blurred the distinction between factual and fictive statements, treating both as symbolic expressions of psychic energy. As a result, an increasing number of critics came to associate autobiography with fiction rather than with biography [see, for example, Leon Edel, "The Novel as Autobiography," in his *The Modern Psychological Novel* (New York, 1955), pp. 103–122].

This association was strengthened by the New Critical animus against historical, biographical, and psychological interpretation, which severed the already attenuated connections between autobiography and historiography and left the genre a freestanding literary form, to be read like any other narrative [see Alfred Kazin, "Autobiography as Narrative," in *To the Young Writer*, ed. A. L. Bader (Ann Arbor, Mich., 1965), pp. 181–93]. Since 1970, critical attention has focussed more and more intently on the text. [Even psychologically informed critics are now less apt to psychoanalyze the writer through the text than to show how a text can be complicated by the author's knowledge of psychoanalysis. See, for example, Bruce Mazlish, "Autobiography and Psycho-analysis: Between Truth and Self-Deception," *Encounter* 35 (1970): 28–37; and Christine Downing, "Re-Visioning Autobiography: The Bequest of Freud and Jung," *Soundings* 60 (1977): 210–28.] And with each deeper penetration into the workings of the text, the connections between autobiography and what it appears to describe have become increasingly problematical, and the differences between autobiography and other written forms correspondingly indistinct, until there no longer seems to be anything that either is or is not autobiography [see, for example, Michel Butor, "L'usage des pronoms personnels dans le roman," *Essais sur le roman* (Paris, 1969), pp. 81–86].

The displacement of critical emphasis from life to mind to text in the study of autobiography can be attributed partly to the development of literary criticism as a whole, which has shifted its interests along the same lines over the past half century; partly to the work of scholars outside the field of autobiography, whose growing interest in the autobiographical aspects of nineteenth- and twentieth-century poetry and fiction has not been impeded by received opinions concerning the boundaries of the genre [see, for example, Robert Langbaum, *The Poetry of Experience* (New York, 1957; repr. 1963); *Romanticism and Consciousness: Essays in Criticism*, ed. Harold Bloom (New York, 1970); Meyer Abrams, *Natural Supernaturalism: Tradition and Revolution in Romantic Literature* (New York, 1972); Charles Rosen, "What Did the Romantics Mean?" *New York Review of Books* 1 Nov. 1973: 12–17; and David De Laura, "The Allegory of Life: The Autobiographical Impulse in Victorian Prose," *Wascana Review* 12 (1977): 3–20]; and partly to such modern literary developments as "confessional poetry," the "non-fiction novel," and autobiographies (especially Sartre's *Les Mots*, Nabokov's *Speak, Memory*, and Leiris' *La Règle du jeu*) which call attention to the problematic character of their own logical status.

Whatever its causes may be, the critical trend from facticity, to psychology, to textuality has not been unilinear, a steady progress through these stages by all parties in concert. Rather it has occurred by way of a continuing debate among the parties concerning the relative position of autobiography to historiography on the one side and poetry on the other. In keeping with the terms of this evolving debate, the remaining materials in this general survey are subdivided into two sections, one dealing with studies of autobiography as a source of information and one on studies of autobiography as a literary form.

V. AUTOBIOGRAPHY AS A SOURCE OF INFORMATION

A. Biography

The predominantly anecdotal character of the myriad autobiographies published during the first half of this century and the historiographical bias of literary scholarship in the same period conspired to place autobiography in the general category of biographical literature, where it served mainly as a source of gossipy entertainment for the common reader and of documentary data for biographers and historians. Its status in this category was by no means secure, however. On the one hand, many scholars found it too subjective, too self-serving to be a trustworthy source of information. On the other hand, these were the very qualities that made autobiography popular, and all the while that the scholars were dissociating it from biography, the literary journalists were treating it as a more or less distinct literary form, lying somewhere between biography and fiction.

Neither the scholars nor the journalists were in full agreement on these matters, however. While some book-reviewers agreed with the scholars that most autobiography is too personal to be of value, either as literature or as a source of information, a number of scholars held with the journalists that subjectivity constitutes its special merit as a biographical document. This latter view arose partly from the long-standing opinion that a proper biography should include the subject's interior experiences [see Dr. Johnson's "Idler No. 84," in *The Yale Edition of the Works of Samuel Johnson* 2, ed. Walter Jackson Bate et al. (New Haven, Conn., 1963): 261–64; and Carlyle's "Jean Paul

Friedrich Richter Again," in *The Works of Thomas Carlyle,
Centenary Edition* 27 (New York, 1901): 96–159] and partly
from the increasing interest in psychology that led to such
early separate studies of autobiography as Anna Burr's. The
idea that subjectivity makes autobiography a particularly
valuable source of biographical information was first ad-
vanced in this century by Gamaliel Bradford [*Biography
and the Human Heart* (Boston, 1906), pp. 239–70], who argued that the subjectivity of these writings more than com-
pensates for their factual distortions. Again, not every student of biography agreed. "Facts," Joseph Collins argued
["Autobiography," in his *The Doctor Looks at Biography*
(New York, 1925), pp. 43–60], "are as necessary to autobiography as they are to biography . . . , for on them truth, the
greatest quality of art, is founded" (p. 47). Dean Inge
concurred ["Diaries," in W. R. Inge, *Lay Thoughts of a
Dean* (New York, 1926), pp. 71–77], adding that it is through
reminiscence that subjective distortions invade the record.

On the other side, James C. Johnston [*Biography: The
Literature of Personality* (New York, 1927), pp. 51–65;
143–51] not only made subjectivity an essential element of
good biography but, by tracing that quality back to St. Augustine, made autobiography the source rather than a by-
product of biography. Still, as long as autobiography was
lumped together with biography, its relative weakness as a
source of facts would continue to overshadow its strengths
as a distinct form of literary expression [see Harold
Nicolson, *The Development of English Biography* (New
York, 1928), pp. 14–16; André Maurois, "Autobiography,"
in his *Aspects of Biography*, pp. 131–60; Edgar Johnson,
One Mighty Torrent: The Drama of Biography (New York,
1937), pp. 97–120; and Amy Loveman, "Autobiography and
Facts," *Saturday Review of Literature* 23 (1941): 8].

By mid-century, enough had been written about the literariness of autobiography and the complexities of literature to make biographers cautious about either merely dismissing autobiography as untrue or using it naively. John Garraty [*The Nature of Biography* (New York, 1958), pp. 149–58, 177–89] offered scholars who might use autobiographies some advice on how to decode them. R. D. Altick [*Lives and Letters: A History of Literary Biography in England and America* (New York, 1965), pp. 94–102] suggested that, for biographical purposes, autobiographies present a better picture of the author at the time of writing than at the times written about. And Donald Greene ["The Use of Autobiography in the Eighteenth Century" in *Essays in Eighteenth-Century Biography*, ed. Phillip B. Daghlian (Bloomington, Ind., 1968), pp. 43–66] acknowledged the rising stock of the genre in proposing that autobiographies provide better information about that period than any biography can. The struggle of autobiography for independence from biography is by no means complete, however. One notes, for example, that in *The New Encyclopedia Brittanica: Macropedia* (Chicago, 1974) Paul M. Kendall discusses autobiography under the heading of "Biographical Literature" (2: 1006–14, esp. 1009–10). [See also Kendall's *The Art of Biography* (New York, 1965), pp. 29–31, 51–70.]

B. Historical Periods and National Cultures

The idea that autobiography could provide information about something more than the writer's biography had its first systematic formulation in Dilthey's philosophical writings. Reacting to the failure of Positivism to achieve the status of a natural science, Dilthey argued that human life, far from being merely biological, has a reality of its own. This reality, however, is not transcendent but purely historical and social, being an agglomeration of all the individual lives in the history of mankind. Consequently, it cannot be comprehended from some external point of absolute ontology; it must be approached empirically through the individual lives that have contributed to the endlessly evolving structure of human existence, lives recorded in autobiography.

Although Dilthey applied his own theories in studies of various German writers, it was Georg Misch who fully demonstrated the value of autobiography as an "instrument of knowledge," in the first volumes of his *Geschichte der Autobiographie*. This work initiated what is perhaps the largest single movement in the study of autobiography: the use of these documents as evidence of the spirit or character of human life in particular times and places. Because it is often difficult to distinguish between studies of this sort and those which aim merely to describe the nature of autobiography in a certain era or country, the following survey lumps both types together under the periods and nations they treat.

Misch's studies in antiquity are amended by Ulrich von Wilamowitz-Moellendorf, "Die Autobiographie im Altertum" [*Internationale Wochenschrift für Wissenschaft, Kunst, und Technik* 1 (1907): 1105–14]; G. Funaioli, "L'autobiografia nell' antichità" [*Atene e Roma* 9 (1908): 332–46] and J.W. Thompson, "Lost Memoirs of Antiquity" [in his *Byways in Bookland* (Berkeley, 1935), pp. 163–79]. Saul K. Padover's *Confessions and Self-Portraits: 4600 Years of Autobiography* (New York, 1957) includes several selections from the ancient works identified by Misch.

Studies of autobiography in the Middle Ages have invariably addressed the question of whether or not the genre can be said to have existed in that period. Adopting Misch's very broad definition of autobiography, Adolf Rein ["Über die Entwicklung der Selbstbiographie im ausgehenden Mittelalter," *Archiv für Kulturgeschichte* 14 (1909): 195–215] and Friederich von Bezold ["Über die Anfänge der Selbstbiographie und ihre Entwicklung im Mittelalter," in his *Aus Mittelalter und Renaissance: Kulturgeschichtliche Studien* (Munich and Berlin, 1918), pp. 196–219] had no serious doubts about the matter, although von Bezold did find the medieval accounts of mystical visions to be more conventional than personal. Leo Spitzer, on the other hand, took this impersonality to preclude the possibility of autobiography ["Notes on the Poetic and Empirical 'I' in Medieval Authors," *Traditio* 4 (1946): 414–22]. Ernst R. Curtius followed with many examples of medieval poetry showing that impersonality was by no means the rule in the period ["Mention of the Author's Name in Medieval Literature," in *European Literature and the Latin Middle Ages*, trans. Willard Trask (New York, 1953), pp. 515–18], and Paul Lehman found in several major Latin texts clear evidence of an autobiographical impulse ["Autobiographies of the Middle Ages," *Transactions of the Royal Historical Society* 5th ser., 3 (1953): 41–52]. While one might think that the five husky volumes Misch published on the subject between 1955 and 1969 would have laid all doubts to rest, the question has persisted. In 1973, Paul Zumthor employed the techniques of discourse analysis to measure the degree of individuality implied by the first-personal pronoun in medieval texts, finding, as many had found before, that while this degree increases toward the end of the period it never reaches the level we have since come to expect of true autobiography ["Autobiography in the Middle Ages?"

Genre 6 (1973): 29–48]. Starting from another modern critical idea—that autobiography and fiction are indistinguishable—Evelyn B. Vitz found the autobiography of the period in its fictions ["The *I* of the Roman de la Rose," trans. Barbara De Stefano, *Genre* 6 (1973): 49–75]. That is, Vitz takes the conventionality of medieval writing not as an obstacle to autobiographical interpretation but as a warrant for it. [See also Vitz's "Type et individu dans l'autobiographie médiéval," trans. Philippe Lejeune, *Poétique* 24 (1975): 426–45.]

Three essays trace the emergence in the Renaissance of a more personal and humanistic autobiography out of conventional and religious sources in the Middle Ages: T. C. Price Zimmerman's "Confession and Autobiography in the Early Renaissance" [in *Renaissance Studies in Honor of Hans Baron*, ed. A. Molho and J. A. Tedeschi (De Kalb, Ill., 1971), pp. 119–40], Josef Ijsewijn's "Humanistic Autobiography" [in *Studia Humanitatis: Ernesto Grazzi zum 70. Geburstag*, ed. Eginhard Hora and E. Kessler (Munich, 1973), pp. 209–19], and Jonathan Goldberg's "Cellini's 'Vita' and the Conventions of Early Autobiography" [*Modern Language Notes* 89 (1974): 71–83].

Comparative studies for later periods seem to be relatively scarce. In the Enlightenment, there is Ralph-Rainer Wuthenow's *Das erinnerte Ich: Europäische Autobiographie und Selbstdarstellung im 18. Jahrhundert* (Munich, 1974); and in the twentieth century, Gerhard Masur's essay "The Confident Years" [in his *Prophets of Yesterday* (New York, 1961), pp. 252–97], a study of H. G. Wells, Stefan Zweig, Gustav Hillard, and Fedor Stepun as autobiographers typical of the period before World War I. Stephen Spender ["Confessions and Autobiography," in his *The Making of a Poem* (New York, 1962), pp. 63–72] observes that what is revealed and repressed in any autobiography comments on the values of the writer's age, and Patricia Meyer Spacks ["Stages of Self: Notes on Autobiography and the Life Cycle," *Boston University Journal* 25 (1977): 7–17] notes the tendency of autobiographers of different periods to concentrate on different stages of life: eighteenth-century writers on fulfilled adulthood, nineteenth-century writers on vanished childhood, and twentieth-century writers on the uncertainties of adolescence. And Jacques Borel identifies trends in the writing and criticism of modern autobiography in "Problèmes de l'autobiographie" [in *Positions et oppositions sur le roman contemporain*, ed. Michel Mansuy (Paris, 1971), pp. 79–90].

One recent comparative study attests to the continuing influence of Dilthey's theories and Misch's example. Karl Joachim Weintraub's *The Value of the Individual* uses autobiographies to trace the history of the idea of individuality in Western civilization. This marvelous book is disappointing only in its failure to pursue the subject through the nineteenth and twentieth centuries, where, as Weintraub himself observes, the problems of both individuality and autobiography become particularly difficult and interesting.

British autobiography has been extensively studied, both in general and in particular periods. The major bibliography of primary materials is William Matthews's *British Autobiographies: An Annotated Bibliography of British Autobiographies Published or Written Before 1951* (Berkeley and Los Angeles, 1955). General surveys from the beginnings through the nineteenth century include Wayne Shumaker's *English Autobiography* and John N. Morris's *Versions of the Self: Studies in English Autobiography from John Bunyan to John Stuart Mill* (New York, 1966). The beginnings of autobiography in England are variously identified by Alois Brandl, "Anfänge der Autobiographie in England" [*Sitzungsberichte der Königlich Preussischen Akademie der Wissenschaften zu Berlin* 34 (1908); Dorothea Hendrichs, *Geschichte der englischen Autobiographie von Chaucer bis Milton* (Weimar, 1925); Donald Stauffer, "The Autobiography" [in his *English Biography before 1700* (Cambridge, Mass., 1930), pp. 175–216]; James M. Osborn, *The Beginnings of Autobiography in England* (Los Angeles, 1962); and Leslie P. Fairfield, *"The Vocacyon of Johan Bale* and Early English Autobiography" [*Renaissance Quarterly* 24 (1971): 327–40].

The practice of spiritual autobiography by English Dissenters in the seventeenth century is examined in J. D. Lerner, "Puritanism and the Spiritual Autobiography" [*The Hibbert Journal* 55 (1957): 373–86]; Margaret Bottrall, *Every Man a Phoenix*; Paul Delany, *British Autobiography in the Seventeenth Century* (New York, 1969), with an extensive primary bibliography, pp. 175–85; Dean Ebner, *English Autobiography in the Seventeenth Century: Theology and the Self* (New York, 1971); and William Matthews, "Seventeenth-Century Autobiography" [in *Autobiography, Biography, and the Novel: Papers Read at a Clark Library Seminar, May 13, 1972*, ed. W. Matthews and R. Rader (Los Angeles, 1973)].

For the eighteenth century, see Donald A. Stauffer's *The Art of Biography in Eighteenth-Century England*, pp. 258–59, where he discusses the influence of autobiography on biography in this period; two articles in *Essays in Eighteenth-Century Biography*, ed. Philip B. Daghlian (Bloomington, Ind., 1968): Donald Greene's "A Reading Course in Autobiography" (pp. 111–17) and Robert E. Kelley's "Studies in Eighteenth-Century Autobiography and Biography: A Selected Bibliography" (pp. 96–110); G.

Bibliographical Essay

A. Starr's *Defoe and Spiritual Autobiography* (Princeton, N.J., 1965), which shows the strong appeal this religious genre held for secular writers; and Patricia Meyer Spacks, *Imagining a Self: Autobiography and Novel in Eighteenth-Century England* (Cambridge, Mass., 1976), which traces related developments in the two genres. The *Bibliographical Supplement* to Stauffer's *Art of Biography* lists among its primary materials many autobiographies written or translated in England, 1700–1800.

Ernst Keller discovers "the spirit of the age" through its autobiographies in *Kulturbilder aus Victorianischen Autobiographien* ["Schweizer Anglistiche Arbeiten," vol. 29 (Bern, 1951)]. A much more precise sense of that spirit is conveyed by Keith Rinehart's "The Victorian Approach to Autobiography." Michael G. Cooke's "Modern Black Autobiography in the Tradition" [in *Romanticism: Vistas, Instances, Continuities*, ed. David Thorburn and Geoffrey Hartman (Ithaca, N.Y., 1973), pp. 255–80] concentrates on the autobiographical tradition of the nineteenth century, with its recurring problems of truth and fictionality, uniqueness and typicality, self-discovery and self-invention.

The vagaries of modern life and autobiography in twentieth-century England are observed in Mary M. Colum's "Personality and Autobiography" [*Forum* 93 (1935): 83–87], a study of fragmented and unified personality in the writings of H. G. Wells, J. C. Powys, and Frieda Lawrence; Bonamy Dobrée's "Some Literary Autobiographies of the Present Age" [*Sewanee Review* 64 (1956): 689–706], on Osbert Sitwell, Herbert Read, John Lehman, and Victor Gollancz; R. Hoggart's "A Question of Tone: Some Problems in Autobiographical Writing" [*Critical Quarterly* 5 (1965): 73–90], on the tendency of modern writers to evade the problems of self-analysis by adopting con-

ventional voices; Bernard Bergonzi's "Retrospect I: Autobiography" [in *Heroes' Twilight: A Study of the Literature of
the Great War* (New York, 1966), pp. 146–70], on the autobiographical tactics employed by Read, Edmund Blunden,
Robert Graves, and Siegfried Sassoon to make sense of their
experiences; and Thomas F. Staley's "The Artist as Autobiographer" [*Journal of Modern Literature* 2 (1972): 576–81],
on the literary merits of autobiographies by modern British
writers.

Although recent developments in the theory of autobiography arise in large part from various French schools of
criticism, French autobiography itself does not appear to
have received anything like the attention given to its British, German, and American counterparts. Henri Peyre offered a very cursory survey of the field in Chapter Seven of
his *Literature and Sincerity* (New Haven, Conn., 1963),
and Philippe Lejeune emphasized the modern period in
L'autobiographie en France (Paris, 1971). The great
seventeenth-century introspectives—like the German Pie-
tists and the English Dissenters—have been widely studied, but more often in works like A. J. Krailsheimer's *Studies in Self-Interest from Descartes to la Bruyère* (Oxford,
1962), which do not deal directly with autobiography; or in
treatments of such individual writers as Descartes, Pascal,
and Montaigne; or in examinations of the *journal intime*;
than in period studies of autobiography. Two exceptions to
this rule are Georg Misch's "Die Autobiographie der
französische Aristokratie des 17. Jahrhunderts" [*Deutsche
Vierteljahrschrift für Literaturwissenschaft und Geistesgeschichte* 1 (1923): 172–213] and, for the next century,
Jacques Voisine's "De la confession religieuse à l'autobiographie et au journal intime: Entre 1760 et 1820"
[*Neohelicon* 2 (1974): 337–57]. Jeffrey Mehlman offers "a

structural history of a significant strand of French thought in the twentieth century" in *A Structural Study of Autobiography*. [For some help with this difficult book, see Michael Ryan's "Self-De(con)struction," *Diacritics* 6 (1976): 34–41.] Several essays dealing with individual modern French autobiographies—especially Michel Leiris's *La Règle du jeu*—contribute to the theory of the genre as a whole and are listed in the appropriate sections below.

German autobiography, on the other hand, has been widely studied, both in general and in its various periods, since the beginning of this century. Happily, a list of this voluminous literature is already available in Ingrid Aichinger's detailed historical survey and extensive secondary bibliography, "Selbstbiographie," in the *Reallexikon der deutschen Literaturgeschichte* [2nd ed. by Klaus Kanzog et al., 3 (Berlin, 1977): 801–19]. The only additions I can make to this list are, first, the twelve monographs by various authors issued under the running title *Deutsche Selbstzeugnisse* [vols. 1–9 ed. by Marianne Beyer-Fröhlich, vols. 10–12 by Ernst Volkmann (Leipzig, 1930–1970); installment number 25 in the series "Deutsche Literatur: Sammlung literarischer Kunst und Kulturdenkmäler in Entwicklungsreihen"] and, second, two essays by Derek Bowman—*Life into Autobiography: A Study of Goethe's Dichtung und Warheit* (Bern, 1971) and "The Path of Life: Attitudes to the Bible in Some Autobiographies of the Seventeenth and Eighteenth Centuries" [in *Essays in German and Dutch Literature*, ed. W. D. Robson-Scott (London, 1973), pp. 65–88].

The handiest general treatment of Italian autobiography is Carlo Calcaterra's article in the *Enciclopedia italiana di scienze, lettere ed arti* [5 (Rome, 1949): 539–40], where a list of modern Italian autobiographies follows a historical survey of the subject based on the scheme devised by Georg Misch. See also, Giorgio Rossi, *Le Autobiografie* [sic] *e gli epistolari* (Milan, 1912), and for the Italian Renaissance: Hans-Jürgen Daus, *Selbstverständnis und Menschenbild in der Selbstarstellungen Giambattista Vicos und Pietro Giannones: ein Beitrag zur Geschichte der italienischen Autobiographie* (Geneva, 1962), and Marziano Guglielminetti, *Memoria e scrittura: L'autobiografia da Dante a Cellini* (Turin, 1977). Glauco Cambon considers the implications of Guglielminetti's theories in "L'autobiografia, poesia e verità," [*Forum Italicum* 11 (1977): 155–63]. For some observations on the nineteenth century, see Neuro Bonifazi, "L'operazione autobiografica e la *Vita* di V. Alfieri" [*L'Approdo Letterario* 75–76 (1976): 115–42]. Vittorio Alfieri's *Vita* was written in 1804 and translated into English in 1877 by William Dean Howells.

In the United States, autobiography has been repeatedly examined for evidence of the national *geist*. Louis Kaplan, James T. Cook, Clinton L. Colby, Jr., and Daniel C. Haskell list primary works written before 1945 in *A Bibliography of American Autobiographies* (Madison, Wis., 1961), and R. G. Lillard lists works written after 1900 in his *American Life in Autobiography* (Stanford, Calif., 1956). A more sharply focussed list is Mary Sue Carlock's "American Autobiographies, 1840–1870: A Bibliography" [*Bulletin of Bibliography* 23 (1961): 118–120]. For Canada, see William Matthews's *Canadian Diaries and Autobiographies* (Berkeley and Los Angeles, 1950), and J. Macpherson's "Autobiography," in *The Literary History of Canada*, ed. C. F. Klinck (Toronto, 1965), pp. 616–23. Two collections of autobiographical writings, Mark Van Doren's *An Autobiography of America* (New York, 1929) and J. B. Mussey's *Yankee Life by Those Who Lived It* (New York, 1947; orig.

We Were New England . . . , 1937) are interesting mainly as early symptoms of the idea, now widespread, that America is to be found in its subjective soul rather than in its bustling exterior.

General studies of the subject date back to Brander Matthews's "American Autobiography" [*Munsey's* 49 (1913): 988–92], which gives autobiography a primary role in America's literary rebellion against England. Dana K. Merrill's inclusion of autobiography in *The Development of Biography in America* (Portland, Me., 1932) evinces the growing interest in subjectivity as a source of cultural data. James Cox ties the genre even more closely to the American spirit when he suggests that autobiography proper was invented by the American and French revolutions (in the persons of Franklin and Rousseau) ["Autobiography and America," *Virginia Quarterly Review* 47 (1971): 252–77; also in *Aspects of Narrative: Papers from the English Institute*, ed. J. Hillis Miller (New York, 1971), pp. 143–72]. In "Autobiography and Images of Utopia" [*Salmagundi* 19 (1971): 18–37], Robert F. Sayre uses selected American autobiographies to argue that these works adumbrate the utopian dreams of their authors. Two essays recommend aubiography to students of American culture: Albert E. Stone's "Autobiography and American Culture" [*American Studies, an International Newsletter* 11 (1972): 22–36] and Robert F. Sayre's "The Proper Study —Autobiographies in American Studies" [*American Quarterly* 29 (1977): 241–62]. G. Thomas Couser's *American Autobiography: The Prophetic Mode* (Amherst, Mass., 1979) appeared too late for review in this survey.

The major studies of particular periods are: for the seventeenth century, Daniel B. Shea, Jr., *Spiritual Autobiography in Early America* (Princeton, N.J., 1969), on the

New England Puritans and Quakers; for the eighteenth and nineteenth centuries, Robert F. Sayre, *The Examined Self: Franklin, Adams, James* (Princeton, N.J., 1964); and for the nineteenth and twentieth centuries, the anonymous essay entitled "The Reflecting Mirror" in *The American Imagination* [(New York, 1960), pp. 50–55], Thomas Cooley's *Educated Lives: The Rise of Modern Autobiography in America* (Columbus, Ohio, 1976), and Mutlu K. Blasing's *The Art of Life: Studies in American Autobiographical Literature* (Austin, Texas, 1977).

C. THE SCHOLARLY DISCIPLINES

Dilthey's arguments concerning the unique value of autobiography as an instrument of knowledge have prompted many scholars to consider the usefulness of the genre in the practice of their own disciplines. Its place in the study of history is the subject of Hans Glagau's *Die moderne Selbstbiographie als historische Quelle* (Marburg, 1903), H. W. Gruhle's "Die Selbstbiographie als Quelle historischer Erkenntnis" [in *Hauptprobleme der Soziologie: Erinnerungsgabe für Max Weber*, ed. Melchior Palyi (Leipzig, 1923)], and Hans H. Muchow's "Über den Quellenwert der Autobiographie für die Zeitgeistforschung" [*Zeitschrift für Religions– und Geistesgeschichte* 18 (1966): 297–310]. Jean N. Cru brings great methodical rigor to an evaluation of autobiographical information about World War I in *War Books: A Study in Historical Criticism* [trans. of Cru's *Du témoignage* (1930) by S. J. Pincetl, Jr., and E. Marchand (San Diego, Calif., 1976)], and Erich Ebstein presents materials for the history of medicine in *Ärtze-Memoiren aus vier Jahrhunderten* (Berlin, 1923).

Relations between autobiography and the study of philosophy are proposed in two practical studies from *Studia Humanitatis: Ernesto Grazzi zum 70. Geburtstag* (Munich, 1973): Eckhard Kessler's "Autobiographie als philosophisches Argument: Ein Aspekt des Philosophierens bei Cicero und die gegenwärtige Praxis der Philosophie" (pp. 173–87), and Stephan Otto's "Zum Desiderat einer Kritik der historische Vernunft und Zur Theorie der Autobiographie" (pp. 221–35).

The role of autobiography in the social sciences in general is defined in *The Use of Personal Documents in History, Anthropology, and Sociology*, by Louis Gottschalk, Clyde Kluckhohn, and R. Angell (New York, 1945). Definitions of its role in particular branches of social science include: for psychology, Gordon W. Allport, *The Use of Personal Documents in Psychological Science* (New York, 1942); Arthur P. Annis, "The Autobiography: Its Uses and Value in Professional Psychology" [*Journal of Counseling Psychology* 14 (1967): 7–19]; Bruce Mazlish, "Autobiographie und Psychoanalyse" [in *Psycho-Pathographien: Schriftseller und Psychoanalyse*, ed. Alexander Mitscherlich (Frankfurt, 1972), pp. 261–87]; and Carl Murchison's *The History of Psychology in Autobiography* [4 vols. (Worcester, Mass., 1930–1952); vol. 4 ed. Edwin G. Boring et al.]; for political science, G. P. Gooch, "Political Autobiography" [in his *Studies in Diplomacy and Statecraft* (London, 1942), pp. 227–90] and *The Difficult Art of Autobiography*, by Richard A. B. Butler (Lord Butler of Saffron-Walden) (Oxford, 1968); and for economics and corporate law, Robert Müller, "Zur autobiographischen Literatur" [in his *Neue Perspektiven aus Wirtschaft und Recht* (Zurich, 1966), pp. 509–30]. Autobiography is treated as a datum for the study of education in Kurt S. Uhlig, *Die Autobiographie als erziehungswis-*

senschaftliche Quelle (Hamburg, 1936); Erika Hoffman, *Kinheitserinnerungen als Quelle pädagogischer Kinder-hunde* (Heidelberg, 1960); and Jurgen Hennigsen, "Autobiographie und Erziehungswissenschaft" [*Göttinger Bulletin für Kultur und Erziehungswissenschaft* 2 (1962): 450–61]; and as a pedagogical tool in Elizabeth A. Straub, "Approach of Autobiographies" [*English Journal* 38 (1949): 559–63], and in four textbook collections—Theodore Baird's *The First Years: Selections from Autobiography* (rev. ed., New York, 1935); Marston Balch's *Modern Short Biographies and Autobiographies* (New York, 1940); Roger J. Porter and H. R. Wolf, *The Voice Within: Reading and Writing Autobiography* (New York, 1973); and Robert Lyons's *Autobiography: A Reader for Writers* (New York, 1977).

D. CLASSES OF PEOPLE

In her essay, "The Lives of the Obscure" [*The Dial* 78 (1925): 381–90], Virginia Woolf expressed an interest, shared by many readers then and since, in autobiography as a source of information about certain sorts of people who might otherwise remain unknown. Among groups that have been studied this way are:

Women: Orlo Williams, "Some Feminine Autobiographies" [*Edinburgh Review* 231 (1920): 303–17]; R. Pierre, "Apple Pie Among the Rajputs: An Analysis of Ten Feminine Personal Experience Books" [*Saturday Review of Literature* 36 (1953): 24–26]; Estelle C. Jelinek, "Teaching Women's Autobiographies" [*College English* 38 (1976): 32–45]; Patricia Meyer Spacks, "Women's Stories, Women's Selves" [*Hudson Review* 30 (1977): 29–46]; and Suzanne Juhasz, " 'Some Deep Old Desk or Capacious

Hold-All': Form and Women's Autobiography" [*College English* 39 (1978): 663–70].

Blacks: Russell C. Brignano, *Black Americans in Autobiography: An Annotated Bibliography of Autobiographies and Autobiographical Books Written Since the Civil War* [to early 1973] (Durham, N.C., 1974); Sidonie A. Smith, *Where I'm Bound: Patterns of Slavery and Freedom in Black American Autobiography* (Westport, Conn., 1974); and Houston A. Baker, "The Problem of Being: Some Reflections on Black Autobiography" [*Obsidian* 1 (1975): 18–30].

American immigrants: Hamilton Holt, *Life Stories of Undistinguished Americans as Told by Themselves* (New York, 1906); and Grace W. Wood, "Autobiographies of Foreign-Born Americans" [*Library Journal* 49 (1924): 420].

Asian Indians: Amarantha Jha, *Some Autobiographies* (Calcutta and London, 1937); and John B. Alphonso-Karakala, "Indo-English Biography and Autobiography" [*World Literature Written in English* 20 (1971): 83–103].

Jewish survivors of the holocaust: William W. and Sarah S. Schack, "The Books of Doom" [*Commentary* 22 (1956): 336–43, 424–32].

Journalists: R. E. Woolseley, "The Journalist as Autobiographer" [*South Atlantic Quarterly* 42 (1943): 38–44].

Homosexuals: Daniel Guérin, *Autobiographie de jeunesse* (Paris, 1972).

VI. AUTOBIOGRAPHY AS A LITERARY FORM

While Dilthey and Misch were interested in autobiography mainly as a source of information about something other than autobiography, implicit in their contentions regarding the unique value of this source is the idea that the form itself is unique. This idea has led to two sorts of studies— inquiries into the conditions responsible for the peculiar traits of autobiography, and comparisons of the finished product with other literary forms—which have the common aim of defining the distinctive character of the genre but are quite different in their effects.

A. THE GOVERNING CONDITIONS OF AUTOBIOGRAPHY

These conditions have been located both outside the work: in the cultural, social or personal situation of the writer; and inside the work: in its structure, techniques, and language. Georges Gusdorf constructs a complete anatomy of these conditions in "Conditions et limites de l'autobiographie" [in *Formen der Selbstarstellung: Analekten zu einer Geschichte des literarischen Selbstporträts*, ed. Günter Reichenkron and E. Haase (Berlin, 1956), pp. 105–23], and Barrett J. Mandel employs several items from Gusdorf's list in "The Autobiographer's Art" [*Journal of Aesthetics and Art Criticism* 27 (1968): 215–26].

Among those who have located the conditions of autobiography primarily in the writer's cultural situation are Robert Kanters ["Du nu en littérature," *Revue de Paris* 72 (1965): 104–12], W. C. Spengemann and L. R. Lundquist ["Autobiography and the American Myth," *American Quarterly* 17 (1965): 501–19], Barrett Mandel ["Basting the Image with Certain Liquor: Death in Autobiography," *Soundings* 57 (1973): 175–88], and Karl J. Weintraub ["Autobiography and Historical Consciousness," *Critical Inquiry* 1 (1975): 821–48, a preliminary version of the ideas taken up in *The Value of the Individual*.

Those who find the necessary conditions of autobiography in the writer's relations with society at large or the audience in particular include P. Mansell Jones ["The Paradox of Literary Introspection," *London Mercury* 32 (1935): 446–50], Roy Pascal ["Autobiography as an Art Form," in *Stil- und Formprobleme in der Literatur*, ed. Paul Böckmann (Heidelberg, 1959), pp. 114–19], Phillip O'Connor ["On Writing an Autobiography," *The Listener* 68 (1962): 215], and Irving Louis Horowitz ["Autobiography as the Presentation of Self for Social Immortality," *New Literary History* 9 (1977): 173–79]. Two earlier critics emphasize the writer's personal situation and motives: Anna Robeson Burr ["Sincerity in Autobiography," *Atlantic Monthly* 104 (1909): 527–36] and Clennell Wilkinson ["The Confessional," *London Mercury* 24 (1931): 532–37]. Bernd Neumann finds the public and personal situations equally important in *Identität und Rollenswang: Zur Theorie der Autobiographie* (Frankfurt, 1970).

Among those critics who have discovered the definitive conditions of autobiography in the text proper, some stress the relations of text and writer [Louis A. Renza, "The Veto of the Imagination: A Theory of Autobiography," *New Literary History* 9 (1977): 1–27]; some stress its relation to the reader [A. von Harnack, "Die Selbstbiographie—ihr Wesen und ihr Wirkung," *Universitas* 10 (1955): 689–98; and Philippe Lejeune, *Le Pacte autobiographique*]; some emphasize its relation to the genre [H. Oppel, "Vom Wesen der Autobiographie," *Helicon* 4 (1942); Jean Starobinski, "The Style of Autobiography," in *Literary Style: A Symposium*, ed. Seymour Chatman (New York, 1971), 285–96 —also in *Poétique* 3 (1970): 257–65; and Barrett J. Mandel in two essays: "Autobiography—Reflection Trained on Mystery and Frank Conroy's *Stoptime*," *Prairie Schooner*

46 (1972): 323–38; and "Darwin's Crisis With Time," *Soundings* 60 (1977): 179–93]; some concentrate on its relations with literature in general (as noted in the next section), and some on its relations with the structures of the language [Philippe Lejeune, *Lire Leiris: Autobiographie et Langage* (Paris, 1975) and "Autobiography in the Third Person," *New Literary History* 9 (1977): 27–50].

B. Autobiography in Relation to Other Literary Forms

The fundamental assumption beneath all these treatments of autobiography as a thing in itself is that the genre is more imaginative—which is to say, literary—than passively reportorial. This assumption is the explicit point of a number of essays: Donald Pizer's "Hamlin Garland's *A Son of the Middle Border:* Autobiography as Art" [in *Essays in American and English Literature Presented to Bruce R. McElderry, Jr.*, ed. Max F. Schulz (Athens, Ohio, 1967), pp. 76–107], Stephen A. Shapiro's "The Dark Continent of Literature: Autobiography," Ingrid Aichinger's "Probleme der Autobiographie als Sprachkunstwerk" [*Österreich in Geschichte und Literatur* 14 (1970): 418–34], William Howarth's "Some Principles of Autobiography" [*New Literary History* 5 (1973): 363–81], János Szávai's "La Place et le rôle de l'autobiographie dans la littérature" [*Acta Litteraria Academiae Scientiarum Hungaricae* 18 (1976): 398–414], and Janet V. Gunn's "Autobiography and the Narrative of Temporality as Depth" [*Soundings* 60 (1977): 194–209].

Autobiography made its way from the realm of historiography to that of literature by a slow process that began years ago. The first steps in this removal may be seen in such studies of biography as Waldo H. Dunn's *English Biography* [(New York, 1916), pp. 130–56, 200–212], Dana K. Merrill's *The Development of American Biography*, pp. 7–11, and Vivian da Sola Pinto's *English Biography in the Seventeenth Century* [(London, 1951), pp. 32–33], where autobiography is treated not as a sub-category of biography but as something essentially different from, and even an influence on, that more historiographical form. This generic distinction has recently been extended by Peter De Mendelssohn ["Biographie und Autobiographie: Grenzlinien mit Wegweisen," in his *Von deutscher Repräsentanz* (Munich, 1972), pp. 9–47] and made the explicit basis for treating autobiography as a literary form by John Sturrock, ["The New Model Autobiographer," *New Literary History* 9 (1977): 51–65].

The relations between autobiography and fiction have been considered in two ways: historically, as a matter of generic development over time, and philosophically, as a matter of similarities and differences between modes of representation. The historical relations between autobiography and fiction are treated summarily by Lionel Trilling ["Freud and Literature," in *The Liberal Imagination* (New York, 1953): 44–64, esp. 46–47] and Northrop Frye [*Anatomy of Criticism* (Princeton, N.J., 1957; repr. New York, 1965), p. 307]. For studies of particular periods see Rudolf Gottfried, "Autobiography and Art: An Elizabethan Borderland" [in *Literary Criticism and Historical Understanding: Selected Papers from the English Institute, 1967* (New York, 1968), pp. 109–34], on Renaissance poetry; Joan Webber, *The Eloquent 'I': Style and Self in Seventeenth-Century Prose* (Madison, Wis., 1968); Patricia Meyer Spacks, *Imagining a Self: Autobiography and Novel in Eighteenth-Century England*; Jerome H. Buckley, "Autobiography in the English *Bildungsroman"* [in *The Inter-pretation of Narrative: Theory and Practice*, ed. Morton Bloomfield (Cambridge, Mass., 1970), pp. 93–104]; Lothar Köhn, "Entwicklungs- und Bildungsroman: Ein For-schungsbericht" [*Deutsche Vierteljahrschrift für Litera-turwissenschaft und Geistesgeschichte* 42 (1968): 427–73]; Georg Misch, *Geschichte der Autobiographie*, vol. 4, part 2: on the *Schelmenroman* (pp. 641–66) and on the novel and religious autobiography (pp. 739–76); John C. Major, *The Role of Personal Memoirs in English Biography and Novel* (Philadelphia, Penn., 1935), on Defoe, Fielding, and Scott; Wayne Shumaker, *English Autobiography*, on the seventeenth (pp. 110–11) and the nineteenth and twen-tieth centuries (p. 140); Robert Langbaum, *The Poetry of Experience*, esp. pp. 35, 146, on the later Romantics and the early modernists; and, on the twentieth century: W. Müller-Seidel, "Autobiographie als Dichtung in der neueren Prosa" [*Der Deutschunterricht für Ausländer* 3 (1951): 29–50] and Helmut Heissenbüttel, "Anmerkungen zu einer Literatur der Selbstenblösser" [*Merkur* 20 (1966): 568–77].

Theoretical questions regarding the relations between autobiography and fiction have figured prominently in the criticism of certain writers, especially Defoe [see Ian Watt, *The Rise of the Novel* (Berkeley and Los Angeles, 1962), pp. 112ff.; George A. Starr, *Defoe and Spiritual Autobiogra-phy*; and Leo Braudy, "Daniel Defoe and the Anxieties of Autobiography," *Genre* 6 (1973): 76–97]. On E. T. A. Hoffman, see Wulf Segebrecht, *E. T. A. Hoffman: Autobiographie und Dichtung in seinem Werk* (Stuttgart, 1967), and Irving Massey, "Narcissism in 'The Sandman': Nathanael vs. E. T. A. Hoffman" [*Genre* 6 (1973): 114–20]. Ramon Fernandez's "L'autobiographie et le roman: L'example de Stendhal" [in his *Messages* (Paris, 1926),

pp. 78–109] is the earliest study I know that treats this relation as a purely rhetorical, rather than a biographical or
psychological, matter. On Henry James, see David K.
Kirby, "Henry James: Art and Autobiography" [*Dalhousie
Review* 52 (1972/3): 637–44), which emphasizes the artistry
of James's autobiographies; and Charles Feidelson, "James
and the 'Man of Imagination' " [in *Literary Theory and
Structure: Essays in Honor of William K. Wimsatt*, ed.
Frank Brady, et al. (New Haven, Conn., 1973), pp. 331–52],
which emphasizes the autobiographicality of the fiction.
And on Conrad, see Edward W. Said, *Joseph Conrad and
the Fiction of Autobiography* (Cambridge, Mass., 1966).
Barbara C. Gelpi treats the relation as a matter of direct
influence in "The Innocent I: Dickens' Influence on Victorian Autobiography" [in *The Worlds of Victorian Fiction*,
ed. Jerome H. Buckley (Cambridge, Mass., 1975), pp.
57–71].

Autobiographies are said to be the prototypes of fiction
in three studies: David L. Minter's *The Interpreted Design
as a Structural Principle in American Prose* [(New Haven,
Conn., 1969), esp. pp. 69–136]; Peter M. Axthelm's *The
Modern Confessional Novel* (New Haven, Conn., 1967);
and Ross Miller's "Autobiography as Fact and Fiction:
Franklin, Adams, Malcolm X" [*Centennial Review* 16
(1972): 221–32].

Studies which discuss the modal relations between autobiography and fiction or poetry generally take the line
that, while all literature is essentially autobiographical,
fiction and poetry are less personal, more "objective" or
"universal" than autobiography per se. For instances of this
argument see Georg Misch, *The History of Autobiography
in Antiquity*, 1: 9; August Derleth, "Marginal Notes: On
Autobiography as Fiction" [in his *Writing Fiction* (Boston,
1946), pp. 168–73]; Mark Schorer, "Technique as Discov-

ery" [*Hudson Review* 1 (1948): 67–87]; D. S. Savage, *The Withered Branch* [(London, 1950), esp. pp. 10–11]; Leon Edel, *The Modern Psychological Novel* (pp. 103–22); and Roy Pascal, "The Autobiographical Novel and the Autobiography" [*Essays in Criticism* 9 (1959): 134–50].

In virtually all the studies listed in this section, the critics' perception of relationships between autobiography and poetry or fiction depends on a prior recognition of differences between these literary forms. And this recognition of differences, in turn, normally rests on the assumption that literary language refers to something outside itself. Francis R. Hart, for example, has maintained that autobiography refers primarily to the author's historical identity, while fiction refers primarily to the author's "meaning" [see "Notes for an Anatomy of Modern Autobiography," p. 501; and for an application of Hart's rule, see Albert E. Stone, "The Sea and the Self: Travel as Experience and Metaphor in Early American Autobiography," *Genre* 7 (1974): 279–306]. Once that assumption about referentiality is called into question—as it is in Jean Thibaudeau's "Le Roman comme autobiographie" [*Tel Quel* 34 (1968): 67–74] and Michel Butor's "L'usage des pronoms personnels dans le roman"—the last distinction evaporates, and the long migration of autobiography from fact to fiction is complete.

VII. NOTES TO THE CHAPTERS

CHAPTER ONE: THE FORMAL PARADIGM

The Confessions of St. Augustine

While one hesitates to generalize about the "criticism" of a work that has been in the hands of scholars for over 1500 years, the inference to be drawn from Pierre Courçelle's monumental *Recherches sur les Confessions de saint Augustin* (Paris, 1950) and the somewhat less intimidating checklist in Carl Andresen's *Bibliographia Augustiniana* [(Darmstadt, 1973), pp. 44–52] is that before the 1950s commentary on *The Confessions* dealt mainly with the biographical events and theological ideas to which Augustine refers and seldom, if ever, with the mode of reference he employs. This inference is supported by Courçelle himself, who placed at the head of his list of topics needing further study in 1950 the formal problems of genre (pp. 46–48) and *"voix"* (pp. 291–310).

The principal exception to this rule is a body of criticism to which neither Courçelle nor Andresen pays very close attention: writings on autobiography. The earliest major studies of the genre, both in German (Misch's *Geschichte der Autobiographie*, 1907) and in English (Burr's *The Autobiography*, 1909) called attention to the formal properties of *The Confessions* by setting the work in this context, and since then Augustine's literary artistry has received increasing scrutiny as the study of autobiography has turned from the writer to the text.

This is not to say that historians of the genre have always agreed about Augustine's pre-eminence, or even his membership, in it. Those who have considered spiritual introspection an essential element in the tradition have generally traced modern autobiography back to *The Confessions* [see, for example, James C. Johnston, *Biography: The Literature of Personality*, p. 54]. On occasion, however, critics have started from the same assumptions and either dismissed Augustine as a mere precocity, "with no serious successors or imitators" for a thousand years [Saul K. Padover, *Confessions and Self-Portraits*, p. ix], or, if their subject is English autobiography, ignored him because he was not English [see, for example, John Morris, *Versions of the*

Self; W. H. Dunn, *English Autobiography* (New York, 1916), pp. 130–56; and Donald Stauffer, *English Biography Before 1700*, pp. 175–76]. Historians who attribute the rise of modern autobiography more to the burgeoning secularism of the Enlightenment than to medieval religiosity have also tended to leave Augustine out of account [Wayne Shumaker, *English Autobiography*, p. 5]. And critics who have approached the genre ahistorically, as James Olney does in *Metaphors of Self*, have generally seen no particular significance in the fact that *The Confessions* came first.

Nevertheless, precisely to the degree that any study of autobiography includes among its generic criteria the act of self-scrutiny and attends to the literary methods of representing that act, it tacitly acknowledges the patriarchy of Augustine, who made self-reflection the subject of autobiography and devised the various methods that all subsequent autobiographers have used to depict it. The case for including *The Confessions* in the study of later autobiographies is made by Meyer Abrams in *Natural Supernaturalism* (p. 498, n. 88) and is supported by his entire discussion. Augustine's importance in (mainly French) literary and intellectual history is documented, with the author's customary attention to detail, in Pierre Courçelle's *Les Confessions de saint Augustin dans la tradition littéraire* (Paris, 1963) and discussed in J. Pépin's essay, "Les Confessions de saint Augustin, leurs antécédants et leur influence" [*Journal des savants* 4 (1964): 261–83].

Outside the study of autobiography, *The Confessions* first came under close literary scrutiny in the 1950s, in H. Fugier's two essays, "Le style imagé des *Confessions*" [*Revue des études Latines* 32 (1954): 53–55] and "L'image de Dieu-Centre dans les Confessions de saint Augustin" [*Revue des études Augustiniennes* 1 (1955): 379–95]. After a brief turn on the couch [C. Klegman, "A Psychoanalytic Study of the *Confessions of St. Augustine*," *Journal of the American Psychoanalytic Association* 5 (1957): 469–84], Augustine continued his movement into literary circles with Christine Mohrman's *"The Confessions* as a Literary Work of Art" [*Études sur le latin des chrétiens* 1 (1958): 378–81] and H. Kuhn's "Die Bekenntnisse des heiliges Augustins als literarisches Werk" [*Stimmen der Zeit* 181 (1968): 223–38]. This movement came to its logical conclusion in a brilliant, maddening essay by Eugene Vance ["Augustine's *Confessions* and the Grammar of Selfhood," *Genre* 6 (1973): 1–28; also "Le moi comme langage: saint Augustin et l'autobiographie," *Poétique* 14 (1973): 163–77]. To explain the function of Books X–XIII, Vance deconstructs the preceding books, thereby removing their ostensible references to Augustine's life and turning them into a meditation on language, and the "conversion" into a movement from corporeal (i.e., referential) to "pure" language—"the self as language" (p. 25).

Several matters mentioned in my essay have received detailed attention elsewhere. As Vance's essay suggests, the relation of Books X–XIII to *The Confessions* as a whole has always been a vexed question. Courçelle reviews the debate in his *Recherches* (pp. 21ff.), as does John O'Meara in *The Young Augustine* [(London, 1954), pp. 17–18]. Among the critics of autobiography, only James Olney (*Metaphors of Self*, pp. 44–45) finds the partition of the work significant. John C. Cooper ["Why Did Augustine Write Books XI–XIII of the *Confessions?*" *Augustinian Studies* 2 (1971): 37–46] connects the narrative of conversion and the meditations to two different meanings of the word "confession," and Fr. Bonnén Aquiló ["Análysis theologico-literaro del libro XIII de las 'Confessiones' de

San Agostino," *Augustinus* 10 (1965): 181–98] treats the final book as different from all preceding ones.

The fundamental conflict between eternal being and temporal becoming in the narrative of conversion is discussed by É. zum Brunn in "Le dilemme de l'être et du néant chez saint Augustin: Des premiers dialogues aux 'Confessions'" [*Recherches Augustiniennes* 6 (1969): 7–102]. Further light on this topic can be derived from Norman Grabo's excellent analysis of the same problem in "Jonathan Edwards' *Personal Narrative*: Dynamic Stasis" [*Literatur in Wissenschaft und Unterricht* 2 (1969): 141–48]. The theological foundations of this problem are clearly outlined in three studies of the morphology of conversion: Norman Pettit's *The Heart Prepared: Grace and Conversion in Puritan Spiritual Life* (New Haven, Conn., 1966); David L. Parker's "Petrus Ramus and the Puritans: The 'Logic' of Preparationist Conversion Doctrine" [*Early American Literature* 8 (1973/4): 140–62]; and C. C. Goen's Introduction to *The Great Awakening* [vol. 4 of *The Works of Jonathan Edwards* (New Haven, Conn., 1972)]. These studies provide invaluable assistance in understanding the differences between the autobiographical methods of Augustine and his Puritan successors.

The failure to observe such differences, I believe, leads to serious errors in the interpretation of *The Confessions* and, hence, of any subsequent autobiography to which that work is compared. By including *The Confessions* in his discussion of *The Prelude*, Meyer Abrams (*Natural Supernaturalism*, pp. 83–87) gains a distinct critical advantage over John Morris, whose *Versions of the Self* leaves Augustine out of account. However, in saying that Augustine's question about the source of evil "is answered in his discovery that evil issues in a greater good, in his own life as in the history of mankind" (p. 86), Abrams fails to recognize how often Augustine explicitly denies any such value to temporal process. When Abrams then compares *The Confessions* to *The Prelude*, which does give authority to temporal experience, he fails to indicate how far from Augustine's views autobiography had drifted in the intervening centuries.

The significance of Augustine's question, "Who can so hold the mind of man . . . ?" and its bearing on the autobiographical writings of Montaigne, Pascal, Rousseau, Proust, and T. S. Eliot are fully treated by Georges Poulet in *Studies in Human Time* [trans. Elliot Coleman (Baltimore, Md., 1956)]. Joseph Mazzeo explains Augustine's ideas about the relation of words to truth, in "St. Augustine's Rhetoric of Silence: Truth vs. Eloquence and Things vs. Signs" [in his *Renaissance and Seventeenth-Century Studies* (London, 1964), pp. 1–28, esp. pp. 16–23].

CHAPTER TWO: HISTORICAL AUTOBIOGRAPHY

La vita nuova

The reviews of modern criticism of *La vita nuova* in Umberto Cosmo's *A Handbook to Dante Studies* [trans. David Moore (Oxford, 1950), pp. 38–44], in the bibliographical notes to Maria Luisa Carloni's *Commento alla Vita nuova di Dante Alighieri* (Udine, 1958), and Mario Pazzaglia's essay, "Vita Nuova" in the *Enciclopedia dantesca* [5 (Rome, 1976): 1086–96] reveal a familiar shift of critical interest over the years from the author's life to his text. True, the shift is somewhat less abrupt in this case than in that of less apparently artful autobiographies. Dante's fame as a poet, his use of poems and remarks on style in *La vita nuova*, the allegorical mode of the work, and its association with the

Divine Comedy, all helped to draw critical attention to his methods from the beginning. Nevertheless, until the 1950s criticism dealt mainly with the problem of separating fact from allegory in the work, and only since that time has it concentrated primarily on the formal properties of the work itself. The earlier stage of this movement is reflected in Pino Da Prati's *Realtà e allegoria nella "Vita Nuova" di Dante* (San Remo, 1958), and the latter phase is anticipated with admirable sensitivity in Charles S. Singleton's *An Essay on the Vita Nuova* (Cambridge, Mass., 1949).

To historians of autobiography, *La vita nuova* has often seemed to hover on the threshold between medieval impersonality and Renaissance self-assertion. While one might expect this liminal position to have attracted considerable attention, its effect appears to have been exactly the opposite. Scholars engaged in the debate over the existence of autobiography in the Middle Ages have tended to locate *La vita nuova* in the Renaissance, while those who have emphasized the emergence of individuality in the Renaissance have tended to place the work back in the Middle Ages. As a result, in the history of autobiography, the work has been more often referred to than closely examined. One notes, for example, that *La vita nuova* falls between the stools of the "High Middle Ages" and the Renaissance in Georg Misch's *Geschichte der Autobiographie*, receiving only scattered references in the volumes devoted to those periods.

Two recent essays are of particular interest in relation to my discussion of Dante's autobiography. Mark Musa's introduction to his translation of *La vita nuova* (New Brunswick, N.J., 1957; Bloomington, Ind., 1962) describes the allegorical structure of the work in great detail, and John Freccero, in his Introduction to *Dante: A Collection of*

Critical Essays [(Englewood Cliffs, N.J., 1965), pp. 1–8] points up the difference between the self-judging narrator of *La vita nuova* and the self-exculpating narrator of Rousseau's *Confessions* (p. 5), without seeming to realize, however, that Dante's methods and their enabling beliefs were not available to Rousseau.

Grace Abounding . . .

The standard text is *Grace Abounding to the Chief of Sinners, by John Bunyan,* ed. Roger Sharrock (Oxford, 1962).

Bunyan's work has often been discussed in relation to autobiography, especially the rise and development of the genre in England. In this context, it has generally served as a classic example of the transition from religious to secular autobiography in the seventeenth century. [See the period studies listed in section V, part B, above; also William York Tindall's *John Bunyan, Mechanick Preacher* (New York, 1934), pp. 31–41, and the Introduction to Sharrock's edition, pp. xxvii–xxxiii.] For considerations of *Grace Abounding* in the larger context of autobiography in general, see Misch's *Geschichte der Autobiographie*, vol. 4, part 2: 795–800; and Elizabeth Bruss's *Autobiographical Acts*, pp. 33–60.

The artistic potential of Bunyan's autobiographical methods is demonstrated in Roger Sharrock's essay "Spiritual Autobiography in the *Pilgrim's Progress*" [*Review of English Studies* 24 (1948): 102–19] and G. A. Starr's *Defoe and Spiritual Autobiography,* while Barrett Mandel emphasizes the artistry of *Grace Abounding* itself ["Bunyan and the Autobiographer's Artistic Purpose," *Criticism* 10 (1968): 225–43]. Dennis Taylor discusses Bunyan's waverings between self-typification and self-individuation as common to works of this sort ["Some Strategies of Religious Autobiography," *Renascence* 27 (1973): 40–44].

The Autobiography of Benjamin Franklin

The standard text is *The Autobiography of Benjamin Franklin*, ed. Leonard W. Labaree, Ralph L. Ketcham, Helen C. Boatfield, and Helene H. Fineman (New Haven, Conn., 1964). Equally reliable for general purposes is Russell B. Nye's edition in *Autobiography and Other Writings by Benjamin Franklin* (Boston, 1958).

The two topics most often debated by readers of the *Autobiography* are its mixture of truth and artifice and its degree of structural coherence. Among those who have emphasized Franklin's conscious artistry are Charles Sanford ["The Art of Virtue," in his *The Quest for Paradise* (Urbana, Ill., 1961), pp. 114–34], Bruce I. Granger [*Benjamin Franklin, an American Man of Letters* (Ithaca, N.Y., 1964), pp. 209–45], David Levin ["The Autobiography of Benjamin Franklin: The Puritan Experimenter in Life and Art," *Yale Review* 53 (1964): 258–75], Paul M. Zall ["A Portrait of the Autobiographer as Old Artificer," in *The Oldest Revolutionary: Essays on Benjamin Franklin*, ed. J. A. Leo Lemay (Philadelphia, Penn., 1976), pp. 53–65], and Janette S. Lewis [" 'A Turn of Thinking': The Long Shadow of the *Spectator* on Franklin's *Autobiography*," *Early American Literature* 13 (1978/9): 268–77].

Coherence or the lack of it in the *Autobiography* is the subject of Robert F. Sayre's chapter on Franklin in *The Examined Self*, A. O. Aldridge's "Form and Substance in Franklin's *Autobiography*" [in *Essays on American Literature in Honor of Jay B. Hubbell*, ed. Clarence Gohdes (Durham, N.C., 1967), pp. 47–62], James A. Sappenfield's *"The*

Autobiography of Benjamin Franklin: The Structure of Success" [*Wisconsin Studies in Literature* 6 (1969): 90–99], and Hugh J. Dawson's "Franklin's 'Memoirs' in 1784: The Design of the *Autobiography*, Parts I and II" [*Early American Literature* 12 (1977/8): 286–93].

These and a number of other studies of the *Autobiography* are reviewed by J. A. Leo Lemay, in "Franklin and the *Autobiography*: An Essay on Recent Scholarship" [*Eighteenth-Century Studies* 1 (1967/8): 185–211], and by Bruce Granger, in "Benjamin Franklin" [*Fifteen American Authors Before 1900: Bibliographic Essays on Research and Criticism*, ed. Robert E. Rees and Earl N. Harbert (Madison, Wis., 1971), pp. 200–203]. To these excellent surveys I would add one observation: whether existing studies deal with the artistry or the coherence of the *Autobiography*, none has sufficiently noticed how consistent Franklin's attitudes are throughout the work, both to his audience and to his subject, given the number of years that elapsed between the writing of the three parts and the change in the author's circumstances during those years. This truly remarkable consistency, it seems, was made possible partly by Franklin's having had his autobiographical intentions taken out of his own hands after Part I and returned to him in the form of public instructions about how to proceed, partly by the close conformity between his narrative posture in the work and his public reputation, and partly by his apparent determination to make the *Autobiography* a public document rather than an exercise in personal introspection or expression.

This point has been touched upon by a number of Franklin scholars. Betty Kushen ["The Three Earliest Published Lives of Benjamin Franklin: *The Autobiography* and its Continuations," *Early American Literature* 9 (1974/5):

39–52] shows that the Franklin portrayed in the *Autobiography* not only arose from, but contributed to, the public image of him. Daniel B. Shea, Jr., [in *Spiritual Autobiography in Early America*, pp. 234ff.] underscores the publicity of Franklin's narrative by showing how much more closely it resembles Puritan biography than autobiography. Earl Fendelman ["Toward Walden Pond: The American Voice in Autobiography," *Canadian Review of American Studies* 8 (1977): 11–25] observes the conflict between Franklin's publicly representative and privately unique selves. Morton L. Ross ["Form and Moral Balance in Franklin's Autobiography," *Ariel: A Review of International English Literature* 7 (1976): 38–52] notices that Franklin effaces his individuality more and more as the autobiography proceeds. And John Griffith ["The Rhetoric of Franklin's 'Autobiography,'" *Criticism* 13 (1971): 77–94] relates the conflict of publicity and privacy to the *personae* of narrator and protagonist, whose identities, Griffith maintains, do not converge at the close of the narrative.

CHAPTER THREE: PHILOSOPHICAL AUTOBIOGRAPHY

The Confessions of Jean-Jacques Rousseau

Of the autobiographies dealt with in this book, Rousseau's is certainly the one most often studied in relation to the development of autobiography. Two recent and especially useful studies of this type are Philippe Lejeune's *Le Pacte autobiographique*, pp. 87–153, which concentrates on the generic properties of the *Confessions*; and Karl Weintraub's *The Value of the Individual*, pp. 294–335, which places the work in its historical setting.

The review of criticism in *The Eighteenth Century*, ed.

Bibliographical Essay

George R. Havens and Donald F. Bond [vol. 4 of *A Critical Bibliography of French Literature*, D. C. Cabeen, gen. ed. (Syracuse, 1951) and *Supplement*, ed. Richard Brooks, 1968] shows that along about 1920 biographical interpretations of the *Confessions* began to give way to psychological readings [see esp. V. Demole, "Analyse psychiatrique des Confessions de J. J. Rousseau," *Schweizer Archiv für Neurologie und Psychiatrie* 2 (1918): 270–304], and that after 1950 critical attention turned increasingly to the artistic qualities of the work. Notable in this regard are Mark J. Temmer, "Art and Love in *The Confessions of Jean-Jacques Rousseau*," [*PMLA* 73 (1958): 215–20], which argues that the work is to be valued as art rather than as fact; Madeleine B. Ellis, *Rousseau's Venetian Story: An Essay Upon Art and Truth in "Les Confessions"* (Baltimore, Md., 1966), which shows that apparent factual inaccuracies are really the result of Rousseau's aesthetic decisions; and two studies by Marcel Raymond: "Les Confessions" [in *Jean-Jacques Rousseau*, by S. Baud-Bovy et al. (Neuchâtel, 1962)] and "Jean-Jacques Rousseau et la problème de la connoissance de soi" [*Studi francesi* 6 (1962): 457–62], which treat the work as a poetic act of self-knowledge.

Two studies deal directly with the internal conflicts outlined in my essay. Although Jean Starobinski's *Jean-Jacques Rousseau, la transparence et l'obstacle* (Paris, 1959) describes this conflict in psychological terms, as a struggle between the desire for spiritual union and the wish to keep the self separate, the essential drift of his discussion is continued in my remarks concerning Nature and experience, going back and going ahead, true being and consanguinity, uniqueness and typicality. Christie Vance ["Rousseau's Autobiographical Venture: A Process of Negation," *Genre* 6 (1973): 98–113] reads the *Confessions* along with the *Dialogues* and the *Reveries* in order to describe Rousseau's struggles with the problem of knowing the self immediately—apart from society on the one hand and language on the other. She concludes that what appear to be unintentional conflicts are in fact strategies devised by Rousseau to define himself by negation. Two additional essays deal with the complexity and temporality of the self that Rousseau discovered in his search for simple unity: Jean Starobinski, "Rousseau et le péril de la réflexion" [in his *L'oeil vivant* (Paris, 1961)], and Lionel Gossman, "Time and History in Rousseau" [*Studies on Voltaire and the Eighteenth Century* 39 (1964): 311–49]. Margery Sabin [*English Romanticism and the French Tradition* (Cambridge, Mass., 1976)] compares the *Confessions* and *The Prelude* to show how these two treatments of autobiography are symptomatic of the cultures out of which they arose. Like many critics who have recently taken up the subject, however, Sabin relates neither the particular autobiographies she is studying to the genre as a whole nor her own work to existing scholarship in the field.

The Prelude

Because *The Prelude* was read as a poem among poems long before it was studied as an autobiography among autobiographies, it came to generic criticism already equipped with literary associations of a sort that prose-narratives like Franklin's and Rousseau's have only recently begun to acquire, as critics have come to recognize how much the genre is subject to literary, as well as biographical, conditions. Indeed, this trend toward literariness in the criticism of autobiography is closely tied to the inclusion of works like *The Prelude* in the genre: our willingness to think of Wordsworth's poem as an autobiography simultaneously reflects and heightens our inclination to think of autobiography as a species of poetry.

This is not to say that the literary status of *The Prelude* has exempted it from biographical interpretation. Many of Wordsworth's early critics, equating autobiography with biography, and poetry with information, mined his "Autobiographical Poem" for information about the poet's past life. It is also true, however, that critical interest turned from the data recollected to the poetic methods of recollection much earlier in this case than in the study of autobiography as a whole. In 1929, Janette Harrington compared two poetic renditions of the same biographical event, in "Wordsworth's 'Descriptive Sketches' and 'The Prelude,' Book VI" [*PMLA* 44 (1929): 1144–58], to show that the report in each poem is conditioned less by the facts reported than by the mood of the poet at the time he composed it and that each poem is a surer reflection of his present than of his past situation. Nor was Harrington's essay atypical, for at least three other essays in the thirties also saw the autobiographical element of the poem in its present action rather than its past events. Bennett Weaver ["Wordsworth's 'Prelude': An Intimation of Certain Problems in Criticism," *Studies in Philology* 31 (1934): 534–40] first insisted that the poem should not be interpreted biographically, since there intrudes between fact and report the act of reflection, which is internal and hence not independently verifiable; and then went on in a later essay ["Wordsworth's 'Prelude': The Poetic Function of Memory," *Studies in Philology* 39 (1937): 552–63] to maintain that when the memory functions poetically it creates, instead of merely recalling, the past, thereby producing a unique variety of truth. The autobiography and artistry of the poem were still more closely identified by Phyllis Bartlett, whose essay "Annette and

Albertin" [*Sewanee Review* 45 (1937): 12–23] remains less interesting for its argument concerning the omission of Annette Vallon from *The Prelude* than for its very early suggestion that the poem can best be understood in relation to a work like Proust's *Remembrance of Things Past*, another autobiography whose contents are determined more by artistic than by biographical intentions and requirements.

The next important steps in this transfer of critical emphasis from the poem's external references to its internal action were taken by critics like Donald Davie and Geoffrey Hartman, who were able to describe rather precisely the methods by which the poem reflects upon its own cognitive processes. Davie's essay "Syntax in the Blank-Verse of Wordsworth's *Prelude*" [in *Articulate Energy* (London, 1955), pp. 106–16] points out the extent to which the language of the poem emphasizes meditation—which is to say present action—over explanation, while Hartman, in *Wordsworth's Poetry, 1787–1814* (New Haven, Conn., 1971), makes consciousness itself the primary subject of the poem.

My treatment of *The Prelude* was anticipated years ago by Charles Williams's discussion in *The English Poetic Mind* (Oxford, 1932). The poem, Williams argues, is not a self-biography but a typically Romantic attempt to solve a personal spiritual problem poetically. In this case, Williams goes on to say, the attempt is unsuccessful because Wordsworth, unable to trust his poetry to arrive at its own solution, imposed upon it external solutions from philosophy, religion, and politics. In "The Evolution of Soul in Wordsworth's Poetry" [*PMLA* 82 (1967): 265–72] Robert Langbaum notes the modernity of both Wordsworth's attempt to find spiritual significance in a world constructed from personal experience rather than given and of his equation of soul with imagination, which makes the poems themselves instruments of soul-making rather than merely reports of a process occurring elsewhere.

Meyer Abrams was the first critic, I believe, to set *The Prelude* in the tradition of spiritual autobiography presided over by Augustine's *Confessions*. Abrams, however, reads the poem as a fully realized structure which returns to its own origins on a new, higher plane of comprehension, rather than as a failure to achieve a final justifying form, with a largely rhetorical conclusion tacked on to cover that failure. Here as elsewhere in his book, Abrams's determination to connect the Romantics with Augustine and to dissociate them from the modernists leads him to underemphasize both Augustine's repeated disparagement of processual experience and the Romantics' inability to achieve a final form of knowledge through process. That inability (which Augustine explicitly predicted) leads both to the unsupported assertions that conclude so many Romantic works (betraying a passion for the absolute that clearly links them to Augustine) and to the gradual acceptance of process as something valuable in itself (a tendency that links them to the modernists).

Cyrus Hamlin's "The Poetics of Self-Consciousness in European Romanticism" [*Genre* 6 (1973): 142–77] fills in the philosophical background of Romantic ideas about the self as absolute, dynamic, and self-creating, and then compares Hölderlin's *Hyperion* and *The Prelude* as parallel attempts, under the influence of Rousseau's *Confessions*, to comprehend the self through poetic reconstructions of experience. For Hamlin (as for Abrams, whom he does not mention), *The Prelude* is an imaginative experience in the life of the narrator, who is changed by it.

Frank D. McConnell's *The Confessional Imagination: A Reading of Wordsworth's Prelude* (Baltimore, Md., 1974) also considers the poem in relation to the confessional tradition that extends from Augustine to English Dissenters of the seventeenth and eighteenth centuries. Like many people who theorize about the confession, however, McConnell distinguishes it from something called "conventional autobiography" without ever providing a definition of the latter that would make the distinction clear. In any case, McConnell's discussion of the confession proceeds on a level of generalization so far above the works in question (the conflict between "holistic or organic" and "*daemonic*" theories of human development) that his quest for Wordsworth's predecessors takes him outside the genre altogether, to *Paradise Regained.*

My point concerning Franklin and Rousseau as exemplars of the two divergent strains of modern autobiography is made, albeit in a very different context, by James M. Cox's essay "Autobiography and America."

Confessions of an English Opium Eater

The only detailed treatment of De Quincey's writings in the context of autobiography, so far as I know, is Elizabeth Bruss's discussion in *Autobiographical Acts* (Baltimore, Md., 1976). Bruss's larger aim is to liberate the idea of autobiography as a genre from prescriptive, formal definition by viewing it as an action—at once cultural, literary, and personal—that both arises out of these conditions and alters them, and thus as a dynamic, evolving genre rather than as a static form to which every autobiographer must adhere. In choosing only first-person narratives of the author's own lives for analysis, however, and especially in selecting De Quincey's *Autobiographical Sketches* rather than the whole of what he called his "Confessions," Bruss limits herself to describing changes within that conventional form and fails to follow what seems to me the most significant movement in the whole history of autobiography, the transition from biographical to fictive metaphor enacted in the *Suspiria de Profundis*. Indeed, Bruss's reason for ignoring these fictional portions of the *Confessions*—that their symbolic pursuit of the absolute self makes De Quincey's biographical anecdotes seem trivial by comparison (p. 96)—strikes me as the best possible reason for considering them very closely. Committed by habit, if not by her theory, to identify autobiography with biography, Bruss misses the boat in which the genre set sail, with De Quincey at the helm, for new shores.

Outside the study of autobiography, there are a few essays that bear more or less directly on the ideas proposed in my essay. Virginia Woolf's impressions of "De Quincey's Autobiography" [*The Common Reader: Second Series* (London, 1932), pp. 132–39] neatly capture De Quincey's poetic, interior (as opposed to prosaic, public) approach to autobiography and, hence, his attraction for the truly modern novelist. Peter Quennell, in the process of complaining about De Quincey's tendency to conceal with an air of revealing, rather accurately identifies the ironic properties of the symbolic method ["Books in General," *New Statesman and Nation* 40 n.s. (1950): 429–30]. Two excellent attempts to disentangle the compositional history of the *Confessions* are: Ian Jack, "De Quincey Revises His *Confessions*" [*PMLA* 72 (1947): 122–46], and David F. Clarke, "On the Incompleteness of the *Confessions of an English Opium Eater*" [*Wordsworth Circle* 8 (1977): 368–76].

CHAPTER FOUR: POETIC AUTOBIOGRAPHY

Sartor Resartus

Autobiographical interpretation of *Sartor Resartus* began in earnest with *Diogenes Teufelsdröckh und Thomas Carlyle* (Leipzig, 1913), by A. C. Lorenz, who announced that Book II is purely autobiographical in that it contains material drawn from Carlyle's own past life. Assisted by C. F. Harrold's detailed biographical footnotes in his 1937 edition of the work, this biographical view of the matter remained much in evidence until the 1950s, when it retired under the withering stare of the New Criticism. In 1965, G. B. Tennyson's *"Sartor" Called "Resartus"* (Princeton, N.J.) attempted to deflect the aim of autobiographical interpretation from Carlyle's life to the text itself. "Regrettably," Tennyson concludes after discrediting all previous attempts to discover the facts behind the fiction, "scholarship has been quicker at pointing out possible private allusions in *Sartor* than in examining their operation in terms of their relationships within the book itself" (p. 191n.). Like the fact-hunters he so justly condemns, however, Tennyson seems to identify autobiography with biographical data. Consequently, his banishment of these data dispatches the idea of autobiography as well, leaving him no way to pursue the somewhat vague but highly suggestive alternative he has posed.

Working under both the New Critical interdict against the biographical interpretation of literature and the received opinion that autobiography is, first of all, biographical, James Morris could not bring himself to call *Sartor Resartus* an autobiography, even though he could discern some enticing resemblances between the thematic movements in Carlyle's prose-narrative and in Bunyan's and

231

Mill's autobiographies. Five years later, however, Meyer Abrams succeeded in realizing the value of both Tennyson's suggested alternative and Morris's insights simply by relating *Sartor Resartus* to autobiography on formal rather than material grounds (*Natural Supernaturalism*, p. 130). With this single, deft stroke, Abrams made what is to my mind the key connection between the biographical and fictive modes of autobiography.

In the few years that have passed since Abrams's book appeared, critics have found it increasingly easy to think of autobiography in other than biographical terms—to hear, that is, what Carlyle himself was saying. In 1954, Wayne Shumaker explicitly rejected both *Sartor Resartus* and *David Copperfield* as autobiographies (*English Autobiography*, pp. 104–05). In 1976, however, Burton Pike could say, without much fear of critical reprisal, that "Autobiography, at least beyond the naïve level, does not necessarily consist of remembered personal experiences" ("Time in Autobiography," p. 327). Between the widely separated positions of Shumaker and Pike falls a great deal of criticism that bears on our understanding of a work like *Sartor Resartus* as an autobiography. Part of this criticism is the work of such nineteenth-century scholars as Marshall Brown, whose essay "Humboldt and the Meditation Between Self and World" [*Genre* 6 (1973): 121–41] explains how Romantic writers sought a universal meaning for the self through the techniques of allegory, thus moving autobiography away from naturalistic documentation toward the metaphors of poetry. Another part of this criticism comprises such studies in the relations between fiction and nonfiction as Käte Hamburger's *Die Logik der Dichtung* [2nd ed. (Stuttgart, 1968)], Gérard Genette's "Vraisemblance et motivation" [in his *Figures II* (Paris, 1969)] and "Discours du récit"

[*Figures III* (Paris, 1972)], Robert Champigny's *Ontology of the Narrative* (The Hague, 1972), Johannes M. Anderegg's *Fiktion und Kommunikation: ein Beitrag zur Theorie der Prosa* (Göttingen, 1973), and two essays in *New Literary History* 6 (1975): John R. Searle's "The Logical Status of Fictional Discourse" (pp. 319–32) and Roland Barthes's "An Introduction to a Structural Analysis of Narrative" (pp. 237–72).

Two studies establish the position of *Sartor Resartus* in relation to modernism: Morse Peckham's *Beyond the Tragic Vision: The Quest for Identity in the Nineteenth Century* [(New York, 1962), pp. 179–86] and Albert J. La Valley's *Carlyle and the Idea of the Modern* [(New Haven, Conn., 1968), pp. 69–118]. The essay by Burton Pike noted above offers a good general account of the problem of time in autobiography and the influence of that problem on the disintegration of the genre in the twentieth century.

Regarding Carlyle's statement that the most valuable books are the "Lives of heroic god-inspired men," see Keith Rinehart, "The Victorian Approach to Autobiography," p. 177 n. 2, which explains that Carlyle often used the words "biography" and "autobiography" interchangeably; and Patrick Brantlinger, " 'Romance,' 'Biography,' and the Making of *Sartor Resartus*" [*Philological Quarterly* 52 (1973): 108–18], which shows that the ideas Carlyle attached to these two words were often similarly overlapping.

David Copperfield

Autobiographical criticism of *David Copperfield* has developed in concert with the criticism of autobiography in general, shifting its attention over the years from the novel's rendition of biographical data, to its expression of the author's psychological state, to its active participation in the creation of the life it records. John Forster opened the investigation in 1872, by including in his *Life of Charles Dickens* [ed. J. W. T. Ley (London, 1928), pp. 22ff.] portions of the autobiography that Dickens had abandoned to write *David Copperfield* and then pointing out details from the fragment that reappear in the novel (pp. 5, 547, 551, 553, and 557). For the next one hundred years, Dickens's readers sifted and weighed this information, until Phillip Collins, in surveying all the accumulated evidence and adjudicating all previous disputes, uttered what surely must be the last word on the subject [*"David Copperfield*: A Very Complicated Interweaving of Truth and Fiction," *Essays and Studies by Members of the English Association* 23 (1970): 71–86].

While the biographical critics were pondering the facts (without considering, however, that the source of these facts might itself be a fiction), psychological criticism was uncovering a deeper connection between the novel and its author. To be sure, this method was sometimes very crudely employed. Leonard F. Manheim's essay, "The Personal History of David Copperfield: A Study in Psychoanalytic Criticism" [*American Imago* 9 (1952): 20–43], displays the customary peppering of quotation marks, exclamation points, and italics—those diacritical nudges and winks to the reader, who, coming after Freud, can be spared the steep condescension shown to poor, benighted Dickens. But in more sensitive hands, the instrument could dissect the novel without murdering it. Concentrating on David rather than the author, Mark Spilka attributed the power of the novel to David's tendency to project his own fears, hostilities, and guilt into his account of the external action, noticing that this "projective method" falters badly when David enters his "new life" [*"David Copperfield* as Psy-

chological Fiction," *Critical Quarterly* 1 (1959): 292–301].
Graham Greene emphasized the novel's importance to
Dickens as a way of confronting the unresolved traumas of
his childhood ["The Young Dickens," in *The Lost Childhood and Other Essays* (London, 1951), pp. 53–54]. More
recently, Sylvia Manning has contended that *Oliver Twist*,
David Copperfield, and *Great Expectations* are all psychologically autobiographical and that *Great Expectations*, the
least biographical of the three, is the most revealing
["Masking and Self-Revelation: Dickens' Three Autobiographies," *Dickens Studies Newsletter* 7 (1976): 69–74]. She
does not explain, however, why Dickens might have found
fiction more satisfactory than biography for his autobiographical purposes. And, in "The Fictions of Autobiographical Fiction" [*Genre* 9 (1976): 73–86] Avrom Fleischman
comes very close to saying that the novel is an action
through which Dickens attempts to transcend, rather than
merely to report factually or express symbolically, the problems of his childhood.

J. Hillis Miller was the first to treat *David Copperfield*
as an autobiographical action in its own right, rather than a
reflection of biographical or psychological actions performed elsewhere, when he said that in the novel ". . . the
author may be seen going away from himself into an imagined person living in an imagined world in order to return
to himself and take possession by indirection of his own
past self and his own past life" ["Three Problems of Fictional Form: First-Person Narration in *David Copperfield*
and *Huckleberry Finn*," in *Experience and the Novel: Selected Papers from the English Institute, 1967*, ed. Roy
Harvey Pearce (New York, 1968), pp. 21–48; quotation is
from p. 33]. Miller, however, locates the union of the narrator and protagonist at the end of the novel, rather than in

Chapter Fourteen, as I do. Barry Westburg goes even farther than Miller in detaching the novel from Dickens's past
life. *Oliver Twist, David Copperfield,* and *Great Expectations,* Westburg argues, are all "confessions," with each
successive work achieving a greater degree of objectivity
until *Great Expectations* becomes a "confession about the
nature of both the fiction-making activity and its product,
the novel per se" [*The Confessional Fictions of Charles
Dickens* (De Kalb, Ill., 1977), p. 203].

Two additional points in my essay—the apparent break
in the novel at Chapter Fifteen and Mr. Dick's relation to
Dickens—have been raised before. Not everyone, it must
be said, shares my opinion about the respective merits of
the two parts of the novel—or even that there are two parts.
J. Hillis Miller [*Charles Dickens: The World of His Novels*
(Cambridge, Mass., 1958), pp. 150–59] and Robin Gilmour
["Memory in *David Copperfield,*" *The Dickensian* 71
(1975): 30–42] prefer what I call the latter, weaker part.
Gilmour, however, notices David's feeling, in Chapter
Eighteen, that his "old life" is not really his, but someone
else's. Furthermore, both Gilmour and Miller locate the
thematic center of the novel in a relationship between David and another character (Agnes and Steerforth, respectively) that is not developed in the first part. To that extent at
least, these treatments recognize the partition that they are
otherwise at pains to deny.

Barry Westburg considers and partially decodes Mr.
Dick's name (*The Confessional Fictions of Charles Dickens,* pp. 192–93), apparently unaware that the job had already been done more thoroughly by Stanley Tick ["The
Memorializing of Mr. Dick," *Nineteenth-Century Fiction*
24 (1969): 142–53]. Tick's essay notices and documents
many connections between character and author but does

not explain why Dick appears in this place, at this time, and in this guise.

The Scarlet Letter

The brooding, introspective tenor of Hawthorne's prose has invited autobiographical interpretation of one variety or another from the very beginning. Hawthorne himself appears to have sanctioned this line of inquiry when he wrote to his publisher concerning the tales selected for *Mosses from an Old Manse*, "My past self is not very much to my taste, as I see myself in this book" [James T. Fields, *Yesterdays with Authors* (Boston, 1879), p. 75], thus implying that his "past self" is plainly visible there. The writer's presence in his work was evidently apparent to his contemporary readers as well. In "At the Saturday Club," Oliver Wendell Holmes first portrayed the author as

> An artist Nature meant to dwell apart,
> Locked in his studio with a human heart,
> Tracking its caverned passions to their lair,
> And all its throbbing mysteries laying bare;

and then said of the works,

> Count it no marvel that he broods alone
> Over the heart he studies,—'tis his own;
> So in his page, whatever shape it wear,
> The Essex wizard's shadowed self is there,—
> The great ROMANCER, hid beneath his veil
> Like the stern preacher of his sombre tale;
> Virile in strength, yet bashful as a girl,
> Prouder than Hester, sensitive as Pearl.

[*The Complete Poetical Works of Oliver Wendell Holmes*, Cambridge Edition (Boston and New York, 1895), p. 271.]

237

The other side of this equation between author and work is supplied by Alcott's allegorical reading of Hawthorne's character (quoted in my text), and by Lowell's nearly identical diagnosis in "A Fable for Critics":

> When Nature was shaping him, clay was not granted
> For making so full-sized a man as she wanted,
> So, to fill out her model, a little she spared
> From some finer-grained stuff for a woman prepared,
> And she could not have hit a more excellent plan
> For making him fully and perfectly man

[*The Complete Poetical Works of James Russell Lowell*, Cambridge Edition (Boston and New York, 1896), p. 135.]

It was some time, however, before Hawthorne's critics began to pursue these rich suggestions. The earliest "autobiographical" studies concentrated upon resemblances between fictive details in the stories and novels and presumably factual statements in the notebooks and prefaces. Bliss Perry's "Hawthorne at North Adams" [in *The Amateur Spirit*, (Boston, 1904), pp. 117–39] described the supposed process by which Hawthorne transformed certain prior experiences into "Ethan Brand." In her essay, "Self-Portraiture in the Works of Nathaniel Hawthorne" [*Studies in Philology* 23 (1926): 40–54], Amy Louise Reed noted a number of similarities between male characters in the romances and remarks Hawthorne had made about himself elsewhere, and Julian Hawthorne's "The Making of *The Scarlet Letter*" [*Bookman* 74 (1931): 401–11] revealed that Pearl was modeled on his sister Una. Ostensibly significant resemblances between Hawthorne's recorded experiences at Brook Farm and the contents of the *Blithedale Romance* were noted in Arlin Turner's "Autobiographical Elements in Hawthorne's *Blithedale Romance*" [*Univer-*

sity of Texas Studies in English 15 (1935): 39–63], in Lina
Bohmer's *Brookfarm und Hawthornes Blithedale Romance*
(Jena, 1936), and in Oscar Cargill's "Nemesis and Nathaniel
Hawthorne" [*PMLA* 52 (1937): 848–62] and then disputed
or revised by W. P. Randel ["Hawthorne, Channing, and
Margaret Fuller," *American Literature* 10 (1939): 472–76]
and Austin Warren ["Hawthorne, Margaret Fuller, and
'Nemesis,' " *PMLA* 54 (1939): 615–18]. In the forties and
fifties, three major critical studies—Mark Van Doren's
Nathaniel Hawthorne [(New York, 1949; repr. 1957), p.
260], E. H. Davidson's *Hawthorne's Last Phase* [(New Haven, Conn., 1949), pp. 137–38], and Hyatt Waggoner's
Hawthorne: A Critical Study [(Cambridge, Mass., 1955;
rev. ed., 1963), p. 230]—identified the hero's family in the
abortive *Dolliver Romance* with Hawthorne's, on the evidence of biographical resemblances. And in 1965, Sidney
Moss ("A Reading of 'Rappaccini's Daughter,' " *Studies in
Short Fiction* 2: 145–56) listed the "raw biographical data"
that are "projected" and "disguised" in the tale.

   Although objections to calling Hawthorne's work "auto-
biographical" were raised throughout these years, by
Randall Stewart [in the Introduction to his edition of *The
American Notebooks* (New Haven, Conn., 1932), p. lxii], F.
O. Matthiessen [*American Renaissance* (New York, 1941),
p. 229 and n.], Roy Male [*Hawthorne's Tragic Vision*
(Austin, Texas, 1957; repr. New York, 1964), p. 86], Arlin
Turner [*Hawthorne: An Introduction and Interpretation*
(New York, 1961), pp. 22 and 81], and Millicent Bell [*Hawthorne's View of the Artist* (New York, 1962), pp. 135ff.],
their objections had less to do with the equation of Hawthorne's life and art than with the inability of the word "autobiography," as they understood it, to express the range
and depth of that equation. Agreeing with Keats, that "they

are very shallow people, who take everything literal" and that "A Man's life of any worth is a continual allegory," which "very few eyes can see" [*The Letters of John Keats, 1814–1821*, 2 vols., ed. H. E. Rollins, 2 (Cambridge, Mass., 1958): 67], these critics sensed that Hawthorne's extra-literary actions and statements were no less allegorical than his fictions and so could not be considered the "reality" to which his fictions referred.

A good deal of the impetus behind this perception that the life and work are equally symbolic clearly came from psychological criticism, which regarded all the writer's overt actions as symbolic of deeper psychic structures. The interpenetrations of Hawthorne's life and writings were de-scribed in more or less doctrinaire psychological terms by Newton Arvin [*Hawthorne* (Boston, 1929)], Austin Warren [Introduction to *Nathaniel Hawthorne: Representative Se-lections* (New York, 1934), esp. p. xiii], Malcolm Cowley ["Hawthorne in the Looking Glass," *Sewanee Review* 56 (1948): 545–63; and his Editor's Introduction to *The Porta-ble Hawthorne* (New York, 1948)], J. E. Hart ["*The Scarlet Letter*: One Hundred Years After," *New England Quarterly* 23 (1950): 381–95], Frederick Crews [*The Sins of the Fa-thers: Hawthorne's Psychological Themes* (New York, 1966)], Barton L. St. Armand ["Hawthorne's 'Haunted Mind': A Subterranean Drama of the Self," *Criticism* 13 (1971): 1–25], and Robert Penn Warren ["Hawthorne Revis-ited: Some Remarks on Hellfiredness," *Sewanee Review* 81 (1973): 75–111]. While these treatments are far more sen-sitive to the uniqueness of Hawthorne's work than are such rigid formulations as Joseph Levi's "Hawthorne's *The Scar-let Letter*: A Psychoanalytic Interpretation" [*American Imago* 10 (1953): 291–306], which describes the work as an expression of the author's Oedipus complex, they all share with biographical interpretation an assumption that the referents of Hawthorne's fiction lie outside the fiction—in his personal situation, whether external or internal, rather than in the symbolic actions performed by the fiction itself.

The earliest, and still the best, study of the tales as efforts by Hawthorne to discover his own nature by discovering their sources, processes, and meanings is Jorge Luis Borges's "Nathaniel Hawthorne" [in his *Other Inquisitions*, trans. Ruth L. C. Simms (Austin, Texas, 1965; repr. New York, 1966), pp. 49–69]. A handful of recent studies have expanded upon this idea without connecting Hawthorne's methods to the development of autobiography. Darrel Abel's " 'A More Imaginative Pleasure': Hawthorne on the Play of the Imagination" [*E.S.Q.* 55 o.s. (1969): 63–71] notes the tendency of Hawthorne's works to refer to the activity that produced them. In his essay, *"The Scarlet Letter*: Through the Old Manse and the Custom House" [*Virginia Quarterly Review* 51 (1975): 432–47], James Cox makes the crucial point that, for Hawthorne, "the life of art was primary and causal, not secondary and resultant" (p. 432). And Kenneth Dauber's *Rediscovering Hawthorne* (Princeton, N.J., 1977) insists that the fiction must be read as a series of verbal actions, independent of all external references. Only one study has connected this movement in Hawthorne criticism with recent trends in the criticism of autobiography. Timothy D. Adams's essay, "To Prepare a Preface to Meet the Faces That You Meet: Autobiographical Rhetoric in Hawthorne's Prefaces" [*E.S.Q.* 23 n.s. (1977): 89–98], starts from a recognition of the ficticity of autobiography in order to break down the assumed barriers between the "factual" prefaces and the "fictional" tales. All together, these recent developments point toward the eventual realization of the "very great possibilities" Robert

F. Sayre saw, some time ago, "for a kind of 'autobiographical criticism' " that "would not tie itself to the reduction of art to moments of a man's biography, and would not simply chase every fictional episode back to some precedent in 'real life,' " but would "relate each part of a man's writing to his own changing needs for form" and "describe and contemplate the image created" [*The Examined Self*, p. x].

Those of my readers who are at all familiar with the published criticism of *The Scarlet Letter* will readily discern the points where my argument stands on the shoulders, on the toes, or in the shadow of existing studies. Nonetheless, I feel obliged to acknowledge at least some of the critics who have addressed the principal themes touched on in my essay. A number of critics have argued that the main characters represent aspects of the author. Gordon Roper attaches Hester, Dimmesdale, and Chillingworth, respectively, to heart, soul, and mind, the three faculties designated by psychological theory in Hawthorne's own time ["The Originality of Hawthorne's *The Scarlet Letter*," *Dalhousie Review* 30 (1950): 62–79]. J. E. Hart, in *"The Scarlet Letter*: One Hundred Years After," calls the novel a symbolic action performed by characters who represent different sides of Hawthorne's personality. Malcolm Cowley makes the important observation that Hawthorne's "audience" was also a self-projection (Editor's Introduction to *The Portable Hawthorne*, p. 7), and Rudolph Von Abele identifies Chillingworth with the "Paul Pry" that Hawthorne saw in himself [*"The Scarlet Letter*: A Reading," *Accent* 11 (1951): 211–27]. Both J. E. Hart and Anne Marie McNamara ["The Character of Flame: The Function of Pearl in *The Scarlet Letter*," *American Literature* 27 (1956): 537–53] observe that Pearl represents the reconciliation of the several "selves" embodied by the other characters.

Hart and Sister Hilda M. Bonham ["Hawthorne's Symbols *Sotto Voce*," *College English* 20 (1959): 184–86] connect Hester with art, thus distinguishing her from Dimmesdale (religion) and Chillingworth (science); while Von Abele finds Hawthorne's feelings about his art expressed in the Minister [*"The Scarlet Letter:* A Reading," p. 215], and Leslie Fiedler suggests that the scarlet "A" itself stands for "Art" [*Love and Death in the American Novel* (New York, 1960), p. 506]. Among those who have seen in one tale or another a "fable of the artist" are Daniel Hoffmann [*Form and Fable in American Fiction* (New York, 1961), p. 138], Marius Bewley [*The Eccentric Design* (New York, 1959), p. 120], Rudolph Von Abele [*The Death of the Artist: A Study of Hawthorne's Disintegration* (The Hague, 1955), p. 101], F. O. Matthiessen (*American Renaissance*, pp. 223ff.), and Millicent Bell (*Hawthorne's View of the Artist*, passim].

The conflict between Hawthorne's public and private selves has been discussed most thoroughly by Mark Van Doren [*Nathaniel Hawthorne*, passim] and Robert Shulman ["Hawthorne's Quiet Conflict," *Philological Quarterly* 47 (1968): 216–36]. The attendant conflict between discursive statement and symbolic action in his writing has been described by Morton Cronin ["Hawthorne on Romantic Love and the Status of Women," *PMLA* 69 (1954): 89–98], Frederick I. Carpenter ["Scarlet A Minus," *College English* 5 (1944): 173–80], and Charles C. Walcutt ["*The Scarlet Letter* and Its Modern Critics," *Nineteenth-Century Fiction* 7 (1953): 251–64].

Neal F. Doubleday ["Hawthorne's Estimate of His Early Works," *American Literature* 37 (1966): 403–09] documents the writer's insistence upon absolute truth and his hatred of ambiguity. Clark Griffith ["Caves and Cave

Dwellers: The Study of a Romantic Image," *JEGP* 62 (1963): 551–68] notes that the paradigmatic figure of the cave appears in Hawthorne's work whenever he turns to the theme of redemptive sin. Charles Feidelson, Jr., [*"The Scarlet Letter,"* in *Hawthorne Centenary Essays*, ed. R. H. Pearce (Columbus, Ohio, 1964), pp. 31–77] defines very precisely the functions of Hawthorne's inquisitive narrators and the reasons for their participation in his fictive actions (esp. p. 34). N. F. Adkins ["The Early Projected Works of Nathaniel Hawthorne," *Papers of the Bibliographical Society of America* 39 (1945): 119–55] shows that Hawthorne was expecting one of his tales to develop into a full-blown romance; the breakthrough, during the composition of *The Scarlet Letter*, is described in the Introduction to the Centenary Edition of the novel (Columbus, Ohio, 1962), pp. xx–xxii.

AFTERWORD

The critical fate of *The Scarlet Letter* in this century has been described by Seymour L. Gross and Randall Stewart, in "The Hawthorne Revival" [*Hawthorne Centenary Essays*, ed. Roy Harvey Pearce (Columbus, Ohio, 1964), pp. 335–66].

Three useful, although very different, books on the problems of selfhood in modern literature and criticism are: Wylie Sypher, *The Loss of Self in Modern Literature and Art* (New York, 1964); Paul de Man, *Blindness and Insight: Essays in the Rhetoric of Contemporary Criticism* (New York, 1971); and Robert Langbaum, *The Mysteries of Identity: A Theme in Modern Literature* (New York, 1977).

The tendency of recent work on autobiography to cancel out both itself and its subject is apparent in the two issues that the journal *Genre* devoted to that subject (March and June, 1973). In her Introduction to this collection of essays, Christie Vance, having noticed the wide variety of forms examined by the authors, appears to throw up her hands: "We cannot offer a satisfactory, all encompassing formula to account for the nature of these disparate texts. Indeed, the object of this special issue is less to present a unified analysis of the 'autobiographical genre' than to explore the limits of autobiography, to examine its viability as a genre and thereby to question the very concept of the genre itself" (p. iii). In other words, the recent upsurge of critical interest in autobiography coincides, on the one side, with a feeling that the genre is ubiquitous and, on the other, with a doubt that it exists at all. One of the essays in the collection, Alain Finkielkraut's "Desire in Autobiography" (trans. by Vance, pp. 220–32), marks either a logical conclusion or a new departure (I am at a loss to say which) by discussing the possibilities of autobiography without self, without a relation between subjectivity and utterance, and without ultimate meaning.

Wallace Stevens's lines at the end of the chapter are from "The Comedian as the Letter C" and "Chocorua to Its Neighbor," in *The Collected Poems* (New York, 1965), pp. 28 and 300.

SUPPLEMENT (1982)
Important additions to the foregoing survey may be found in the checklist of criticism appended to James Olney's *Autobiography: Essays Theoretical and Critical* (Princeton, N.J., 1980) and in the "Current Bibliography on Life-Writing" published annually in the Fall issue of *Biography,* 1978– . A few studies that do not appear on either of these lists are arranged below according to the scheme of my "Bibliographical Essay."

Period and national studies include Owen C. Watkins, *The Puritan Experience: Studies in Spiritual Autobiography* (New York, 1972); Kingsbury Badger, "Christianity and Victorian Religious Confessions," *MLQ* 25 (1964): 86–101; Phyllis Grosskurth, "Victorian Autobiography—The Very Public Private Voice," *Humanities Assoc. Bulletin* 16 (1965): 5–16; Arnold Krupat, "American Autobiography: The Western Tradition," *Georgia Review* 35 (1981): 307–17; and Gordon O. Taylor, "Voices from the Veil: Black American Autobiography," ibid., pp. 341–61.

Autobiography is considered as a source of psychological information in Thomas C. Greening's "The Uses of Autobiography," in *Therapy and the Arts: Tools of Consciousness*, ed. W. Anderson (New York, 1977), pp. 90–112; and in relation to biography in Anders Damsager's *Erindring—fortegning eller indsigt?* (Aarhus, Denmark, 1978).

The conditions and limits of the genre are examined in Hugh J. Silverman's "Un égale deux: ou l'espace autobiographique et ses limites," *Revue d'Esthétique* 33 (1980): 279–302; Anna Whiteside's "Barthes et l'autobiographie eclatée," *Romance Notes* 21 (1980): 4–9; and Michael Ryan's review of Lejeune's *Le Pacte autobiographique*, "Self-Evidence," *Diacritics* 10 (1978): 2–16.

Identität, a collection of essays by various hands, ed. Odo Marquard and K. Stierle (Munich, 1979), includes three studies bearing on Augustine's place in the autobiographical tradition (by M. Fuhrmann, pp. 685–90; M. Sommer, pp. 699–702; and H. R. Jauss, pp. 708–17).

My treatment of Bunyan as a transitional figure in the generic movement from Augustine to Franklin and Rousseau was anticipated, I now discover, in Robert Bell's "Metamorphoses of Spiritual Autobiography," *ELH* 4 (1977): 108–26.

Index

247

Index

Index

Index